The Learning Portfolio

The Learning Portfolio

Reflective Practice for Improving Student Learning

Second Edition

John Zubizarreta

JOSSEY-BASS
A Wiley Imprint
www.josseybass.com

Published by Jossey-Bass
A Wiley Imprint
989 Market Street, San Francisco, CA 94103-1741—www.josseybass.com

Jossey-Bass books and products are available through most bookstores. To contact Jossey-Bass directly call our Customer Care Department within the U.S. at 800-956-7739, outside the U.S. at 317-572-3986, or fax 317-572-4002.

Jossey-Bass also publishes its books in a variety of electronic formats. Some content that appears in print may not be available in electronic books.

Credits on page 349.

Library of Congress Cataloging-in-Publication Data
Zubizarreta, John.
  The learning portfolio : reflective practice for improving student learning /
John Zubizarreta. — 2nd ed.
      p. cm.
  Includes bibliographical references and index.
  ISBN 978-0-470-38847-1 (pbk.)
  1. Electronic portfolios in education.   2. Reflective learning.   I. Title.
  LB1029.P67Z83   2009
  371.39—dc22
                                                                          2008045997

Printed in the United States of America

SECOND EDITION

PB Printing   10   9   8   7   6   5   4   3   2

The Jossey-Bass Higher and Adult Education Series

Contents

About the Author

JOHN ZUBIZARRETA is professor of English and director of honors and faculty development at Columbia College in South Carolina. A Carnegie Foundation/CASE professor for South Carolina, he has earned a number of awards for teaching and scholarly excellence from several educational organizations.

John is a frequent conference presenter and consultant on improving college teaching and learning, and he has mentored educators internationally on developing teaching and administrative professional portfolios. His work on portfolios includes many articles and chapters in journal and book publications such as the *Journal on Excellence in College Teaching; The Department Chair; Phi Delta Kappan;* Seldin's *The Teaching Portfolio* (1997, 2004), *Changing Practices in Evaluating Teaching* (1999), *Improving College Teaching* (1995), and *Successful Use of Teaching Portfolios* (1993); Roth's *Inspiring Teaching* (1997); and Wright's *Teaching Improvement Practices* (1995). He also has contributed to Seldin and Higgerson's *The Administrative Portfolio* (2002) and Seldin and Miller's *The Academic Portfolio* (2009).

John is president-elect of the National Collegiate Honors Council, the nation's premier professional association for honors education. He has contributed essays to the organization's journals, and he is coauthor of *Inspiring Exemplary Teaching and Learning: Perspectives on Teaching Academically Talented College Students* (2008).

In addition to his scholarship on teaching and learning, John has published widely on modern American and comparative literatures. Foremost among his disciplinary publications is his coedited *Robert Frost Encyclopedia* (2001).

John is also a moonstruck husband and father of two girls who keep him busy outside the ivied walls. When the academic life becomes too hectic, John is an avid telemark skier and fisherman, an aching runner, and a former six-time gold medalist champion in national white-water canoe competitions.

About the Contributors

Dorothe J. Bach is an assistant professor and faculty consultant at the University of Virginia's Teaching Resource Center. In addition to facilitating events designed to enhance the university's teaching mission, she supports incoming faculty through the Excellence in Diversity Fellows Program and writes articles about women and minority faculty retention. She teaches literature courses in the university's German department and comparative literature program.

Stephanie Burrell is assistant director of the Center for Academic Excellence at Fairfield University and a visiting assistant professor in curriculum and instruction. A 2008 graduate of the social justice education program at the University of Massachusetts Amherst, Stephanie focused her doctoral research on assessment of educational outcomes of college-level diversity courses. She has faculty development expertise in student outcomes assessment and curriculum design for multicultural/social justice education.

Russell Butson is a lecturer in higher education at the University of Otago in New Zealand. He is involved in exploring learning approaches that have an impact on the learner's life, with a particular interest in more engaging and collaborative learning experiences that are consistent with the idealism, imagination, and expectations of learners in higher education. He has published several articles on the use of technology in higher education.

Vicki Chan provides technical support and counsel as an educational development officer at the City University of Hong Kong.

Helen L. Chen is a research scientist at the Stanford Center for Innovations in Learning at Stanford University. She is a founding member and cofacilitator of the Electronic Portfolio Action and Communication network, a community of practice focusing on pedagogical and technological issues related to e-portfolios broadly defined. She also serves on the advisory board for the Association of American Colleges and University's Valid Assessment of Learning in Undergraduate Education initiative. Her current research interests focus on the design and evaluation of social software and innovative learning spaces to support portfolio-related activities and student learning in higher education.

Hokling Cheung is an educational development officer at the City University of Hong Kong, where she promotes creative and pedagogical applications of technology for teaching and learning. She is also a lecturer on Internet communication for the university's master of arts in communication and new media program. Currently, she is the coinvestigator of two government-funded projects, one on e-portfolios for English language learning and one on podcasting technology for student learning.

Jennifer Marie Cook is an assistant research fellow in the faculty of dentistry at the University of Otago in New Zealand. She graduated in 2004 with a BA in cultural anthropology from the University of Western Ontario. She began her career as a science and development manager at the Economic and Social Research Council in the United Kingdom. In 2007, she joined the University of Otago to work on the e-portfolio project. She has coauthored *Professional ePortfolio Project: Bridging the Divide Between Student and Practicing Professional* (2007) and *The Development of an ePortfolio for Lifelong Reflective Learning and Auditable Professional Certification* (2008).

Ann C. Cunningham is an associate professor in the Department of Education at Wake Forest University. She holds a PhD in instruction and teacher education from the University of South Carolina. She specializes in cross-disciplinary technology-enhanced instructional design and currently teaches elementary and secondary undergraduate and graduate technology courses to preservice teachers. Her education and scholarly interests include teacher leadership, electronic portfolios, technology integration, and assessment.

Marilyn Drury is director of educational technology at the University of Northern Iowa. She has taught in higher education throughout the state of Iowa for ten years and has spent more than twenty years in information technology leadership roles in higher education. She has served on national advisory councils for Apple, IBM, and Gateway.

Ronald J. O. Flores is an associate professor of sociology and director of the Center for Civic Engagement and Leadership at St. Lawrence University. His research interests include immigrant adjustment experiences in New York City and educational attainment patterns and differentials among Latino groups. He is currently teaching several courses that examine active citizenship in an increasingly complex and diverse society.

M. Heather Hartley is a documentary filmmaker and assistant professor in the Department of Communication Studies at the University of Windsor, teaching film and video production courses. She taught for several years at the Pennsylvania State University, where she completed her most recent documentary, *Linciati: Lynchings of Italians in America*. Her current projects include a documentary on the ninety-nine-day automotive workers' strike in Windsor, Ontario, shortly after World War II.

Emily Hauck is an alumna of Agnes Scott College. She was one of the first participants in the college's Dana Design program, a curriculum reserved for the most promising art students and aimed at providing real-world experience in graphic design. She most recently served as a mentor for other Dana Design students, providing direction and leadership for their studies.

John C. Ittelson is director of instructional technologies for the K–20 California Educational Technology Collaborative, a new consortium focused on helping students prepare for and stay in college. He also serves as the principal investigator for the Verizon Foundation–supported Thinkfinity California Project, bringing high-quality, standards-based Internet content to California's K–12 classrooms. He is also working with the California State University chancellor's office on a National Science Foundation grant.

Rosemary Kardos is a senior teaching fellow in the faculty of dentistry at the University of Otago in New Zealand and director of the bachelor of oral health degree. She is also a member of the university's Committee for the Advancement of Teaching and Learning.

Frank Linnehan is associate dean for undergraduate programs at Drexel University's LeBow College of Business and a professor of organizational behavior and human resources in the Department of Management. His research interests include school-to-work transitions for high school and college students, adult-youth mentoring, affirmative action, equal employment, and workforce diversity initiatives.

Olivia White Lopez is a rising senior at Agnes Scott College, majoring in studio art and anthropology. She plans to pursue a graduate degree in either visual anthropology or documentary photography studies.

Laurence Miners is director of the Center for Academic Excellence at Fairfield University. An associate professor of economics, he primarily focuses his research interests on economic pedagogy and course design. He has led faculty development workshops at other colleges and universities and made presentations at regional and national pedagogy conferences. Each June, he and others at Fairfield University lead a conference on pedagogy, technology, and course redesign.

Kathryn Nantz is an associate professor of economics at Fairfield University. She has spent much of her career working on innovative teaching projects and using technology in the economics department. In recent years, she has served on the staff of Fairfield's Center for Academic Excellence, helping facilitate work on a university-wide strategic planning initiative involving integrative teaching and learning. Her contributions to *College Teaching* and *The History Teacher* reflect her keen interest in making connections across disciplinary boundaries. She is an associate editor of the journal *Perspectives on Economics Education Research*, and she is on the board of Omicron Delta Epsilon, the international honor society for economists.

Leslie Ortquist-Ahrens is founding director of the Center for Teaching and Learning and an associate professor of German at Otterbein College. Her work on faculty learning communities and facilitating faculty dialogue has appeared in *New Directions for Teaching and Learning*, *To Improve the Academy*, and *College Teaching*. She has also published articles on German film.

Elizabeth Regosin is an associate professor of history at St. Lawrence University. She is the author of *Freedom's Promise: Ex-Slave Families and Citizenship in the Age of Emancipation* (2002) and *Voices of Emancipation: Understanding Slavery, the Civil War, and Reconstruction through the U.S. Pension Bureau Files* (coedited with Donald Shaffer, 2008).

Donna Reiss is professor emeritus of English at Tidewater Community College, where, over twenty-five years, she taught writing and literature and directed the writing center and writing across the curriculum, online learning, and distributed teaching and learning. From 2005 to 2008, she was a lecturer and coordinator of the LitOnline faculty development project at Clemson University. She has been writer and editor of popular and scholarly articles, book chapters, and collections, and has given talks and workshops in North America, Europe, Australia, and New Zealand with a focus on online learning, electronic communication, and digital portfolios for active learning (http://wordsworth2.net).

Rachel Spronken-Smith is a senior lecturer in the Higher Education Development Centre at the University of Otago in New Zealand. She works mainly as an academic staff developer but also continues to lecture in geography and environmental science. While lecturing in geography at the University of Canterbury, she was awarded a University Teaching Award and nominated for a National Innovation in Teaching Award. Her research interests in higher education include the use of inquiry-based learning, the teaching-research nexus, and the student experience.

Sarah Stein is a senior lecturer in the Higher Education Development Centre at New Zealand's University of Otago, where she works as an academic staff developer. She researches and publishes in the areas of design and technology education, science education, and teacher professional development at the school and higher education levels.

Roben Torosyan is associate director of the Center for Academic Excellence and assistant professor of curriculum and instruction at Fairfield University. He has facilitated faculty development workshops at thirty conferences and at institutions including New York University, Rensselaer Polytechnic Institute, LaGuardia Community College, and The New School. His transdisciplinary scholarship interests include critical thinking, resistance, popular culture, and philosophy. He earned his BA and MA at New York University and his PhD in philosophy and education at Teachers College, Columbia University.

Fiona Williams is a senior tutor in the English Language Centre at City University of Hong Kong. She teaches undergraduates in English language enhancement courses and manages a team of teachers. She is responsible for the Self-Access Centre and independent learning initiatives. From 2005 to 2007, she was the principal investigator of a government-funded project on e-portfolios for English language learning.

Alan Wright is an educational developer with broad teaching, research, and administrative experience in universities in the Canadian provinces of Nova Scotia, Quebec, and Ontario. He has been an active board member of the Professional and Organizational Development Network in Higher Education and the Society for Teaching and Learning in Higher Education, for which he is publications chair. As vice provost at the University of Windsor, he has the mandate to develop the institution's focus on learning and effective teaching.

Shannon Yarbrough is a senior studio-art major at Agnes Scott College.

Foreword to the Second Edition

BECAUSE THE LEARNING portfolio operates on so many levels, I consider it one of the most powerful learning and assessment tools to emerge in the past quarter century. Its most telling feature is the student reflection that forms the "heart" of an effective portfolio.

Self-reflection—sometimes called "metacognition"—is arguably the new frontier in teaching. Bransford, Brown, and Cocking (2000), for example, regard metacognition as one of three key learning principles (the other two are prior learning and deep foundational knowledge based on concepts). John Zubizarreta repeatedly emphasizes the value of reflection and the crucial role it plays in portfolio creation and student development. He notes that reflective thinking is "the linchpin of lifelong, active learning, the key to helping students discover and understand what, how, and why they learn." Students typically reflect on what should be included in their portfolio, on the meaning and value of each "artifact" in the appendixes, and on the ways that the portfolio will lead to continued learning. The terms *learning how to learn* or *lifelong learning* are virtually clichés, but without intentional, focused planning, too many students may regard the portfolio only as a postmortem look back at the "ghost of learning past."

Another facet of learning that John Zubizarreta explores in this seminal book is the power of learning through writing. For example, students typically compose, as a guiding principle, their philosophy of learning. The writing-across-the-curriculum movement is fueled by the power of writing to learn. Zubizarreta encourages both writing and reflection through his careful question prompts, such as these initial ones:

- What have I learned? Why did I learn?
- When have I learned? In what circumstances? Under what conditions?
- How have I learned or not, and do I know what kind of learner I am?
- How does what I have learned fit into a full, continual plan for learning?

- Has my learning been connected, integrated, coherent?
- Is my learning relevant, applicable, practical?

Because reflection and writing to learn are synergistic ideas that inform portfolios, an integrated approach typically emerges. Zubizarreta and the contributing authors in the "models" section stress that such integration is related to the portfolio's central purpose, which could be for improvement, a job search, or other reasons. All the elements should support the primary purpose.

This integration is often achieved, Zubizarreta postulates, through a collaborative approach with students working together or with portfolio mentors. The research on collaboration and cooperation as learning tools is ongoing and convincing. The research on deep learning in particular is relevant here. The four premises of deep learning as outlined by Rhem (1995) focus on four components: motivation, active learning, interaction with others, and a deep foundational knowledge base built around concepts (that last component is also one of Bransford, Brown, and Cocking's key learning principles). Because portfolios get students into a rich and deep knowledge base focused on their own learning experiences, portfolios are highly motivating. Collaboration with others deepens these individual experiences by allowing probing questions, socially constructed knowledge, and alternative viewpoints. Such approaches often lead to significant critical thinking as part and parcel of the deep processing.

John Zubizarreta's integrated portfolio model itself is inspiring, but the book is greatly enhanced by the contributions of informed practitioners who provide practical examples of how to use student learning portfolios for a variety of programs and purposes. The disciplines addressed include humanities, composition and literature, business, education, and oral health. Chapters provide in-depth looks at topics such as scaffolding critical thinking through learning portfolios, integrating learning portfolios with a course management system, getting started with learning portfolios, facilitating change and development in faculty beliefs and practices, and taking a second look at the learning portfolio. Best of all, Zubizarreta has collected articles from around the world with contributions from the United States, Hong Kong, New Zealand, and Canada.

Because these authors are different from those contributing to the original edition, readers interested in learning portfolios will need to treasure both editions.

• • •

Barbara J. Millis
Director, TEAM Center
University of Texas at San Antonio

References

Bransford, J. D., Brown, A. L., & Cocking, R. R. (Eds.). (2000). *How people learn: Brain, mind, experience, and school* (Expanded ed.). Washington, DC: National Academy Press.

Rhem, J. (1995). Close-up: Going deep. *The National Teaching & Learning Forum, 5*(1), 4.

Foreword to the First Edition

NOT LONG AGO, an academic friend came into my office. He asked me how he could *really* tell what students had learned in his class. Examination scores, he said, were an obvious way to measure student learning: the higher the grade, the greater the learning. I told my friend that it was an obvious way but that it struck me as more likely that examination scores or course grades were a measure of what students have retained, not necessarily what they have learned. True, a low test score might reflect inadequate learning, but it might also be no more than a reflection of the student's inability to articulate the full level of learning. Or the particular test might not be the best vehicle for the student to demonstrate learning.

My friend pondered what I had told him. OK, he said, if examination scores or course grades are flawed approaches to measuring deep student learning, is there a better way? I said that there is. It is the learning portfolio. My friend was not familiar with the concept and asked how he could learn more about it. *The Learning Portfolio: Reflective Practice for Improving Student Learning*, I told him, is the book you need. It covers just about everything you should know about print and electronic portfolios, gives models of successful use, and then provides sample learning portfolios and practical materials. Read it through, I advised; use it to understand what the learning portfolio is, how it can be used, and what might go into it; and then decide how you can build it into your teaching. If you do that, you'll be able to tell better what students have *really* learned in your class.

The learning portfolio concept has gone well beyond the point of theoretical possibility. It has been used for more than fifteen years. Today it is being adopted or pilot-tested in various forms—paper-based or multimedia/online—by faculty in different disciplines in a rapidly increasing number of colleges and universities.

To create portfolios, students do three things. First, they collect their work, including notes for presentations, drafts of assignments, journals, homework, lab reports, class projects, critical essays, course Listserv entries, research papers, and creative displays/performance. Then they select from this archive exhibits that demonstrate stipulated criteria, such as best work, critical thinking, successive drafts, affective learning, practical application, and leadership. Finally, students reflect on their work by considering important guiding questions, such as what they learned, why their learning is important, how they can apply key concepts in local and global contexts, how their learning has developed over the course of the term, and how they have used reflection to improve their performance.

All this underscores a key point: in learning portfolios, students assume responsibility for documenting and interpreting their own learning. Through reflection, students make their thinking visible.

Since I use student learning portfolios in my own teaching, I asked the students in my organizational behavior class what they saw as the benefits of portfolios. Interestingly, their answers parallel those found in the literature. The students suggested the following benefits:

- Portfolios capture intellectual substance and deep learning in ways that other methods of evaluation cannot.
- They support the development, demonstration, and valid assessment of a wide range of personal, professional, and academic capabilities.
- They encourage students to take on important new roles in the documentation, observation, and review of their learning.
- They encourage improved student performance.
- They support the integration of learning from different parts of a course or program of study.
- They place some responsibility for assessing learning in the hands of the students instead of relying only on the judgment of others.
- They engage students in what they are learning so that transformation and internalization can take place.
- They lead students to relate new concepts to existing experience and critically evaluate and determine key themes.
- They show deep analysis of evidence and learning that stems from deep reflection.

A word about the importance of deep reflection: as college and university professors, we encourage our students to be reflective and to adopt reflective practices. But too often, such practices are passive and are no more than a "navel-gazing" activity. Perhaps the most commonly accepted means of recording student reflective practice is to retain a learning log. But merely recording what a student has learned is not sufficient. It does not indicate that deep reflection has taken place.

As John Zubizarreta points out in *The Learning Portfolio*, deep reflection—not a learning log—is at the very heart of the learning portfolio. It is the deliberate and systematic attention to a student's self-reflective, metacognitive appraisal of why and—more importantly—how learning has occurred. Deep reflection allows students to focus on learning in a new way: it makes sense of the artifacts in a learning portfolio by converting the tacit knowledge in the evidence into explicit knowledge related to the student and his or her learning. The evidence is drawn together into a coherent tale of learning, of sense made, of new ideas developed, tested, and sometimes discarded. Through deep reflection, students explain what the evidence shows about what they have learned. They tell their own stories, assess their own strengths and weaknesses as learners, evaluate their products and performances, reflect on past learning, and think about paths for future learning.

How do students react to engaging in deep reflection as part of their learning portfolios? Consider these comments from students in my organizational behavior class:

I confess that I was very skeptical at first. But when I reviewed the things that I put in my portfolio since the beginning of the semester, it became clear to me that some things were good and other things were not. I could really see how my understanding had developed during the course.

· · ·

My hypertext presentation made it easy to make references back and forth between reflection and evidence. The reflective part made the evidence come alive.

· · ·

I believe that all students can improve their learning by preparing a learning portfolio, especially if they include a significant reflective section.

· · ·

Though my students today are quite supportive of learning portfolios, my understanding of portfolios has come late in my teaching career. And much of that understanding has come through trial and error. Because there was no reliable guide available, I had to experiment and struggle to find answers to questions such as these: What does the term *portfolio* mean in a course? What kinds of student work should be included? How closely should the instructor specify the form, structure, size, and content of a learning portfolio? How much time does it take to put one together? What is the role of reflection? How does a mentor help?

Had *The Learning Portfolio* been available earlier, it would have answered virtually all of my questions. Clearly, this book has much to offer college professors who want to know more about portfolios. A particular strength is that it reviews generic issues in student learning portfolios that will be common to most practitioners, and it explores practices in a range of institutions.

The book draws together the accumulated knowledge and wisdom of John Zubizarreta and a host of worthy contributors from a wide range of institutions around the world. The book offers an array of specific models of portfolio use across disciplines, courses, and programs, and the models can easily be adapted to different campuses.

The book also includes sample learning portfolios and practical materials. Because each portfolio is an individual document, varying importance has been assigned by different students to different items. Some students discuss an item at length; others dismiss it with just a sentence or two or even omit it. That is as it should be. Although there is a general template for learning portfolios, much of what goes into them is determined by specific factors such as academic discipline, level of course or program, and personal preferences of the individual students who prepare them.

This book is unusually good. Clear, comprehensive, and immediately useful, it should be read by every faculty member who wants to know what students have *really* learned.

• • •

Peter Seldin
Distinguished Professor of Management
Pace University

Preface to the Second Edition

THE SECOND EDITION of *The Learning Portfolio: Reflective Practice for Improving Student Learning*, like the first, is an effort to lodge the concept of learning portfolio development more firmly and higher on the agenda of higher education. The learning portfolio is a rich, convincing, and adaptable method of recording intellectual growth and involving students in a critically reflective, collaborative process that augments learning as a community endeavor and refines their educational experience. This book, then, is organized into four sections to offer readers both an academic understanding of and rationale for learning portfolios and practical information that can be tailored to suit many disciplinary, pedagogical, programmatic, and institutional needs.

In the second edition, I have expanded and updated the section on electronic portfolios because of the explosive surge of interest in how digital media contribute to the learning potential of portfolios and to the seemingly easy, seamless capabilities of electronic tools to make the information in portfolios accessible for assessing and evaluating programs, majors, and institutions. I have also explored the topic of reflection more generously, an outgrowth of my own interest in what I consider the true heart of any substantive portfolio agenda.

I have changed a few other details from the first edition, adding and deleting some information, hoping to make the volume even more useful and more of a springboard for finding resources on the value and implementation of learning portfolios. Since finding diverse models of actual student portfolios is now just a click away on the Internet, where hundreds of student portfolios are viewable through many institutions' portfolio programs, I have retained only a choice few from the first edition and added a modest selection of new examples of students' reflective work in learning portfolios.

The models are all new. Read the second edition alongside the first edition to double the excellent examples of how portfolios are used by a variety of faculty, students, and administrators around the globe to stimulate significant learning.

Overview of the Contents

"Part 1: About Student Learning Portfolios" offers a foundation for and review of the value of reflective practice in student learning and how learning portfolios support reflection, sound assessment, and collaboration. I include an expanded and updated section on electronic portfolios in the second edition, sharing more information about how electronic media choices enhance the development, archiving, and public display of learning portfolios. Still, I remind readers that pedagogy and deep learning should always come before technology, a personal philosophy that drives my emphasis not on the particular medium used in the production of portfolios but rather on the principles, practice, and powerful rationale for portfolios—the common theoretical and practical learning issues that underlie portfolio development whether the product is paper or digital. Also, an expanding collection of academic organizations dedicated to electronic portfolios, many college faculty development centers and education department Web sites, and a continuing proliferation of educational technology consultants have posted Internet sites and published monographs and handbooks about electronic portfolios, and the topic is well covered elsewhere. A staggering amount of information on electronic portfolios is increasingly available on the Web, and the most helpful contribution I believe this book can make is to reaffirm the electronic portfolio's grounding in fundamental principles of learning portfolio development and to point the reader to some of the numerous, useful Internet and print resources.

- Chapter 1 offers a general background of the student portfolio movement and a rationale for implementing learning portfolios to improve and assess student learning, stressing the importance of reflection, documentation, and collaboration or mentoring.
- Chapter 2 defines the learning portfolio; addresses practical issues of time, length, and content; suggests a versatile, adaptable model; emphasizes the importance of writing in portfolio development across disciplines and portfolio presentation choices; and offers tips for managing portfolio projects.

- Chapter 3 elaborates on the foundational value of reflective inquiry; collection, selection, and organization of evidence; and collaboration and mentoring in the process of developing and revising learning portfolios. The three crucial components of learning portfolios work together to promote improvement and sound, rigorous assessment of learning.

- Chapter 4 addresses the rapidly growing trend of electronic portfolios, discussing briefly the various ways in which multimedia and hypermedia technologies have transformed the development of learning portfolios in the digital age. The chapter also balances advantages and disadvantages, reminding us of the fundamentals inherent in print or electronic portfolios, and shares a list of useful resources on electronic portfolios. Most of the institutions on the list include links to numerous student portfolios available on the Web.

"Part 2: Models of Learning Portfolios" includes diverse contributions from practitioners who implement portfolios in a variety of ways, including the ubiquitous use of digital technology. The array of specific models of how to use portfolios across disciplines, courses, and programs provides many practical ideas that can work on different campuses.

- Chapter 5: Dorothe J. Bach describes her use of learning portfolios as alternatives to final exams to help develop students' reflective learning skills in upper-level literature courses at the University of Virginia.

- Chapter 6: Stephanie Burrell, Laurence Miners, Kathryn Nantz, and Roben Torosyan share firsthand experiences and wise, practical counsel from implementing a successful portfolio program at Fairfield University.

- Chapter 7: Russell Butson, Jennifer Marie Cook, and Rosemary Kardos offer a strong model of marshaling the power of reflection, application, and professional development in learning portfolios in the field of oral health at New Zealand's University of Otago.

- Chapter 8: Helen L. Chen and John C. Ittelson relate the history of the Electronic Portfolio Action and Communication network, a community of practice focused on state-of-the-art use of electronic portfolios around the world.

- Chapter 9: Ann C. Cunningham discusses the value of electronic portfolios at Wake Forest University in improving and assessing student teachers' professional training and their ability to meet reflection, technology, and other standards in teacher certification requirements.

- Chapter 10: Marilyn Drury reveals the benefits of using common easy-to-use course management systems to build a culture of reflection and portfolio assessment in a pilot e-portfolio program at the University of Northern Iowa.

- Chapter 11: Emily Hauck, Olivia White Lopez, and Shannon Yarbrough, students at Agnes Scott College, demonstrate how portfolio strategies involving creative interview and film work in the art major engaged them in meaningful reflection, skills development, and appreciation for the quality of their education.

- Chapter 12: Frank Linnehan describes the innovative, complex My LIFEfolio e-portfolio model used in the LeBow School of Business at Drexel University to prompt students to demonstrate competencies in key areas of learning in their major discipline and beyond.

- Chapter 13: Leslie Ortquist-Ahrens details the successful use of learning portfolios to strengthen students' reflection and writing skills in a midlevel composition and literature course at Otterbein College.

- Chapter 14: Elizabeth Regosin and Ronald J. O. Flores of St. Lawrence University showcase the use of learning portfolio strategies in fostering a culture of reflective learning in a service-oriented first-year undergraduate course built around pedagogies of civic engagement and the democratic classroom.

- Chapter 15: Donna Reiss discusses her considerable experience in using the Webfolio as an alternative tool for deep learning and end-of-course assessment throughout her years of teaching composition and undergraduate general education courses in literature and the humanities at Tidewater Community College and Clemson University.

- Chapter 16: Rachel Spronken-Smith and Sarah Stein of New Zealand's University of Otago share their successful use of portfolio assessment in preparing tertiary teachers for professional careers, helping those teachers develop skills of reflection and integration.

- Chapter 17: Fiona Williams, Vicki Chan, and Hokling Cheung offer a glimpse at the English language e-portfolio at the City University of Hong Kong, showing how electronic portfolios support language acquisition, reflection, integration, and evaluation of learning outcomes.

- Chapter 18: Alan Wright and M. Heather Hartley reflect on the success and challenges of ongoing portfolio programs in various departments at Canada's University of Windsor.

"Part 3: Sample Learning Portfolio Selections" presents a collection of representative and adaptable examples of actual selections from learning portfolios.

- Chapter 19: Robyn Allen (Wake Forest University) offers excerpts from a portfolio that demonstrates the usefulness of Web-based portfolios in prompting students' reflections on learned skills and how best to communicate their learning against stated technology competencies and standards for teacher certification.
- Chapter 20: Alicia I. Gilbert's (Arizona State University) portfolio includes reflections on educational history and progress and a reflective analysis of academic and career values.
- Chapter 21: Diana Lynde (Columbia College) is a first-year student who provides reflections in a learning portfolio for an introductory literature and composition course.
- Chapter 22: Lindsay Perani's (University of North Florida) portfolio demonstrates how strategies can be implemented in PowerPoint to provide a teacher education student with an effective means of offering multisourced evidence of personal accomplishments and student outcomes in an internship.
- Chapter 23: Connie Thackaberry's (Kent State University) final reflection essay reviews her development through four years of college as an honors student with shifting disciplinary interests.
- Chapter 24: Josee Vaillant (Dalhousie University) offers an example of a student's reflections on the purpose and value of the career portfolio process.

"Part 4: Practical Materials" includes a wealth of practical assignment sheets, guidelines, criteria, evaluation rubrics, and other materials used in developing learning portfolios from across disciplines, programs, and types of institutions in higher education.

- Chapter 25: The self-assessment guide from Albion College is tailored for students developing digital portfolios and can help them reflect on and write about learning and career or academic goals.
- Chapter 26: Albion College's four-year portfolio development plan offers students detailed instructions and exercises for developing each year's portion of their digital portfolio.
- Chapter 27: Arizona State University's portfolio evaluation form contents checklist is an evaluation and scoring rubric for print portfolios in an interdisciplinary program course.
- Chapter 28: This showcase/electronic portfolio evaluation form from Arizona State University is an evaluation and scoring rubric for e-portfolios in an interdisciplinary program course.

- Chapter 29: Clemson University's Webfolio assignment provides students with detailed instructions for an e-portfolio in an undergraduate course.
- Chapter 30: The learning portfolio project assignment from Columbia College offers criteria and guidelines for a project in an upper-level literature course.
- Chapter 31: Columbia College's online reflective writing assignment guides students writing in a Web-based threaded discussion and blog environment designed to develop reflection, integration, and application skills for a learning portfolio.
- Chapter 32: The portfolio reflections assignment from Dalhousie University details the purpose and value of reflection in a portfolio.
- Chapter 33: The honors senior portfolio option document from Kent State University contains a contract form and guidelines for developing an honors capstone senior assessment portfolio.
- Chapter 34: The criteria for evaluating learning portfolios document from Otterbein College is a rubric for evaluating learning portfolios in a sophomore literature and writing course.
- Chapter 35: Otterbein College's assignment sheet for double-column notes models a tool for developing reflective learning through critical-reading skills.
- Chapter 36: Otterbein College's learning portfolio assignment comes from a portfolio project in an undergraduate literature and writing course.
- Chapter 37: This collection of sample student reflections from Otterbein College comes from a sophomore-level composition and literature course.
- Chapter 38: Tidewater Community College lays out the components of a Webfolio project in this document on the review and revision process and submission letter for Webfolios.
- Chapter 39: Tidewater Community College's rubric details how Webfolio projects are scored.
- Chapter 40: The University of Oklahoma's reflective writing assignment includes instructions for reflection on course content and integration of skills in an undergraduate engineering program.
- Chapter 41: These report guidelines from the University of Saskatchewan are a guided exercise for portfolio reflections on experiential work in a technical field.
- Chapter 42: The University of Virginia's intentional learning assignment promotes intentional reflective learning in a portfolio project in an undergraduate humanities course.

- Chapter 43: This evaluation rubric for reflective essays from the University of Virginia explains to an undergraduate humanities class how essays will be assessed and evaluated.
- Chapter 44: Wake Forest University's reflections in technology portfolio offers brief guidelines for meaningful reflection in an electronic portfolio designed to partially meet requirements for technology competencies in teacher certification.
- Chapter 45: This Technology in Education Web page from Wake Forest University is useful for examining diverse student electronic portfolios designed to meet professional education standards for state licensure.

Conclusion

I have witnessed the remarkable growth and transformation of students as they engage in the process of developing their learning portfolios. They reflect in depth on their learning, their achievements and disappointments, and their intellectual goals and professional aspirations. They understand the satisfaction of taking ownership of their own learning and becoming self-directed, reflective learners. And they lay a foundation for their futures as versatile, lifelong learners. The learning portfolio is a rich learning tool. I hope that this book will help others experience firsthand the rewards of the learning portfolio process.

• • •

John Zubizarreta
July 2008

Acknowledgments

PROJECTS OF THIS scope never get done without the boundless energizing inspiration, kind encouragement, and generous support of many faithful souls. I have a myriad of people to thank for this book—from parents who sacrificed much as nurturing, hardworking adopted U.S. citizens from homeland Cuba to help me with my education in this country; to former teachers who fired my passion for teaching, learning, and scholarship; to colleagues whose mentoring and professional collaborations have sustained me and helped me grow as an engaged academic citizen; to personal friends who have cheered my accomplishments, forgiven my lapses, and remained loyal and selfless in our bonds of friendship; to a brother held close to heart (and not just because he provides yearly rest from hard work by skiing with me in the Colorado Rockies each spring); to my wife, Margie, and precious daughters, Anna Ruth and Maria, who regularly give up time with me to support my other devotions, knowing that they are first and foremost in my heart. I owe all of them this book, my sanity, my ambitions, my values, my love.

I want to thank also the students I have had the privilege of teaching and knowing as I have restlessly sought ways to make them as excited about learning as I am. Much of my thinking on the topics of reflection, significant learning, and portfolios is an outgrowth of my rich and transforming relationships with them. I especially thank Mary Jewel Waddell, a former student who spent two years as my administrative assistant, patiently helping me with the initial editing of the volume. More recently, Amanda Bowman, a current student and my new office hand, has put up with my rush to bring the book to press, and I am grateful for her skills and dedication.

Finally, I acknowledge, of course, the various contributors to this book. Their additions to the volume are strong signs of the power of learning portfolios and the ingenuity and care of the teachers who implement them uniquely in courses and programs. The models they share are useful and easily adapted to enhance student learning. This book belongs to them and their students, as much as it is mine and my students'.

The Learning Portfolio

Part One

About Student Learning Portfolios

PART 1 OFFERS a foundation for and review of the value of reflective practice in student learning and how learning portfolios support reflection, sound assessment, and collaboration. It presents information about developing portfolios and answers to common concerns.

Chapter 1

An Overview of Student Learning Portfolios

THE CONCEPT OF THE STUDENT PORTFOLIO has been widely known and implemented for some time in academic fields such as English, journalism, and communications. Similarly, portfolios have been a staple form of documentation of performance skills in the fine arts, providing students and teachers with a method for displaying and judging evidence of best practice and samples of the full range of students' talents. Another popular application has been to provide a device for demonstrating the value of experiential learning or for assessing credit for prior learning in a program of adult education. Some portfolios are shared by students and faculty advisers for the purpose of academic advising and career counseling, a use strongly advocated by the National Academic Advising Association, which provides on its Web site (www.nacada.ksu.edu/AAT/NW26_1.htm) a rationale and a number of sample guidelines for advising portfolios as well as models derived from institutions such as Indiana University–Purdue University Indianapolis, the Pennsylvania State University, and the University of Denver (www.nacada.ksu.edu/Clearinghouse/AdvisingIssues/portfolio examples.htm). Also, in business and teacher education, portfolios have been used as effective tools for career preparation. The contribution in this volume of Drexel University's LeBow College of Business portfolio project is a good example of the practical benefits of a thoughtful portfolio system. In teacher education, for accreditation purposes, the National Council for Accreditation of Teacher Education advocates the portfolio model as an effective tool for showcasing a representative breadth of acquired skills for professional success and career preparation, using specified licensure competencies and professional standards as benchmarks against which to measure achievements signified by portfolio artifacts (www.ncate.org).

Such applications predominately have targeted the portfolio's efficacy in gathering judiciously selected products of student work to display content mastery or job readiness. Writing portfolios, for example, have been used generously in composition, creative writing, and other types of communication courses to present a diverse profile of a student's creative and technical skills. Used in this way, the portfolio is an enhancement to a writing, speech, business, leadership, or computer-information-systems teacher's comprehensive assessment of a student's growth during a particular course or at the end of an enrichment program, an academic major, or a general education core with goals, objectives, and competencies in writing and other areas. Undoubtedly, the portfolio is both an intellectually stimulating process and a product with keen utilitarian properties.

Yet, despite the history of portfolios in certain disciplines, the portfolio approach to gauging student accomplishments and growth in learning—while not entirely new in higher education—has historically received more attention in the K–12 arena. In English and a few other disciplines in college classes, portfolios, journals, and more recently, digital storytelling strategies have been employed with some regularity, but remarkably, higher education has lagged behind the grade schools in innovating and refining such persuasive learning tools. Today, following the groundswell of interest in teaching, administrative, course, and institutional portfolios, learning portfolios are attracting significant attention in college and university settings. Now the numerous Web sites that provide information on portfolios—and that especially offer rich and diverse models of how electronic or digital portfolios are used for multiple purposes—are coming predominantly from colleges and universities around the world. Countries such as Australia, Britain, Canada, Finland, France, Hong Kong, Japan, Mexico, the Netherlands, New Zealand, Poland, Portugal, Singapore, and of course, the United States—just to name a few—are home to institutions with student portfolio programs designed to help with systematic learning-outcomes assessment plans. Arter and Spandel (1992); Gordon (1994); Wright, Knight, and Pomerleau (1999); and Cambridge (2001) are a few print resources that demonstrate the interest in portfolios in higher education. Helen Barrett (www.electronicportfolios. com); the ePortConsortium (www.eportconsortium.org); the Multimedia Educational Resource for Learning and Online Teaching (www.merlot. org); the Electronic Portfolio Action and Communication network (http:// eportfolio.merlot.org); the Inter/National Coalition for Electronic Portfolio Research (http://ncepr.org); EDUCAUSE (www.educause.edu); the Europortfolio (www.europortfolio.org) consortium; EPICS-2 (www.eportfolios. ac.uk), a collaboration of several UK institutions dedicated to e-portfolio development, with strong emphasis on medical education; and other Web sites are among the numerous sources for online information on electronic portfolios in colleges and universities around the world. Following Seldin's

(2004) work on teaching portfolios, learning portfolios are clearly now main-stream in higher education.

A Focus on Learning

In addition to the diverse applications already mentioned, Burch (1997) suggests a few other uses of portfolios: "They can reveal, in the aggregate, the state of an academic program; they can provide valuable insights into what students know and how they construct that knowledge; they can provide institutional barometers, if you will, that suggest programmatic highs and lows, strengths and weaknesses" (p. 263). His comment hints that often what is left out of the formula in student portfolios is an intentional focus on learning, the deliberate and systematic attention not only to skills development and career readiness but also to a student's self-reflective, metacognitive appraisal of how and, more importantly, why learning has occurred. This is not to assert, of course, that learning does not happen at all when portfolios are used only as collection and organizing devices, that a student does not benefit simply from the thoughtful act of choosing representative samples of accomplished work and making sense of the materials as a display. But more significant learning is likely to occur if the student is encouraged to come to terms self-consciously over the duration of an academic endeavor—for example, a semester course, the culmination of an honors program, the achievement of general education goals, or the completion of a degree—with essential questions about learning itself:

- How have such products as those collected in a portfolio over time contributed to significant higher-order learning?
- What has the student learned from the process of generating the work and from collecting it, selecting it, analyzing its value, pondering its integration and future applications?
- How does the work fit into a larger framework of lifelong learning that goes beyond simply completing graded assignments?
- Why was the work valuable in the student's overall cognitive, social, ethical, spiritual development?

Imagine how such an opportunity for mentored, critical reflection and for immediate assessment of learning grounded in direct outcomes or products can benefit all our students, especially after carefully and intentionally integrating reflective learning pedagogies into our courses and programs of study. Imagine, too, how such work can benefit an academic organization looking for ways to demonstrate the value-added dimension of its influence on students' learning. More importantly, imagine the impact of such an opportunity on students' appreciation for and understanding of the visible, recorded, shared evidence of the outcomes of their reflective learning.

Such directed probing of the sources, coherence, and worth of learning—especially when combined with the power of collaboration and mentoring in making learning a recorded and shared community endeavor—is sometimes missing from the model of the student portfolio as simply an individual repository of selected artifacts. To the point, analogously, the same vital components frequently are lacking in what many faculty describe as their teaching or professional portfolios, prodigious folders that often are not much more than elaborate personnel files submitted confidentially at critical junctures in a professor's professional career.

Student portfolios, too, largely have been used to collect and evaluate students' work at key points in their progress, usually at the end of an academic endeavor; in a sense, the portfolio has been used primarily as a capstone product, sometimes even unintentionally minimizing the crucial learning process along the way in favor of the finished document, especially when the shine of fancy covers and graphics or the glitz of digital enhancement becomes the student's focus, luring the teacher into similar pitfalls. Today, although exciting and positive innovations in electronic portfolios are increasingly emphasizing the importance of reflection (see Chen and Ittelson's piece in this volume, detailing the growth of the Electronic Portfolio Action and Communication network, dedicated to electronic portfolios), the allure and dazzle of electronic media make the temptation toward product rather than process even greater. In "Costs and Benefits of Electronic Portfolios in Teacher Education: Student Voices," for example, Wetzel and Strudler (2006) report how easily even a well-intended focus on reflection in portfolio systems can go awry when students quickly decode the perceived real emphasis on product and "busywork" in a portfolio:

> *The value of reflection differed somewhat from site to site depending on the emphasis, but generally, teacher candidates reported that the connections they made to state and national teaching standards helped them to understand the standards and the attributes of well-prepared teachers. They also thought that reflecting on their teaching practice helped them learn from their experiences. However, the sentiment was almost universal that there could be too much of a good thing and that they were being "reflected to death." They recommended that faculty modify the logistics for reflections; for example, the reflection should be embedded within the*

artifact or inserted separately within the EP [electronic portfolio] system. Requiring both, however, led to redundancy and overload. . . . There was also evidence . . . of what might be described as elaborate, hyperlinked checklists in which faculty assess the EPs based on completeness rather than the quality of the content. In instances where students perceived this to be the case, they expressed great frustration in having worked hard on a component of their portfolio and feeling that it was not even read by faculty. (p. 77)

Nevertheless, in truth, it would be difficult today to find a portfolio system that does not incorporate some element of critical reflection, even if the reflection amounts to rudimentary and form-generated statements about individual exhibits collected in a portfolio developed exclusively as a performance assessment or as a "vitae on steroids," as an acerbic voice once quipped informally about portfolio-based evaluation. One need not be so deprecatingly witty, however, because simply collecting artifacts for presentation and review purposes has the intrinsic worth of at least helping students organize the outcomes of their efforts in a way that communicates accumulated skills and learning. Add a reflective component, and learning portfolios, like teaching portfolios (Seldin, 2004), become "part of a process of monitoring ongoing professional growth," encouraging "greater self-understanding" and serving as "effective tools for goal setting and self-directed learning"; they become, in short, "part of a learning process" (Campbell, Melenyzer, Nettles, & Wyman, 2000, p. 14).

The authors just cited—writing about portfolios with "a focus on product," largely from the utilitarian angle of how such documents serve as an "employment or credentialing tool" for certification in teacher education—also make the strong point that in a well-managed portfolio project, students should realize that their effort is not simply to construct "a scrapbook of college course assignments and memorabilia" (p. 2). Instead, even in a "presentation" portfolio (which the authors distinguish from a "working" portfolio), the product is also a process and should be construed as an "organized documentation of growth and achievement that provides tangible evidence of the attainment of professional knowledge, skills, and dispositions. Each portfolio is goal-driven, original, and reflective" (p. 13).

Survey Responses

Citing responses from a survey administered to students in a teacher-certification program, Campbell et al. (2000) demonstrate how students evidently "became aware of the full range of benefits of portfolio work" (p. 14):

> Question: How have you benefited from the process of portfolio development?
>
> - *"It has helped me to build confidence in myself as an educator."*
> - *"Portfolio development has helped me to identify my strengths and weaknesses. . . ."*
> - *"I have become more aware of what future employers may be looking for. . . ."*
> - *"It is nice to be able to look back at everything I have accomplished throughout my college career."*
> - *"The portfolio has helped me become more organized. It has helped me set goals and achieve them. I have a basis for my future education."*
> - *"By having specific outcomes to accomplish I am able to see exactly what areas of preparation I need to work on. . . ."*
> - *"The development of the portfolio has helped me see the importance of my work."*
> - *"It made me strive to do my best work possible."*
> - *"It helped me see the value of the assignments that I have completed in my classes. I take away more meaning from my work."*
> - *"It has shown me how what I have learned all fits together."*
> - *"The portfolio development itself is a means of becoming professional. . . ."*
> - *"I feel a sense of accomplishment. . . . Being able to see your own growth and achievement is very exciting." (p. 15, from Dorothy M. Campbell et al., Portfolio and Performance Assessment in Teacher Education, published by Allyn and Bacon, Boston, MA. Copyright © 2000 by Pearson Education. Reprinted by permission of the publisher.)*

Other students speak their minds about the value of reflective portfolios just as convincingly. For this volume, three students from Agnes Scott College have contributed a creative piece formatted as a video interview produced for a portfolio assignment, and one of the students offers the following insights, revealing the utility of portfolio work in fostering mature thinking and judgment:

The development of my views of a liberal arts education and what it means to me, my future, and who I am did not even become clear to me until I began the process of reflection. As a part of the project, we wrote reflections on the entire three-month journey. . . . In fact, this very essay for this volume has allowed me to step back and view the project objectively. While writing, I have realized how the project has changed me. The process has been ongoing, and we have shown the video at orientation events, to friends and family, and as a part of a presentation on our work open to the campus. Each time I have presented the video and spoken about the process, my understanding of my learning has become more refined through reflection. (See "The E-portfolio and Liberal Arts Education at Agnes Scott College" in this volume.)

In my own practice, I employ reflective learning strategies in a number of ways, including asking students to engage regularly and meaningfully in reflective writing in an online threaded discussion and in the continuous development of a learning portfolio that is submitted at the end of the course. In the portfolio, students ultimately reflect on their reflections, write about their writing, and critically examine the progressive arc of their learning throughout the semester. An excerpt from the culminating reflections of Amanda Bowman, a highly motivated, nontraditional Columbia College honors student, underscores the value of such work in enhancing metacognition, in establishing a safe and mentored space for creativity and intellectual risk, and in promoting deep learning:

For me, the learning portfolio was more than a mere assignment in an English course; it was an illuminating coda—a review of how I learn. I found that my learning doesn't cease on completion of an assignment or class session but, instead, is an ongoing process that continues to evolve.

While compiling my work, I noticed a common thread that ran through my papers, online reflective writing forum entries, group projects, and class notes: this thread was metamorphosis, a change in my creative and critical thinking. The pages of my portfolio uncover the development of my ideas, the enhancement of my writing skills, and an enrichment of my learning repertoire.

I believe that this personal realization would not have been apparent without the assemblage of a portfolio. I have discovered that the utility of my portfolio is ongoing because it serves as a catapult for my continuing academic improvement. Thus, while the portfolio was the course's grand finale where all the components returned to the stage for curtain, the portfolio, in fact, continues to be called to the stage for encores. (Personal entry in learning portfolio, English 102, Spring 2008).

Undoubtedly, much more has happened to such students than the satisfaction of physically completing the task of collecting and organizing information, though their comments suggest appreciation for how the portfolio prepared them for standards assessment and future careers. The testimonies also reveal a profound sense of the value of reflective inquiry, the intrinsic merit of involving students in the power of reflection, the critically challenging act of thinking about their learning and making sense of the learning experience as a coherent, unified developmental process. Such thinking is the linchpin of lifelong, active learning, the key to helping students discover and understand what, how, and why they learn.

Embracing the efficacy of reflection in promoting significant learning, King (2002), of the University of Portsmouth, argues in a paper delivered at the 4th World Conference of the International Consortium for Educational Development in Higher Education that reflective learning strategies are fundamental to international reform efforts in higher education:

> *Due to the increasing importance of critical reflection as part of the key skills agenda in higher education in the UK, staff and students need to develop an awareness of the stages of reflection and how these may be employed to develop better quality reflective writing and more controlled and informed assessment of that writing if required. . . . The potential for reflection in facilitating learning and understanding in the more unstructured areas of knowledge domains, enabling students to tackle the "messy corners" of even the most structured domains, is one of its most powerful features. (pp. 1–2)*

King also reminds us that "the ability to reflect has been associated with the higher levels of learning in a number of taxonomies of learning objectives" (p. 2), a pivotal point also in the work of Fink (2003), whose seminal book, *Designing Courses for Significant Student Learning*, posits that the learning portfolio is an ideal approach to deepening students' learning.

The Importance of Reflective Inquiry

The crucial element of reflection is the key to marshaling the power of what I call "learning portfolios," and I will return to the theme in Chapter 3. I dwell on reflection precisely because of my emphasis on how reflective thinking and judgment are effective stimuli to deep, lasting learning. Certainly, such reflection is desirable in promoting better learning, but it is also challenging and painful, demanding a level of self-scrutiny, honesty, and disinterestedness that comes with great difficulty. As John Dewey (1910) proclaims:

Reflective thinking is always more or less troublesome because it involves overcoming the inertia that inclines one to accept suggestions at their face value; it involves willingness to endure a condition of mental unrest and disturbance. Reflective thinking, in short, means judgment suspended during further inquiry; and suspense is likely to be somewhat painful. . . . To maintain the state of doubt and to carry on systematic and protracted inquiry—these are the essentials of thinking. (p. 13)

Questions for Reflection in Portfolios

This book argues that the durable value of portfolios in improving student learning resides in engaging students not just in collecting representative samples of their work for assessment, evaluation, or career preparation but in addressing vital reflective questions that invite "systematic and protracted inquiry":

- What have I learned? Why did I learn?
- When have I learned? In what circumstances? Under what conditions?
- How have I learned or not, and do I know what kind of learner I am?
- How does what I have learned fit into a full, continual plan for learning?
- What difference has the learning made in my intellectual, personal, ethical, spiritual development?
- Has my learning been connected, integrated, coherent?
- Is my learning relevant, applicable, practical?
- When, how, and why has my learning surprised me?
- What have been the proudest highlights of my learning? The disappointments?
- What difference has mentoring in the portfolio process made in my learning?

Many more questions come to mind as one begins to fashion a strategy for reflection. Fink (2001), sharing a keen interest in learning portfolios, suggests:

[S]tudents may comment on the way they were challenged to analyze new ideas; or they may report on the excitement generated by mastering complex material; or they may describe how they came away from the class with a new, more positive attitude for the subject matter. In addition, the development of the learning portfolio may ask the students to address such personal issues as: "Was this class enjoyable, exciting, interesting?" or "How did this class relate to your personal beliefs and/or prior knowledge about the subject matter?" (p. 1)

Linking his innovative taxonomy of "higher-level learning" to his understanding of how learning portfolios facilitate metacognitive processes that lead to greater leaps in knowing how and why one has changed as a result of learning, Fink (2001) also provides an example of how carefully formulated questions can yield fruitful reflective learning in the case of students' internships:

> *I recently had occasion to interview a pair of students who had partici-pated in a summer internship in Washington, DC, and who were trying to prepare future interns. During the interview, I posed a series of ques-tions focused on each of the components.*
>
> 1. *During the time you were working as an intern, how did you change, in terms of*
>   - *What you care about differently now, than you did before?*
>   - *What actions you are capable of performing now?*
>   - *What you can connect or integrate now, that you could not before?*
>   - *Your ability to think about problems in political science?*
>   - *What you know?*
>
> 2. *What did you learn about*
>   - *The process of learning about politics?*
>   - *Interacting with other people?*
>   - *Yourself?*
>   - *Some of the major ideas you studied in political science?*
>   - *The phenomena involved (in this case, politics)?*
>
> *The answers from the two students were different from each other, very focused, and very rich. (pp. 127–128)*

In the context of a methods course, Yancey (1997) reports having student teachers respond to questions in portfolios structured to promote their reflections on their learning progress as prospective novice instructors:

- *"What have you learned so far in this class?"*
- *"Is this what you expected to learn?"*
- *"What else do you need to learn?"*
- *"How will you go about learning it?" (p. 252)*

Guiding students toward the metacognitive work necessary for higher-level composition and strong critical-thinking skills, Claywell (2001) begins nearly every section of her book on portfolios with directed questions for reflection on purpose, content, format, process, and evaluation of learning. Here are some examples, slightly modified to make them practical across a variety of disciplines:

- *How will your portfolio be used? Who is the audience for your portfolio? What is the role of that audience? (p. 1)*

- *What have you learned about the subject that you did not previously know? What have you discovered about your learning style? (p. 20)*

- *What are the best examples of your work for this project? The worst? Why? (p. 33)*

- *What do the pieces and the portfolio reflect overall about your learning? (p. 35)*

- *What new learning strategies have you adopted as a result of the portfolio process? (p. 43)*

- *What were the most difficult parts of the process? Why? (p. 49)*

- *In what ways do your reflections reveal what makes your portfolio unique? What specific features of the class were beneficial in your learning? Your personal voice? How do your reflections point to specific changes in the actual revisions in the portfolio? The improved knowledge you have gained? The growth you have made as a scholar? (p. 52)*

- *What has been meaningful about the portfolio process? (p. 65)*

What is particularly instructive and liberating about the questions suggested by Fink, Yancey, Claywell, and others who employ portfolio strategies in improving and assessing student learning is that the queries motivate students to professionalize their responses to the enterprise of education by taking seriously the underlying pedagogical as well as overt methodological reasons for learning. Attaining this professional, objective attitude toward learning is an important lesson in mature and critical thinking for all students. In a sense, students are empowered to know and make sense of the sources and outcomes of their learning, acquiring not just the skills necessary for effective learning and goal setting but essentially a habit of being, an approach to knowing and learning—indeed, to life itself—grounded in critical reflection.

Learning as Community

Such reflection is facilitated best not by leaving students individually to their own devices in thinking about their learning but by using the advantages of collaboration and mentoring in making learning community property. The idea here is not to suggest tactics that would violate personal and legal boundaries of privacy but rather to endorse the premise that learning is enhanced by recognizing its relational values, by helping students connect individual pieces of gained knowledge to a larger puzzle of learning with ever-widening intellectual, material, ethical, social, even spiritual implications. Deep, lasting learning is also relational in the sense that what students learn in the classroom ideally must relate sensibly to their felt lives, must provide avenues for them to connect the abstractions of academic pursuits to the realities of immediate experience. Dewey (1910), once again, provides us with the needed insight:

> *Instruction always runs the risk of swamping the pupil's own vital,*
> *though narrow, experience under masses of communicated material. The*
> *instructor ceases and the teacher begins at the point where communi-*
> *cated matter stimulates into fuller and more significant life that which*
> *has entered by the strait and narrow gate of sense-perception and motor*
> *activity. Genuine communication involves contagion; its name should*
> *not be taken in vain by terming communication that which produces no*
> *community of thought and purpose between the [student] and the race of*
> *which he is the heir. (p. 224)*

In other words, dissemination of facts and delivery of knowledge are acts of instruction that serve an important but hierarchically lower purpose in how we think and learn. Higher-order teaching and learning are the shared acts of a reflective discourse community, a dynamic collaborative of living ideas that transform both teacher and learner.

The relationship with an influential mentor adds the collaborative edge that makes the human difference in moving students (and teachers) along a continuum of learning. Collaborators and mentors—whether peers or teachers (either or both can be helpful catalysts in the process of developing portfolios)—are vital agents in moving students in the right direction toward more meaningful learning, toward knowledge and insights that they can relate to other academic discoveries and to other dimensions of their personal experiences. Recent developments in the available scholarship on student portfolios suggest that more educators are recognizing the acute importance of such reflection in portfolios, and happily, a trend toward emphasizing the reflective, process-oriented component of student portfolios (as opposed to its twin function of collecting selected samples of representative work for assessment) is emerging. I would add to the trend that reflection, an inherently private act, is sharpened by the positive influence of collaboration with a mentor in developing and reviewing a learning portfolio.

Campbell et al. (2000) agree that collaboration is important:

[S]tudents . . . left alone to do portfolio work . . . tend to focus on organizing and justifying documentation of what they have already done well. It takes encounters with peers, faculty facilitators, and members of the larger professional community to challenge progress toward growing and changing, setting new goals, and designing new strategies for professional development. . . . [T]he more collaborative portfolio work becomes, the greater the growth in meeting the standards [of higher-level learning]. (pp. ix–x)

But identifying portfolio mentors can be a significant hurdle. Should the coach be the teacher in a course? Should trained students be enlisted as peer mentors? Can professional or faculty advisers serve as guides? Can students developing electronic portfolios turn to technology staff for mentoring resources? Are there ways to use interactive technology tools to provide virtual opportunities for collaboration? The questions are many, but the answer to each is yes. Context, resources, purpose, and other factors all play a role in helping us figure out ways to connect students with knowledgeable, effective mentors who can assist them in cultivating substantive reflective judgment and the analytical skills needed to develop a purposeful, selective portfolio.

The Argument for Learning Portfolios

This book sheds further light on how and why the portfolio contributes to students' sophisticated learning by exploring how strategies of reflective practice, especially when conjoined with the supportive influence of mentoring, can be applied to improve and document student learning. Engaging students not only in collecting selected samples of their work for assessment, evaluation, and career development but also in continuous, collaborative reflection about the process of learning is a powerful complement to traditional measures of student achievement. In her book on learning journals, kin to the format and function of learning portfolios, Moon (1999) summarizes the various ways in which students benefit from reflective activity and organized assessment; she argues that journals (or portfolios, in my rephrasing) create "conditions that favour learning":

- *Portfolios demand time and intellectual space.*
- *The independent and self-directing nature of the process develops a sense of ownership of the learning in the learner.*

- *Portfolios focus attention on particular areas of, and demand the independent ordering of, thought.*

- *Portfolios often draw affective function into learning, and this can bring about greater effectiveness in learning.*

- *The ill-structured nature of the tasks involved in portfolio development challenges a learner and increases the sophistication of the learning process. (p. 34)*

Moon also suggests that creating frameworks such as learning portfolios for students to reflect progressively on their work provides

an opportunity for a range of forms of learning activities [such as] learning about self (self-development); learning to resolve uncertainty or to reach decisions; learning that brings about empowerment or emancipation. Sometimes the learning that arises from reflection may be unexpected. (p. 34)

Finally, she adds that learning journals or portfolios stimulate and support learning across diverse disciplines by encouraging "reflective thinking and writing, which are associated with deeper forms of learning and better learning outcomes" and by fostering the "metacognition . . . associated with expertise in learning" (p. 35).

Alan Wright, one of the chief players behind the formidable Career Portfolio program at Canada's Dalhousie University, offers apt testimony to the value of such reflective writing even when it is not ostensibly the main purpose of a student's portfolio: "Although the employment parlance is what gets us the grants to do our work at Dal, the practice shows that the reflective component is crucial to the success of the enterprise" (personal communication, July 26, 2001). Again, the crossover lessons of the teaching portfolio's premium on the "special power" of reflection apply to the learning portfolio (Seldin & Associates, 1993, p. 9).

In the next chapter, I will address some of the practical considerations involved in using student learning portfolios, such as the time involved, length, and content.

References

Arter, J. A., & Spandel, V. (1992). NCME instructional module: Using portfolios of student work in instruction and assessment. *Educational Measurement: Issues and Practice, 11*(1), 36–44.

Burch, C. B. (1997). Finding out what's in their heads: Using teaching portfolios to assess English education students—and programs. In K. B. Yancey & I. Weiser

(Eds.), *Situating portfolios: Four perspectives* (pp. 263–277). Logan: Utah State University Press.

Cambridge, B. L. (Ed.). (2001). *Electronic portfolios: Emerging practices in student, faculty, and institutional learning*. Washington, DC: American Association for Higher Education.

Campbell, D. M., Melenyzer, B. J., Nettles, D. H., & Wyman, R. M., Jr. (2000). *Portfolio and performance assessment in teacher education*. Boston: Allyn & Bacon.

Claywell, G. (2001). *The Allyn and Bacon guide to writing portfolios*. Boston: Allyn & Bacon.

Dewey, J. (1910). *How we think*. Boston: D. C. Heath.

Fink, L. D. (2001). Higher-level learning: The first step toward more significant learning. In D. Lieberman & C. Wehlburg (Eds.), *To improve the academy: Vol. 19. Resources for faculty, instructional, and organizational development* (pp. 113–130). Bolton, MA: Anker.

Fink, L. D. (2003). *Designing courses for significant student learning: Making dreams come true*. San Francisco: Jossey-Bass.

Gordon, R. (1994, May). Keeping students at the center: Portfolio assessment at the college level. *Journal of Experiential Education, 17*(1), 23–27.

King, T. (2002, July). *Development of student skills in reflective writing*. Paper presented at the 4th World Conference of the International Consortium for Educational Development in Higher Education (ICED), University of Western Australia, Perth.

Moon, J. A. (1999). *Learning journals: A handbook for academics, students and professional development*. New York: Routledge.

Seldin, P. (2004). *The teaching portfolio: A practical guide to improved performance and promotion/tenure decisions* (3rd ed.). Bolton, MA: Anker.

Seldin, P., & Associates. (1993). *Successful use of teaching portfolios*. Bolton, MA: Anker.

Wetzel, K., & Strudler, N. (2006). Costs and benefits of electronic portfolios in teacher education: Student voices. *Journal of Computing in Teacher Education, 22*(3), 69–78.

Wright, W. A., Knight, P. T., & Pomerleau, N. (1999). Portfolio people: Teaching and learning dossiers and innovation in higher education. *Innovative Higher Education, 24*(2), 89–103.

Yancey, K. B. (1997). Teacher portfolios: Lessons in resistance, readiness, and reflection. In K. B. Yancey & I. Weiser (Eds.), *Situating portfolios: Four perspectives* (pp. 244–262). Logan: Utah State University Press.

Chapter 2

Practical Questions and Issues About Student Learning Portfolios

THE NUMEROUS CONTRIBUTIONS IN PART 2 of this volume attest to the multiple approaches to engaging students in portfolio development. I would venture, however, a model that broadly approximates in the field of student learning what the teaching portfolio offers in the field of teaching performance. In the work of Shore et al. (1986); Edgerton, Hutchings, and Quinlan (1991); Seldin (2004); Zubizarreta (1994, 1995, 1997, 1999); Murray (1995); Hutchings (1998); and other advocates of portfolio strategies, the premium value of teaching portfolios is improvement through the continual process of reflection tied to mentoring, rigorous assessment, and documentation. Likewise, the primary motive of the learning portfolio is to improve student learning by providing a structure for students to reflect systematically over time on the learning process and to develop the aptitudes, skills, and habits that come from critical reflection. Following paradigms of learning found in Dewey's (1910), Kolb's (1984), Schön's (1983, 1987), King and Kitchener's (1994), or Brookfield's (1995) theories of reflection; Bloom's (1956) taxonomy of educational objectives; and Perry's (1970) or Fink's (2001, 2003) experimental models of "intellectual development" and "higher-level learning," such thinking about the process of learning forms the heart of the learning portfolio.

Sharing my values, Annis and Jones (1995) offer a brief definition of student portfolios: "A portfolio can be defined as a multidimensional, documented collection of . . . a . . . student's work put together in an organized way and including a reflective discussion of the materials contained in the portfolio" (pp. 181–182). I suggest the following definition that allows for proper flexibility across disciplinary purposes and designs:

The learning portfolio is a flexible, evidence-based tool that engages students in a process of continuous reflection and collaborative analysis of learning. As written text, electronic display, or other creative project, the portfolio captures the scope, richness, and relevance of students' intellectual development, critical judgment, and academic skills. The portfolio focuses on purposefully and collaboratively selected reflections and evidence for both improvement and assessment of students' learning.

Such a process is a rich, convincing, and adaptable method of recording intellectual growth and involving students in a critically reflective, collaborative process that augments learning as a community endeavor. If we can motivate students to focus on the process of their learning and not just on chalking up grades and credentials, they will find portfolio development challenging and rewarding. The payoff for students will come when they recognize that reflecting on and documenting their progress as learners reinforces the foundational elements of significant learning by teaching them to value formative feedback and to respond positively to incentives for progress. The portfolio, in effect, can help students transform gaps in learning into potential opportunities for improvement.

Time Commitment

Let's cut to the chase. Recognizing that both students and faculty will justifiably resist any methodology or instrument that is nothing more than an add-on to course activities and requirements, I issue a strong word of caution at the outset before pondering a model. As a teacher myself, I know time is a paramount issue. Learning portfolios must be an idea driven by philosophical and pedagogical goals integrated into a course in such a way to contribute qualitatively, not necessarily quantitatively, to the learning/teaching enterprise. Moon (1999) reinforces the message: "Time is an issue," for while learning portfolios create a positive "intellectual space for learners," the considerable time involved "is a major reason for the abandonment" of such projects (p. 79).

Length

Sensitive to the issue of time, I envision a model that is not an unwieldy repository of continually expanding artifacts and reflective commentaries, the type of student portfolio in which students are asked to collect scores of exhibits and write prescribed narratives, prompted by a standardized list of questions for each item. Instead, my sense is that less is better, especially if the portfolio author enlists the aid of a collaborative mentor who helps provide feedback in making decisions about purpose, content, format, and selectivity of appendix materials. The mentor might be an assigned or self-selected peer in a course, a veteran peer in a major or program, a teacher, an academic adviser, or a program director. The mentor is not so much an expert or evaluator as a collaborator who assists the author in identifying the rationale for selectivity of information and in carrying out a thoughtful plan for developing a succinct but sound portfolio that meets the learner's needs. One of the mentor's major responsibilities is to keep the portfolio manageable in size by pressing for concise, reflective narratives plus judiciously selected evidence in a series of appropriate hard-copy appendixes, digital files, Web links, or other means of archiving outcomes or products of student learning.

The parameter of a few narrative pages, plus appendixes, is obviously a flexible benchmark. In any case, the portfolio never outgrows its practical boundaries (whether in print, on disk, or online) for the sake of both the author and the designated audience, if any. In the instance of a portfolio created as a profile of learning over a long period of time, I recommend that as new materials are added, old ones are removed, keeping the act of revision active and refreshing, continually informing the learning process. Conceivably, an anthology of progressive drafts or a bank of smaller course portfolios could be assembled to form a substantive, revealing history of learning. Obviously, the capabilities of digital media easily lure both students and faculty into the trap of regarding the electronic environment as an inexhaustible repository for information, but that tendency can be paralyzing in the end. I offer a strong caution against size. Remember: less can be better, and carefully selected content, a clear purpose, and regular feedback and mentoring are essential.

Content

What are the contents of a learning portfolio? There is no right or complete answer. Portfolios vary in purpose, and different purposes determine the diverse contents. Generally, the learning portfolio I have in mind consists of a carefully reasoned, reflective narrative that, depending on purpose, captures the scope, progress, and value of learning, complemented by an equally representative compilation of concrete evidence. A popular alternative is a number of short reflections on separate or grouped items of evidence, though I prefer the coherence and unity of reflective analysis required in a single reflective statement and overview with keyed references (if paper) or Web links (if electronic) to evidence in an appendix or linked pages.

In Chapter 3, I discuss further the issue of evidence, providing representative examples of items that may be included in a portfolio, but here is a very generic table of contents that is organized by broad categories and that contains items that are certainly not prescriptive or exhaustive. This table of contents is meant to be suggestive, inviting multidisciplinary ideas of what the actual, complex contents of a student portfolio might be, remembering the caveat that purpose will drive final decisions about both reflection and documentation. Remember, too, that the organization and presentation of the contents may vary depending on whether the portfolio is on paper or in electronic form:

Table of Contents
1. *Reflections on Learning* (reflective narrative[s] on philosophy of learning, meaning of learning, value of learning, learning process, learning style)

2. *Achievements in Learning* (transcripts, course descriptions, résumés, honors, awards, internships, tutoring)

3. *Evidence of Learning, or Outcomes* (research papers, critical essays, field experience logs, creative displays/performances, data/spreadsheet analyses, course Listserv entries, lab reports)

4. *Assessment of Learning* (instructor feedback, course test scores, exit/board exams, lab/data reviews, research project results, practicum reports)

5. *Relevance of Learning* (practical applications, leadership experiences, relation of learning to personal and professional domains, ethical/moral growth, affiliations, hobbies, volunteering, affective value of learning)

6. *Learning Goals* (plans to enhance, connect, and apply learning; response to feedback; career ambitions)

7. *Appendixes* (selected documentation)

The general categories of this table of contents, again, are suggestive; each portfolio project will define specific content in different ways, depending on the purpose and learning objectives. But it is worth noting that the categories reflect a logical pattern, one that essentially mirrors sound practice for both improvement and assessment. The flow parallels this order of reflective analysis, complemented by documentation in the appendix:

- What, how, when, why did I learn?
- What have I accomplished with my learning?

- What products and outcomes do I have to demonstrate learning?
- What measures and accounting do I have of my learning?
- What difference has learning made in my life?
- What plans do I have to continue learning?
- How is the evidence of my learning integrated with my reflections and self-assessments in the portfolio?

A brief reflective section of just a few pages, plus appendixes, is a practical investment for the student, who benefits from the efficacy of portfolio development in bolstering learning. The teacher, too, gains a multifaceted means of appreciating, understanding, and assessing a student's learning. The portfolio may range from detailing specific gains made in a single course or designated part of a course to plotting a student's learning in an entire academic program.

The increasing popularity of electronic student portfolios naturally encourages us to rethink the criterion of length or the issue of content because of the awesome capability of the hypertext medium. The point is illustrated by a glance at some of the samples of digitized portfolios in this volume or at the proliferation of student portfolios on the Web (see several references in the "Selected Resources" section of Chapter 4 in this volume). Chapter 4 addresses some of the ways in which analog and digital technologies have contributed to new, exciting models of portfolio development, but even with the marvels of computerization, I emphasize again the cautionary note of keeping the portfolio process manageable and coherent, focused on meaningful reflection and selective evidence rather than on many pages of writing or overwhelming hyperlinks and flashy technical display.

A Model for the Learning Portfolio

Recognizing that student portfolios take many forms, depending on purpose and design (as the diverse summaries and examples included later in this volume demonstrate), I propose a rather simple model for the learning portfolio that is predicated on three fundamental components found also in teaching portfolios (Seldin, 2004):

- Reflection
- Documentation
- Collaboration

The result is a compact, strategically organized print or electronic document that evolves qualitatively to reflect the dynamic nature of engaged learning. Multiple revisions are encouraged as desirable spotlights on progress, each draft tightly structured and manageable, revealing over time a student's individual pattern of intellectual and personal growth. Drafts may be textual revisions, updated documentation, or redesigned Web pages, depending on the type of portfolio and disciplinary preferences, but the nature of ongoing reflection is fundamental to learning portfolios. Instructors need not provide lengthy feedback on each draft, but the insights gained into a student's progress offers teachers opportunities for better assessment and more positive influence on learning through closer mentoring. Hence, feedback, though time consuming, is key to the learning component of portfolio work, as Wetzel and Strudler (2006) indicate:

> *Although data suggest that components of the EP [electronic portfolio] process might be streamlined to be less time consuming, as Shulman (1998) reminds us, the fact remains that "portfolios done seriously take a long time" (p. 35). As could be expected, student comments about the amount of time they needed to devote to the electronic portfolio were frequent and emphatic. There were many complaints about the requirement to scan pupil work samples and the time required to upload lengthy documents. Other expenditures of time were met with more varied responses. Overall, it appears that one major variable that affects students' satisfaction with the process is the degree to which they received thoughtful feedback from faculty on their work. In many instances, students mentioned that the EP process—including meaningful assignments, thoughtful assessments, and subsequent student-faculty interaction—stretched their learning in significant ways. (p. 77)*

Feedback on drafts ensures that students know the teacher takes the portfolio seriously as a meaningful representation of progress in learning. If feedback on a portfolio—no matter whether brief or lengthy—is frequent, focused, and friendly, students will respond positively to the portfolio model.

Not at all prescriptive, then, the model obviously synthesizes the basic, sound elements of the many versions of student portfolio projects represented in Part 3, and it may be adapted in myriad ways to suit individual needs. Flexibility, of course, is key to learning, just as it is to portfolio development. Yancey (1997) underscores this point in her own reflections about her dynamic use of portfolios with teacher protégés in a methods class:

> *[If we think of it] as a professional text, we . . . lose the chance to learn from the portfolio what it can teach us: that the only way that it can teach us is by not being too rigid, too fixed, too . . . professional in its*

FIGURE 2.1

Graphic Model of a Learning Portfolio

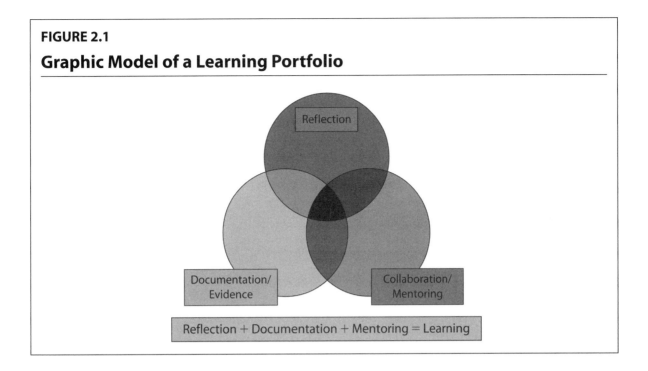

Reflection + Documentation + Mentoring = Learning

construction; that allowing freedom in it provide[s] one way for students' voices to be heard. . . ." (p. 259)

A learning portfolio that is flexible in design, goals, and outcomes; easily adaptable to a variety of disciplines and purposes; and available for constructive feedback and generous mentoring is a strong model. Figure 2.1 graphically conceptualizes a learning portfolio.

Notice in the simple model that maximum learning occurs when reflection, documentation, and collaborative mentoring come together in the center of the design. To be sure, learning occurs even when only one of the domains is activated. For example, a student may gain valuable insight into the quality of a learning experience solely by the private act of thinking critically about his or her progress; by simply gathering and organizing available artifacts or evidence; or by reaping the benefits of collaboration and mentoring inherent in accepting another's challenging insights and perspectives.

When any two of the components of the educational process are tapped, the potential for better learning increases. Hence, the student who joins reflection with evidence to think about how completed work reveals a pattern of positive learning capitalizes on the best features of portfolio designs that combine exhibits of learning with reflective statements about achievements and goals. The student who partners with a peer or faculty mentor to take advantage of directed discourse and feedback about his or her own reflections benefits from the virtues of collaboration in building a learning community.

Arguably, the student who pulls all three domains together stands a greater chance of transforming an incidental learning activity into a deeper, enduring learning process. By providing a structure that is essentially an act of communication—that is, an investment in learning as community— the learning portfolio concept, primarily through the powerful agency of reviewed work, facilitates students' active engagement of the three crucial domains.

Moon (1999, p. 35) offers a much more elaborate and visually complex model of the reflective learning process, and her concept map is a useful complement to the simplicity of the tripartite figure. King (2002) reaffirms Moon's model and adds the following:

> *Students may embark on pieces of reflective writing for many reasons[:] professional portfolio entries, in learning journals or logs or workbooks, as part of personal or professional profiles, for evaluating project work in dissertations, or specifically as part of directed assessments. As a result of reflection a variety of outcomes can be expected, for example, development of a theory, the formulation of a plan of action, or a decision or resolution of some uncertainty. Such outcomes would be likely as a result of some problem-solving activity. In addition, students may experience emotions, leading to self-development, empowerment, and knowledge about their own feelings and emotions. Finally reflection might well provide material for further reflection, and most importantly, lead to learning and, perhaps, reflection on the process of learning. (p. 2)*

King (p. 6) further summarizes Moon's work and offers a simplified version of her diagram of the reflective learning process, as shown in Figure 2.2.

Moon's (1999) design maps a course from initial reflection to resolution, but I would add another step—collaborative mentoring—accounting for the influence of consultation with a mentor (a teacher, course or program peer, senior student, or academic adviser, for instance) who can create a significant spark for reflective learning.

The Power of Writing and Learning Portfolios

The engine that drives much of the success of the learning portfolio and many other strategies of collaborative and cooperative learning, active learning, classroom assessment techniques, problem-based learning, and reflective practice is the power of writing. Moon (1999), relying on key

FIGURE 2.2

Reflective Learning Process

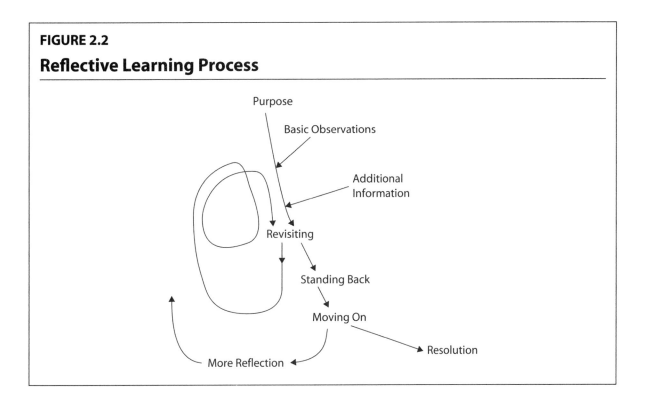

ideas from several sources in the vast literature on process rhetoric and composition, underscores the ways in which writing is "a powerful way of learning":

- *Writing forces time to be taken for reflection.*
- *Writing forces learners to organize and to clarify their thoughts in order to sequence in a linear manner. In this way they reflect on and improve their understanding.*
- *Writing causes learners to focus their attention. It forces activity in the learner.*
- *Writing helps learners to know whether or not they understand something. If they cannot explain it, they probably cannot understand it.*
- *Along similar lines, being asked to write the explanation of something can encourage a deep approach to learning in the manner that the learner anticipates the quality of understanding required for the writing.*
- *Writing an account of something enables the writer to talk about it more clearly.*
- *Writing captures ideas for later consideration.*
- *Writing sets up a "self-provided feedback system."*
- *Writing can record a train of thought and relate it in past, present and future.*

- *The process of writing is creative, and develops new structures. It can be enjoyable.*
- *The pace of writing slows the pace of thinking and can thereby increase its effectiveness. (p. 31)*

Elbow's (1998a, 1998b) formidable work on the integral connections between writing and learning has helped spawn many clever phrases, such as "write to learn" or "think write," the common slogans of composition and rhetoric programs; his scholarship in the field lends sufficient authority to the theoretical assumption that writing is a productive form of thinking and learning. But Elbow's achievement is only one contribution to the movement that has linked writing to thinking and learning. Light (2001), too, has reiterated the strong connection between writing and learning: "The relationship between the amount of writing for a course and students' level of engagement . . . is stronger than the relationship between students' engagement and any other course characteristic" (p. 55).

As an engaged process of learning, the writing that anchors portfolio development—whether the portfolio is a text document, creative project, or Web site with multiple hypertext links—stimulates in the learner not only the conventional aspects of invention, composition, and revision inherent in writing with a purpose but also the complex dimensions of selecting representative samples of one's work, thinking about how and why such information reveals higher-level learning, maintaining currency and vitality in the compilation of materials, and evaluating the relevance and significance of such work. Weiser (1997), focusing on portfolios designed to improve and assess students' writing abilities, adds:

> *Portfolios allow us to consider the writing process in a broader context than the familiar planning, drafting, revising, editing concept of process does. While revision is an inherent part of portfolio approaches, the decision to use portfolios as the means of evaluating students' writing ability and development extends the process to include additional decision-making conditions: the* collection *of writing,* reflection *about that writing, the* selection *of pieces to be further revised for the final evaluation, the* revision *of those pieces, and finally their* evaluation. *Each of these, often overlapping practices, contributes to both students' and teachers' extended understanding of what it means to write. (p. 296)*

Many writing teachers have held tight to such ideas, including, representatively, Emig (1971, 1977), Hayes and Flower (1980a, 1980b), Lindemann

(1982), Hillocks (1995), and Bean (1996). But the foundation established by the composition and rhetoric revolution of the past few decades is equally applicable to other disciplines. The variety of ways in which writing can be used as a tool for disciplinary learning has been at the front of writing-across-the-curriculum programs, and some innovative approaches are described and shared in summaries and models included later in this volume. Such exciting developments in the use of writing for learning across disciplinary lines have been instrumental in triggering and valorizing the numerous pedagogies that rely on writing as a vehicle for reflection, as a structure for learning in a variety of disciplines.

Tips for Managing the Portfolio Process

Already, my readers—faculty, advisers, administrators, students who are all very busy, overcommitted people—are feeling the anxiety of jumping into a portfolio project that seems overwhelming. The good news is that there are steps we can take to control the process as a reasonable endeavor. Burrell, Miners, Nantz, and Torosyan, in this volume, suggest positive ways of implementing a portfolio program without unfortunate, burdensome mistakes. Also, here is a checklist of brief tips that provide some reassurances that the beneficial work that goes into portfolio development can be manageable, especially if we are sensible and realistic in implementation and if we put into place the right kinds of personal, pedagogical, and institutional support needed for success:

- Start slow and small. Some ideas: pilot portfolios in one class; count the portfolio as a portion of a course grade, instead of using it as the sole evaluation; offer simple individual feedback such as check marks on selected portfolio assignments and brief comments; substitute the portfolio for the final exam.
- Streamline feedback. Focus on purposeful items, don't try to respond to all dimensions of a portfolio, and collect a digital bank of common responses for reuse.
- Think of the portfolio as qualitatively different work, not necessarily more work, when designing a course syllabus, assignments, and assessment strategies.
- Use technology. Most Web course management tools include handy feedback and assessment systems.
- Develop scoring rubrics to help make feedback and grading processes clearer and more efficient.

- Large classes? Offer feedback on a schedule to rotating groups; respond to randomly selected individuals throughout the term until all have received at least one communication about their work; rely on structured peer feedback.
- Do you have your own teaching portfolio? You should! The principles, methods, and valuable benefits applicable to your portfolio will help you design an equally powerful and manageable learning portfolio project for students.
- Be careful, clear, and deliberate in planning a portfolio project; have explicit goals, objectives, due dates, length, and assessment criteria. Save time by being organized.
- Incorporate portfolio work into other work in a course—as drafting for a graded paper, project, or lab report, for example. Let the portfolio serve double duty. The majority of the content items in a capstone portfolio should be work that has already been done and graded.

Are the time, effort, work, and mentoring that go into a sound portfolio project worthwhile? A student perspective, offered by Diana Lynde, a Columbia College student who completed a learning portfolio in a first-year literature course, is the best answer:

> *My learning portfolio served as an outlet for me to examine and express my individual growth—in fact, even reflecting on my reflections in my portfolio helped me make further connections. I saw improvement on two levels while working on my portfolio. First, while the lack of a detailed, step-by-step assignment frustrated me, I learned to combine my instructor's assignment with my own experiences and narrow my backwards glance to lessons, experiences, and information that stimulated my growth. The other, more significant area I developed in was the very goal of the learning portfolio—self-reflection. I learned to create links, build connections, and cement my knowledge by taking a step back, much like looking away from the individual links in a puzzle to view it in its entirety. My portfolio stands as a lasting relic of the growth I experienced as a learner and a lasting reminder to take learning a step further to make deeper, more fulfilling connections. (Personal entry in learning portfolio, English 102, Spring 2008)*

More of Diana's reflections about specific activities and assignments in the course are included in Part 3 of this volume. Her *intro*spective and *retro*spective reflections on her learning are inspiring enough to share with other students (and teachers) who wonder why and how learning portfolios make a difference in promoting lasting, significant learning.

References

Annis, L., & Jones, C. (1995). Student portfolios: Their objectives, development, and use. In P. Seldin & Associates, *Improving college teaching* (pp. 181–190). Bolton, MA: Anker.

Bean, J. C. (1996). *Engaging ideas: The professor's guide to integrating writing, critical thinking, and active learning in the classroom.* San Francisco: Jossey-Bass.

Bloom, B. S. (Ed.). (1956). *Taxonomy of educational objectives, handbook 1: Cognitive domain.* New York: Longman.

Brookfield, S. D. (1995). *Becoming a critically reflective teacher.* San Francisco: Jossey-Bass.

Dewey, J. (1910). *How we think.* Boston: D. C. Heath.

Edgerton, R., Hutchings, P., & Quinlan, K. (1991). *The teaching portfolio: Capturing the scholarship in teaching.* Washington, DC: American Association for Higher Education.

Elbow, P. (1998a). *Writing with power: Techniques for mastering the writing process* (2nd ed.). New York: Oxford University Press.

Elbow, P. (1998b). *Writing without teachers* (2nd ed.). New York: Oxford University Press.

Emig, J. A. (1971). *The composing processes of twelfth graders* (NCTE Research Report No. 13). Urbana, IL: National Council of Teachers of English.

Emig, J. A. (1977). Writing as a mode of learning. *College Composition and Communication, 28,* 122–128.

Fink, L. D. (2001). Higher-level learning: The first step toward more significant learning. In D. Lieberman & C. Wehlburg (Eds.), *To improve the academy: Vol. 19. Resources for faculty, instructional, and organizational development* (pp. 113–130). Bolton, MA: Anker.

Fink, L. D. (2003). *Designing courses for significant student learning: Making dreams come true.* San Francisco: Jossey-Bass.

Hayes, J. R., & Flower, L. S. (1980a). The dynamics of composing: Making plans and juggling constraints. In L. W. Gregg & E. R. Steinbert (Eds.), *Cognitive processes in writing* (pp. 31–50). Hillsdale, NJ: Lawrence Erlbaum Associates.

Hayes, J. R., & Flower, L. S. (1980b). Identifying the organization of writing processes. In L. W. Gregg & E. R. Steinbert (Eds.), *Cognitive processes in writing* (pp. 3–30). Hillsdale, NJ: Lawrence Erlbaum Associates.

Hillocks, G., Jr. (1995). *Teaching writing as reflective practice: Integrating theories.* New York: Teachers College Press.

Hutchings, P. (Ed.). (1998). *The course portfolio: How faculty can examine their teaching to advance practice and improve student learning.* Washington, DC: American Association for Higher Education.

King, P., & Kitchener, K. (1994). *Developing reflective judgment.* San Francisco: Jossey-Bass.

King, T. (2002, July). *Development of student skills in reflective writing.* Paper presented at the 4th World Conference of the International Consortium for Educational Development in Higher Education (ICED), University of Western Australia, Perth.

Kolb, D. (1984). *Experiential learning as the science of learning and development.* Englewood Cliffs, NJ: Prentice Hall.

Light, R. J. (2001). *Making the most of college: Students speak their minds.* Cambridge, MA: Harvard University Press.

Lindemann, E. (1982). *A rhetoric for writing teachers.* New York: Oxford University Press.

Moon, J. A. (1999). *Learning journals: A handbook for academics, students and professional development.* New York: Routledge.

Murray, J. P. (1995). *Successful faculty development and evaluation: The complete teaching portfolio* (ASHE-ERIC Higher Education Report No. 8). Washington, DC: George Washington University.

Perry, W. G. (1970). *Forms of intellectual and ethical development in the college years: A scheme.* New York: Holt, Rinehart, & Winston.

Schön, D. (1983). *The reflective practitioner: How professionals think in action.* New York: Basic Books.

Schön, D. (1987). *Educating the reflective practitioner: Toward a new design for teaching and learning in the professions.* San Francisco: Jossey-Bass.

Seldin, P. (2004). *The teaching portfolio: A practical guide to improved performance and promotion/tenure decisions* (3rd ed.). Bolton, MA: Anker.

Shore, B., Foster, S., Knapper, C., Nadeau, G., Neill, N., & Sim, V. (1986). *The teaching dossier: A guide to its preparation and use* (Rev. ed.). Ottawa, ON: Canadian Association of University Teachers.

Shulman, L. (1998). Teacher portfolios: A theoretical activity. In N. Lyons (Ed.), *With portfolio in hand: Validating the new teacher professionalism* (pp. 23–37). New York: Teachers College Press.

Weiser, I. (1997). Revising our practices: How portfolios help teachers learn. In K. B. Yancey & I. Weiser (Eds.), *Situating portfolios: Four perspectives* (pp. 293–301). Logan: Utah State University Press.

Wetzel, K., & Strudler, N. (2006). Costs and benefits of electronic portfolios in teacher education: Student voices. *Journal of Computing in Teacher Education, 22*(3), 69–78.

Yancey, K. B. (1997). Teacher portfolios: Lessons in resistance, readiness, and reflection. In K. B. Yancey & I. Weiser (Eds.), *Situating portfolios: Four perspectives* (pp. 244–262). Logan: Utah State University Press.

Zubizarreta, J. (1994). Teaching portfolios and the beginning teacher. *Phi Delta Kappan, 76*(4), 323–326.

Zubizarreta, J. (1995). Using teaching portfolio strategies to improve course instruction. In P. Seldin & Associates, *Improving college teaching* (pp. 167–179). Bolton, MA: Anker.

Zubizarreta, J. (1997). Improving teaching through portfolio revisions. In P. Seldin, *The teaching portfolio: A practical guide to improved performance and promotion/ tenure decisions* (2nd ed., pp. 167–179). Bolton, MA: Anker.

Zubizarreta, J. (1999). Evaluating teaching through portfolios. In P. Seldin & Associates, *Changing practices in evaluating teaching* (pp. 162–182). Bolton, MA: Anker.

Chapter 3

Important Factors in Developing and Using Student Learning Portfolios

THE MODEL I have proposed for the learning portfolio stresses the interplay among the three vital elements of reflection, evidence, and collaboration or mentoring. As we design portfolio projects for our students that combine the three cornerstones of sound portfolio construction, we should remember that sustaining the process of developing and revising the portfolio is the power of writing as a corollary to thinking and learning as well as a creative and facilitative activity for recording, assessing, improving, and evaluating learning.

The learning portfolio, therefore, consists of written narrative sections in which the student reflects critically about essential questions of what, when, how, and why learning has occurred. In the course of such introspective analysis, the student is guided to think further about how specific acts of learning—for instance, a seminar or lab course, a special writing assignment in a class, a long-term undergraduate research project, a field experience or internship, an interdisciplinary core, or an honors program of study—have contributed to a coherent, developmental, interrelated process of learning. Reflective writing, in other words, is an instrumental feature of effective portfolios for learning.

Reflection

I point out that in the extensive literature about teaching portfolios, critical reflection is cited repeatedly as the main stimulus to improvement of practice. While the teaching portfolio is widely implemented as a "relevant, valid, useful component of a teaching evaluation system" (Zubizarreta, 1999, p. 164), the primary benefit of professional portfolio development is improvement, a chief motivation for "engaging in the reflection and documentation that [compose] a portfolio" (Seldin, Annis, & Zubizarreta, 1995,

p. 60). Such enhancement of teaching performance occurs as a result of the mentoring and systematic self-analysis that characterize the process of reflection in writing a reliable and valid portfolio. Seldin (1997), the leading voice on teaching portfolios, captures the message of the power of reflection: "In truth, one of the most significant parts of the portfolio is the faculty member's self-reflection on his or her teaching. Preparing it can help professors unearth new discoveries about themselves as teachers" (p. 8).

Similarly, learning portfolios emphasize that students' knowledge and, more significantly, their understanding of how and why such knowledge fits into a larger framework of cognitive and emotional development are fundamentally connected to the opportunities that they have to reflect critically on their education. Learning portfolios help students "unearth new discoveries about themselves" as learners.

Moon (2005) underlines the importance of reflection in deep learning:

Reflection is not just an "add-on-extra" to academic learning, but it is an essential component of good quality learning and the representation of that learning. Reflection seems to be a part of the kinds of learning in which learners try to understand material that they encounter and to relate it to what they already knew. Relating new material to what one knows already may mean reflecting on what one knows and modifying it (deep approach). Reflection does not seem to have a role in the learning in which learners try just to retain new information without creating deep links with the new ideas (surface approach). Reflection will also be involved in the process of representing learning—when, for example, a learner's understanding is tested in a format that demands reprocessing of the ideas (e.g., an essay). . . . So reflection is a fundamental feature of a deeper approach to learning. (p. 2)

But students do not automatically know how to reflect; they may lack the skills of reflection, or they may confuse reflective inquiry with untempered emotional unloading. Brookfield's (1995) guidelines for his students' learning journals are excellent reminders of how important it is to approach the use of such learning tools carefully and to be deliberate and clear in expressing expectations to students. Moon (2005) issues similar cautions:

There are some things to think about when asking students to reflect. Some academic colleagues may not understand what place reflective activities have within the curriculum.

Some students will not understand what you want them to do. They will be unused to being asked to process information that is not from a book or given by a lecturer and they may be uneasy about the use of the first person in an academic context. . . . A means of overcoming this seems to be to introduce reflection as a two-part process. Initially students are helped to understand what they should do in a reflective task. Later, when they are at least managing descriptive reflection, they are helped to deepen their reflection to levels from which greater value will develop. A series of exercises will help with both of these stages. (pp. 2–3)

Perry (1997) also warns:

Most importantly, the purpose and audience of any portfolio must be explicit. Moreover, the purpose must be meaningful to the students. All students do not have to assemble portfolios for the same purposes and audiences, but all must have explicit rubrics for scoring. (p. 188)

Rubrics and Assessment of Reflective Learning and Portfolios

Examples of the rubrics mentioned by Perry are shared in Part 4 of this volume, and Campbell, Melenyzer, Nettles, and Wyman (2000, pp. 128–133) offer handy checklists. More evaluation models are found in Martin-Kniep's (1999) book on professional portfolios and in Barrett's (2000) "Evaluating the Electronic Portfolio" section in her online essay "Electronic Portfolios = Multimedia Development + Portfolio Development: The Electronic Portfolio Development Process" (www.electronicportfolios.org/portfolios/EPDevProcess.html#eval). Here are some additional resources on rubrics that are helpful to learning portfolio projects:

- Authentic Assessment Toolbox: http://jonathan.mueller.faculty.noctrl.edu/toolbox. Scroll to "Rubrics" button.
- TLT Group page on rubrics: www.tltgroup.org/resources/flashlight/rubrics.htm.
- University of Wisconsin–Stout's rubrics for assessment: www.uwstout.edu/soe/profdev/rubrics.shtml.
- Rubric for critical thinking: www.insightassessment.com/pdf_files/rubric.pdf.
- For PowerPoint presentations, but adaptable to other uses: www.cgu.edu/pages/762.asp.
- Templates for rubrics: http://rubistar.4teachers.org.
- Andrade, H. G. (2000, February). Using rubrics to promote thinking and learning. *Educational Leadership, 57*(5). See www.ascd.org (follow the "Publications" link to "Educational Leadership" and then to "Archived Issues").
- The following pieces are available at http://pareonline.net: Mertler, C. A. (2001). *Designing scoring rubrics for your classroom;* Moskal, B. M. (2001).

Scoring rubrics: What, when and how?; Moskal, B. M. (2003). *Recommendations for developing classroom performance assessments and scoring rubrics.*

- Nuhfer, E. (2004, October). Developer's diary: Why rubrics? Educating in fractal patterns IX. *National Teaching & Learning Forum* 13(6). See www. ntlf.com.
- Ohio Learning Network, "CourseCheck" Resource Bank: www.oln.org/ teaching_and_learning/coursecheck/resourcebank.php. Includes rubrics to assess Seven Principles of Good Practice. See Principles 2, 4, 5, and 6.
- Illinois Community College Board's *Preparing Technology-Proficient Educators in Illinois:* www.iccb.state.il.us/pt3/res/link.html. Scroll to "Information on Rubrics."

The clarity and useful guidance provided by such detailed expectations and evaluation criteria promote more focused, substantive reflection in students. Without such planning and precision from their teachers, students will have a reduced chance of embracing the challenges and rewards of reflective practice.

Drawing from a portfolio project she helped implement among K–12 instructors, D'Aoust (1992) points out that although many teachers "considered reflection to be a critical component of using portfolios, they also discovered that it was the most difficult 'to teach.' The difficulty was that most students lacked a vocabulary enabling reflection" (p. 44). D'Aoust further reveals how the teachers "found that, in order to initiate and sustain student reflection, they needed to structure specific questions for the students" (p. 44). The following are some examples from D'Aoust's account, freely modified to suggest how such prompts can be used across disciplines for students' self-analysis of their development as learners:

- How am I doing on this lab report or paper assignment?
- Where am I headed in this statistical summary and analysis?
- How does this piece of writing compare with my other writing?
- How did I sustain my interest in collecting this data?
- Did collaborating with peers or with my instructor help me better achieve the learning goals of my practicum?
- How would I describe my progress as a learner in my major, and what evidence can I give in my portfolio?
- Where do I need help as a learner in my chosen field?
- How can a peer mentor or the teacher assist me in becoming a better learner?

D'Aoust's samples are easily adapted to other disciplinary areas, and the underlying advantage of designing such probes in any context is that students begin to develop a vocabulary of reflection, a means for communicating to themselves, to each other, and to external evaluators the individual character and progress of their learning.

Brookfield's (1995) instructions and questions on keeping a learning journal are worth sharing at length, too:

> *The purpose of this journal . . . will give you some insight into your own emotional and cognitive rhythms as a learner. By this, I mean that you will become more aware of how you go about organizing your learning, what kinds of learning tasks you are drawn to, what teaching styles you find most congenial, what tasks you resist and seek to avoid, what conditions encourage you to take risks in learning. . . . If you'd like some structure to help you with the first few weeks' entries, try writing a few lines in response to the following questions:*
>
> - *What have I learned this week about myself as a learner?*
> - *What have I learned this week about my emotional responses to learning?*
> - *What were the highest emotional moments in my learning activities this week?*
> - *What were the lowest emotional moments in my learning activities this week?*
> - *What learning tasks did I respond to most easily this week?*
> - *What learning tasks gave me the greatest difficulties this week?*
> - *What was the most significant thing that happened to me as a learner this week?*
> - *What learning activity or emotional response most took me by surprise this week?*
> - *Of everything I did this week in my learning, what would I do differently if I had to do it again?*
> - *What do I feel proudest about regarding my learning activities this week?*
> - *What do I feel most dissatisfied with regarding my learning activities this week? (pp. 97–98)*

After stating how important it is to give students clear guidelines and ample practice in critical reflection to ensure sound assessment of reflective portfolios, Moon (2005) offers the following list of best-practice strategies before launching into portfolio work:

> - *Express the role of reflection in the learning outcomes for the module or the programme outcomes for the programme (in the programme specification).*

- *Think about the purpose of reflection—and the purpose will guide the writing of learning outcomes and will be a basis for writing assessment criteria.*

- *Think about your strategy for assessment before you give the work to students and tell them not only that the work will be assessed, but how it will be assessed, i.e., the criteria that will be used.*

- *Think, in particular, about whether you are concerned with developing students' ability to reflect or the product of the reflection. If it is the latter, then you can assess by many of the standard means—essay, examination, etc.*

- *If you are concerned about students' learning to reflect, then you will need to assess their ability to reflect—and to think about the criteria that express this. You may need to think about the depth of the reflective activity, for example.*

- *Provide students with examples of reflective writing and encourage them to evaluate what learning is being gained through the process. (p. 3)*

Brookfield, Moon, and others are communicating to students that getting beyond the acquisition of presumably known facts to questioning received knowledge and then to self-examining the complex epistemological process involved in knowing ourselves and our world is the hallmark of critical thinking, higher-order learning, and reflective judgment. The learning portfolio, installed in any of its numerous print or electronic manifestations in a student's educational progress, provides a vehicle for such practiced reflection.

Assessing the value of such reflection is not easy, and both faculty and students struggle with knowing what difference reflection makes in learning. Keeping a systematic stream of frequent, immediate, open, and constructive feedback flowing in a portfolio project is essential in providing both teacher and student (and administrators using portfolio data for institutional purposes) with the kind of information that records and showcases the value-added features of portfolio development. Documented feedback—leading to improvement, coupled with practical application of rubrics and other scoring mechanisms—can yield specific results useful in assessment and evaluation programs. More importantly, students themselves, as principal agents in the process of investigating the impact of reflective practice in deep learning, see their own growth and opportunities for development.

Other means of measuring the role and worth of reflective practice in producing significant learning include well-tested instruments that either directly or indirectly capture students' dispositions for and skill levels in critical reflection. None is the magic bullet that we look for in providing hard data about the value of reflection, but a combination of elements from such standard instruments may be useful. Some examples are the Myers-Briggs Type Indicator, Sociomoral Reflection Measure, Measure of Intellectual Development, Watson-Glaser Critical Thinking Appraisal, Cornell Critical Thinking Test, Measure of Epistemological Reflection, Reflective Judgment Interview, and others. A good review of such resources, including discussion of the relationship between reflection and critical thinking, is found in King and Kitchener (1994, pp. 75–123). Also, a useful article by Baxter Magolda (2001) lends insight into the ongoing research on assessing reflective learning, emphasizing that assessing reflection and students' overall cognitive development is a constructivist project that challenges positivist approaches to data collection. Reflection is hard. Measuring reflection is harder.

Evidence and Outcomes of Learning

Complementing portions of reflective narrative, an appendix of documentary materials balances the portfolio by providing concrete evidence of the student's claims, descriptions, analyses, and reflections. The narrative must include methodical references throughout to documentary materials in the appendix, linking reflection and evidence in a sound representation of the extent, meaning, and value of a student's learning. If, in the course of the reflective narrative, a student suggests gained mastery of a specific skill or aspect of disciplinary content, then a keyed reference to evidence in a corresponding appendix will substantiate what the student has learned. In an electronic portfolio, the reference would be a hypertext link.

No matter the medium of expression, the benefit to the student is an opportunity to engage in self-examination of what has been learned in an assignment, a course, or a program; how it has been applied; why the learning has been valuable; and to what extent the product of learning meets educational standards and goals. The combination of reflection and documentation encourages the student to articulate the core aims of portfolio development:

- Engaging students in a process of inquiry into what they have learned
- Providing students with a model for demonstrating the outcomes of learning
- Establishing a reflective learning environment that helps students go beyond accumulating knowledge to analyzing how, when, and why they have learned
- Promoting thinking about what lies ahead for improvement and future learning

The process of such reflection tied to evidence promotes a sophisticated, mature learning experience that closes the assessment loop from assertion, to demonstration, to analysis, to evaluation, to goals. Such coherence between reflective narrative and materials in the appendix is necessary to stem the potential influence of what Weiser (1997) calls the "schmooze" and "glow" of reflective writing that can skew—in either positive or negative ways—the authenticity of portfolio work (pp. 300–301).

The problems uncovered by Weiser's shrewd analysis are real and common enough to merit some attention here. A portfolio system—relying heavily on qualitative information and on a student's ability to communicate meaningful gains in learning—can easily lose sight of substance. One cause of resistance to implementing student portfolios (the same is true of faculty teaching portfolios) is the complaint that portfolios too easily risk the shine of rhetoric, the potentially blinding effect of persuasive writing, solicitous tone, and perhaps invented achievement. The portfolio may even fabricate the prized outcome of improvement based on falsely engineered products that seemingly detail progress from lesser to greater skills and accomplishments. I have mentored many faculty in developing teaching portfolios, and I have heard the same suspicions about faculty portfolios as ongoing displays of professional improvement. Faculty might ask, "Why articulate lofty, challenging goals when one can set sights lower and demonstrate progress by leaps and bounds?" Students might ask, "Why do my best on an essay assignment or lab project when I can ratchet down a first effort and then produce a much better final endeavor?"

Brookfield (1995) points out yet another fascinating possibility that may happen inadvertently when learning portfolios stress the importance of reflection and students misinterpret the message to mean that they must find ways to hype their self-reporting:

> Student journals, portfolios, and learning logs are all the rage among teachers who advocate experiential methods. Teachers believe that encouraging students to speak personally and directly about their experiences honors and encourages their authentic voices. That this often happens is undeniable. However, journals, portfolios, and logs also have the potential to become ritualistic and mandated confessionals . . . the educational equivalents of the tabloidlike, sensationalistic outpourings of talk show participants. (p. 13)

Such mixed messages are a tricky problem in setting up requirements for a learning portfolio project, and the teacher must be fully aware of students' difficulty in navigating between the "risks of denial and distortion," as Brookfield (1995, p. 33) puts it, and the transformative and liberating benefits of critical reflection. Add to such suspicions and predicaments the fear of how writing skills, glitzy covers and formats, or the digital enhancements of Web pages, presentation software, or CD-ROM technology can color the fair, objective assessment of portfolios, and it is easy to see why some resistance occurs.

The obstacles mentioned here are addressed by the nonnegotiable requirement that learning portfolios must consist of more than the reflective narrative, even though reflection forms the core of the process. Reflective thought must be tied to real evidence, a lesson Brookfield (1995) takes on in a much broader, polemical context, arguing finally that "reflection in and of itself is not enough: it must always be linked to how the world can be changed" (p. 217). In his definition of critical reflection as it applies to improvement of teaching, Brookfield outlines four lenses available to the critically reflective practitioner for viewing and analyzing a teacher's individual performance and hegemonic assumptions about the teaching enterprise: autobiographical reflection, students' eyes, colleagues' perceptions and experiences, and theoretical literature.

Without much force, we can apply virtually the same principles to the successful use of learning portfolios. Students, exactly like faculty, easily buy into the hegemony of improvement—that is, into the collectively accepted notion that what matters most in assessment and evaluation of learning and teaching is the extent to which we can demonstrate positive, ongoing progress and growth. While the principle is admirable and sound in many ways, both students and teachers must guard against the subtle lure to concentrate on reflecting about the outcome of change without critically examining the nature and worth of change itself. Learners must ask themselves key questions about the assumed value of improvement:

- Was change necessary?
- What process did I use to facilitate change?
- How has change affected the way I work?
- Why was the change desirable?
- What evidence do I have that I am a better learner because of change?

The skeptical posture of such reflection goes beyond simply meeting imperatives of improvement. Having critically questioned the very foundation of an assumption that undergirds even this volume—the assumption that reflective inquiry is at the heart of higher-level learning and portfolio development—the practiced reflective learner realizes that a creditable learning portfolio depends on purposefully selected, collaboratively reviewed, and diverse documentation for complete efficacy. To borrow Brookfield's metaphor, we need multiple lenses through which to view and understand the phenomenon of learning, necessitating, among other things, clear, detailed, and thoughtful documentation.

As I suggested earlier in this chapter, the documentation in the appendix is the leveler needed to stem hesitations about the undue influence of form over content. Students clever enough to manufacture work of lesser quality to play against improved work later cannot hide the eventual truth of their actual skill levels within the context of a carefully mentored, collaboratively developed, and diverse compilation of exhibits tied to reflective commentary and judgment. The more angles from which we view learning, the better we see it, and that is the virtue of collaborative portfolio development.

Selectivity

The concrete evidence of learning in a portfolio is collected selectively in an appendix of materials that meets the specific purposes of the portfolio. The appendix in a paper portfolio may be a series of tabbed sections; in a digital portfolio on disk, it may be a collection of electronic files in program subfolders; in a Web-based portfolio, it may be a network of online links. The representation of student work, or products, in the appendix is linked to the reflective component of the learning portfolio and its critical process, and driven by purpose and audience. For example, Table 3.1 suggests some representative ways in which the purpose of a learning portfolio strongly determines the themes of the reflective narrative as well as the types of evidence selected in the appendixes.

The examples given, of course, do not exhaust the numerous possibilities across disciplines and program applications of how learning portfolios can help students make connections between the purposes, goals, actual experiences, and outcomes of their learning. In fact, Campbell, Cignetti, Melenyzer, Nettles, and Wyman (2001), writing for teacher-prep candidates seeking professional employment, offer many of the same items as Table 3.1 but include other potential artifacts that may support a student portfolio. While their items are most relevant to a particular field, a little ingenuity can uncover multiple adaptations to other disciplines; here are a few from their list:

- Article summaries or critiques
- Case studies
- Classroom learning philosophy and work strategies

TABLE 3.1

Purpose, Themes, and Evidence of a Learning Portfolio

Purpose	Themes	Evidence
Improvement	Development, reflective inquiry, focus on goals, philosophy of learning	Drafts, journals, online threaded discussions, e-mails, statement of goals, classroom assessments, research notes
Job Search	Career preparation, versatile skills, ambitions, potential for future contributions, flexibility	Showcase projects, writing and communication samples, résumé, references, internship evaluations, certifications, reports/logs, computer programs, awards, transcripts
Writing	Voice, creativity, diverse and flexible skills, craftsmanship, facility with language, research proficiency	Essay drafts, journal entries, Listserv or threaded discussion entries, research papers, publications, concept maps or outlines
Prior Learning	Mastery of content, readiness for new curriculum and challenges, goals	Products demonstrating skills and competency, references, achievement/placement test scores, interview transcripts
Problem Solving	Critical thinking, creativity, application of knowledge, flexibility, curiosity	Problem-solving logs, lab reports, computer programs, spreadsheet data analyses, art installations, engineering/architecture models
Field Experiences	Application of knowledge, trained skills, adaptability	Field journals, logs, reports, video/audiotapes, photos, project leader evaluations, grant proposals, publications
Assessment of Achievement in Honors Program	Challenge, risk, creativity, reflection, motivation, self-directed learning, preparation for graduate/professional school, higher-level skills, collaboration, service, leadership, value-added education	Applications or first-year essays alongside capstone retrospective essays, senior thesis/project, essays/labs/projects in draft and final forms with feedback and responses, academic presentations (programs, handouts), creative performances (video, audio, programs, reviews), service/leadership records, photos, posters, awards

- Community service learning activities
- Cooperative learning log
- Field trip journal
- Individualized career plan
- Media competencies

(From Dorothy M. Campbell et al., *How to Develop a Professional Portfolio* 2nd ed., published by Allyn and Bacon, Boston, MA. Copyright © 2001 by Pearson Education. Reprinted by permission of the publisher.)

One other suggestion for addressing the topic of selectivity in gathering the evidence necessary for a sound learning portfolio is, once again, to turn to the proven work of the teaching portfolio movement. Seldin (2004), for instance, maintains that documentation gathered to support the reflective portion of a faculty portfolio must come as evenly as possible from three broad areas: (1) information from self, (2) information from others, and (3) products of effective teaching. With only slight modifications, the guidelines are applicable to learning portfolios, reminding us of the importance of both coherence and diversity in balancing the reflective dimension of a portfolio with the numerous and varied artifacts in the appendix. Using the three areas as a framework, students, too, for example, can develop three basic dimensions of their learning portfolios:

- *Information from self:* reflective narratives, personal learning goals, career plan
- *Information from others:* feedback and evaluations from faculty, recommendation letters, statements from advisers, academic awards, scholarships, undergraduate research grants
- *Products of learning:* samples of selected work and achievements appropriate for the purpose of the portfolio

Standards Versus Standardization in Documentation

When gathering the evidence necessary in documenting the sources, extent, meaning, and value of learning in a portfolio, the student and collaborative mentor inevitably will confront the issue of what criteria to use in selecting information for inclusion in the appendixes. Students must decide how much and what kinds of documentation to attach to a portfolio, taking into consideration the purpose of the portfolio and the intended audience. They need to reckon with the internal as well as the external motivations for developing a learning portfolio and with two interconnected questions: (1) What standards should be used to help focus the scope and shape the unity of the portfolio? (2) How should the portfolio be standardized (or should it be standardized?) for reliability of assessment outcomes?

Recalling the admonitions of Brookfield (1995) and others about the importance of supplying students with clear goals, guidelines, and rubrics for the challenges of systematic reflective inquiry, the problem of standards versus standardization raises a provocative debate over the fundamental rationale for portfolios. For example, Murphy (1997) follows the lead of several scholars and practitioners in arguing that portfolios offer an alternative, individualistic means of evaluating students' learning:

> *Portfolios . . . seem to provide the ideal recipe for educational reform because they offer new, more individualized modes of instruction, and because they promise to capture information not easily assessed by other methods. We can use portfolios, for example, to assess students' ability to think critically, articulate and solve complex problems, work collaboratively, conduct research, accomplish long-term, worthwhile projects, and set their own goals for learning. . . . We can use portfolios to assess progress over time and to assess performance under a variety of conditions and task requirements. (p. 72)*

Portfolios should be flexible and dynamic without the homogenizing effect of standardization to achieve "traditional statistical kinds of reliability" (p. 72).

Williams (2000), on the other hand, concedes that "*standardization* is not the same thing as *standards*" but reasons that we should not ignore "the fact that standardization is a necessary factor in establishing standards because it allows for the comparisons that underlie all standards. Rejecting standardization, therefore, commonly results in a failure of standards" (p. 136).

Sunstein (2000) counters with a contention that "by privileging the surface features" and placing too much emphasis on standardization of "style and form" in students' learning portfolios, we "create a demand for a superficial kind of product . . . using curriculum guidelines to shape student texts and ideas." She reinforces her point with this thought: "It is chilling to think of the expression 'Beware of what you ask for because you just might get it' in relationship to our traditional assessment practices . . ." (p. 13).

One potential solution to the quandary of standards versus standardization in creating and assessing learning portfolios is to require all portfolios to share a common set of standards for both content and format but allow each student the individual, creative opportunity to add a prescribed limit of additional elements that capture the exclusive dimensions of a particular student's learning experience. The suggestion assumes, of course, that the portfolio will have an external audience, a condition that makes some degree of standardization practical and helpful. By combining prescribed content and format features with individually relevant components, the learning portfolio—especially when produced with the guidance of a mentor—meets the challenge of standardization for reliable assessment and honors the learner's individuality and the imperative of personal or collective standards in the process of learning.

Collaboration and Mentoring

All the models described in Part 2 highlight the way in which student portfolios have traditionally incorporated, to differing degrees, the fundamental features of reflection and evidence. The role and involvement of the mentor are less clear, but remember that the value of collaboration in constructing knowledge takes many forms, though the common denominator, as Bruffee (1993) has shown, is a reconceptualizing of the authority of knowledge, resulting essentially in a student-centered classroom in which learning is a shared endeavor, the effort of a learning community. Thus, while collaboration and mentoring may not be overt facets of a portfolio project, intentionally identified in the design and written into specified goals, the very nature of portfolio development—with its premium on reflection, sharing of evidential materials, and decentralization of the classroom—presupposes a sense of authorship that suggests audience. Whether that audience is a history class engaged in the continuous discourse of an online threaded discussion, a peer reviewer in a composition course, a teacher providing formative feedback on a business plan assignment, a team of lab partners, or a program adviser, the portfolio author is keenly aware of the other as presence, as collaborator. There is even a sense in which, when a learner is strongly self-aware and highly skilled at reflective inquiry, the purportedly private venture of reflective thinking for oneself still invokes an "other": the critical self as collaborator.

The teacher who facilitates the portfolio-centered class is inevitably a collaborative mentor just by virtue of privileging a community of reflective practice in which the authority of knowledge as a traditional, static monolith gives way to interdependent, active learning or intellectual journeying that stems from reflective thought. Portfolio authors and mentors consequently depend on each other to sustain the dynamism of the reflective classroom and the portfolio project. Learning portfolios foster a version of what Dewey (1910) calls "consecutive discourse" and "systematic reflection" (p. 185), or what Brookfield (1995) calls "systematic inquiry" (p. 39); hence, the "instructor" becomes a genuine teacher (to draw on Dewey's subtle distinction), a mentor who exerts an indelible influence on the student's continual progress of learning and who shares in the construction of that learning.

The faculty member as a mentor who helps guide the development of a learning portfolio is a model that is common and natural enough to embrace. The faculty mentor can be the classroom teacher, an academic adviser, a program director, or other faculty member who can help coach the student's portfolio development.

More challenging, though potentially no less productive and transformative, is rallying students as collaborators in the processes of discovering a learning philosophy or educational plan, assembling relevant and representative products of learning, reflecting on immediate or long-range learning activities, and evaluating the nature and value of learning experiences. In the first edition of this volume (Zubizarreta, 2004), I include good examples of peer portfolio mentoring strategies, such as Herteis's report of the power of teaming fourth-year and third-year students in the portfolio program of the College of Pharmacy and Nutrition at the University of Saskatchewan in Canada or Batterbee and Dunham's description of what Albion College calls its Association Mentors, a trained cadre of student mentors who work with first-year students who are adopting the institution's digital portfolio.

Another model is to adapt the commonly used Small Group Instructional Diagnosis (SGID) process to engage students in reflective small-group conversations not about instructional performance but about their own learning experience (see Black, 1998, for a brief summary of the SGID method). A student consultant/collaborator can help peers delve into their learning by posing critical questions to the group about what, how, when, and why they have learned and then asking students to write a thoughtful list of recommendations they might have for self-improvement and for creating a stronger learning environment. The writing can be included in a portfolio and shared in further mentoring sessions with the teacher or with other students in a learning community. Such peer collaboration, support, and encouragement to think across disciplines about one's learning can be a powerful boost to developing higher-level metacognitive skills and to the concept of learning as community.

Yet another model is that described by Wright and Barton (2001) in a summary of Dalhousie University's successful Career Portfolio program. Students enroll in credit courses to train as mentors, learning about communication concepts and mentoring skills, career development theory, role playing, conflict resolution, group dynamics, and leadership skills. The authors offer a special directive derived from their experiences over two years of working with student portfolio mentors: "We cannot overemphasize the absolute necessity of thorough preparation and training for student mentors. The preparation includes development of knowledge in the area of career orientations as well as knowledge of the communications process" (p. 70). The positive outcomes of such a mentoring program are evident in the responses given by students about the value of portfolios in helping them not only prepare for jobs but deepen their learning through structured reflection and supportive peer mentoring. As the authors reveal:

> *When asked what they liked best about the course, students identified the production of the portfolio itself, the opportunity for self-reflection and growth, and the interaction with the professors and their peers. The students identified five key skills learned in the class: personal reflection, goal setting, teamwork, effective listening, and time management. (p. 70)*

Dalhousie's peer mentoring program for developing career portfolios is a showcase model that demonstrates how students can be employed to help enrich learning and provide the collaboration, objective perspective, and encouragement needed for producing and maintaining a sound learning portfolio. In concluding their piece, Wright and Barton (2001) share several tips for replicating their success on an institutional level:

- *Establish a broad-based task force to discuss implementation . . . and seek early input from all potential stakeholders.*

- *Look to the instructional development center (or committee) on campus for resources.*

- *Survey faculty to discover who might have already used peer mentoring or student portfolios in their classrooms. Invite them to join the committee or to make presentations on their experiences.*

- *Seek out expertise in the student services department regarding . . . portfolio writing . . . and student mentoring.*

- *Be prepared to patiently explain the peer mentoring concept so that the community supports the project.*

- *If academic credit for portfolio writing and mentoring is not provided, devise some other form of recognition or compensation in order to attract students. (pp. 73–74)*

In a classroom situation, peer mentors may be instructor assigned or self-selected classmates whose role is to encourage reflection and assist in purposeful selection of supportive evidence to document learning. Such relationships can be the result of cooperative learning groups established at the beginning of a course, and the thoughtful instructor will develop clear expectations and guidelines for both the peer mentors and their portfolio partners. Outside the classroom, peer mentors may be veteran majors in a discipline or alumni of particular courses or programs. More than just a traditional tutor in a content area, a peer portfolio mentor, especially with some training, offers a balanced, critical perspective on the learning process itself and joins with other students (and the teacher) in creating a community of reflective learners through the shared act of developing learning portfolios.

Access to online coaches and mentoring tools is another way of extending the benefits of collaboration to students engaged in portfolio development without extreme burdens on human and financial resources. An impressive example is the Portfolio Center at Columbia College in Chicago (www. colum.edu/portfolio_center), where students can find many helpful links to live and Web tutorials, "portfolio boot camps," interactive wiki feedback on Web portfolios, personalized consulting on electronic portfolio creations, portfolio mailing lists and connections to other portfolio authors, materials and service vendors, case studies of portfolio development, and more.

The chief point of mentoring as a crucial dimension of portfolios is that regardless of who serves as mentor—teacher, adviser, peer—or whether the mentoring occurs face-to-face or in virtual space, such collaboration, as Hutchings (1990) suggests, results in the "conversation and debate" needed for "human judgment" and "meaning making":

> *Who should be part of that conversation? Much depends on purposes, but fruitful things would surely happen around a table that included the student—let's say a psychology major—his department advisor, a faculty member from his support area in philosophy, and the director of student services with whom he's been working on a peer-advising project. (p. 7)*

Collaboration may even be as loose as an interactive, Web-based set of goals, directions, advice, and models developed as a virtual mentor or guide to portfolio development. One example is the online guide crafted by the University of Lethbridge, in Alberta, for preprofessional student teachers and faculty (www.uleth.ca/edu/undergrad/fe/pdf/portfolioguide.pdf). The particular value of engaging students in the process of collaboration, working in concert with the teacher and helping each other in designing and revising learning portfolios, is summed up again by Hutchings:

> *[W]here students are active partners in the assembly and analysis of portfolios, they can learn a great deal from the method—about putting pieces together, making connections, the need for revision, setting goals for the future. . . . [W]hat's most at stake here are educational values. Choosing portfolios is choosing to enact—and communicate to students—a view of learning as involving, personal, connected, and ongoing. (p. 8)*

References

Barrett, H. (2000). *Electronic portfolios = multimedia development + portfolio development.* Retrieved October 2, 2008, from www.electronicportfolios.com/portfolios/EPDevProcess.html#eval

Baxter Magolda, M. B. (2001, November/December). A constructivist revision of the measure of epistemological reflection. *Journal of College Student Development, 42*(6), 520–534.

Black, B. (1998). Using the SGID method for a variety of purposes. In M. Kaplan & D. Lieberman (Eds.), *To improve the academy: Vol. 17. Resources for faculty, instructional, and organizational development* (pp. 245–262). Stillwater, OK: New Forums Press.

Brookfield, S. D. (1995). *Becoming a critically reflective teacher.* San Francisco: Jossey-Bass.

Bruffee, K. A. (1993). *Collaborative learning: Higher education, interdependence, and the authority of knowledge.* Baltimore, MD: Johns Hopkins University Press.

Campbell, D. M., Cignetti, P. B., Melenyzer, B. J., Nettles, D. H., & Wyman, R. M., Jr. (2001). *How to develop a professional portfolio: A manual for teachers* (2nd ed.). Boston: Allyn & Bacon.

Campbell, D. M., Melenyzer, B. J., Nettles, D. H., & Wyman, R. M., Jr. (2000). *Portfolio and performance assessment in teacher education.* Boston: Allyn & Bacon.

D'Aoust, C. (1992). Portfolios: Process for students and teachers. In K. B. Yancey (Ed.), *Portfolios in the writing classroom: An introduction* (pp. 39–48). Urbana, IL: National Council of Teachers of English.

Dewey, J. (1910). *How we think.* Boston: D. C. Heath.

Hutchings, P. (1990). Learning over time: Portfolio assessment. *AAHE Bulletin, 42*(8), 6–8.

King, P., & Kitchener, K. (1994). *Developing reflective judgment.* San Francisco: Jossey-Bass.

Martin-Kniep, G. O. (1999). *Capturing the wisdom of practice: Professional portfolios for educators.* Alexandria, VA: Association for Supervision and Curriculum Development.

Moon, J. A. (2005, November 28). *Guide for busy academics: No. 4. Learning through reflection.* The Higher Education Academy. Retrieved October 2, 2008, from www.heacademy.ac.uk/resources/detail/id69_guide_for_busy_academics_no4_moon

Murphy, S. (1997). Teachers and students: Reclaiming assessment via portfolios. In K. B. Yancey & I. Weiser (Eds.), *Situating portfolios: Four perspectives* (pp. 72–88). Logan: Utah State University Press.

Perry, M. (1997). Producing purposeful portfolios. In K. B. Yancey & I. Weiser (Eds.), *Situating portfolios: Four perspectives* (pp. 182–189). Logan: Utah State University Press.

Seldin, P. (1997). *The teaching portfolio: A practical guide to improved performance and promotion/tenure decisions* (2nd ed.). Bolton, MA: Anker.

Seldin, P. (2004). *The teaching portfolio: A practical guide to improved performance and promotion/tenure decisions* (3rd ed.). Bolton, MA: Anker.

Seldin, P., Annis, L., & Zubizarreta, J. (1995). Answers to common questions about the teaching portfolio. *Journal on Excellence in College Teaching*, 6(1), 57–64.

Sunstein, B. S. (2000). Be reflective, be reflexive, and beware: Innocent forgery for inauthentic assessment. In B. S. Sunstein & J. H. Lovell (Eds.), *The portfolio standard: How students can show us what they know and are able to do* (pp. 3–14). Portsmouth, NH: Heinemann.

Weiser, I. (1997). Revising our practices: How portfolios help teachers learn. In K. B. Yancey & I. Weiser (Eds.), *Situating portfolios: Four perspectives* (pp. 293–301). Logan: Utah State University Press.

Williams, J. D. (2000). Identity and reliability in portfolio assessment. In B. S. Sunstein & J. H. Lovell (Eds.), *The portfolio standard: How students can show us what they know and are able to do* (pp. 135–148). Portsmouth, NH: Heinemann.

Wright, W. A., & Barton, B. (2001). Students mentoring students in portfolio development. In J. E. Miller, J. E. Groccia, & M. S. Miller (Eds.), *Student-assisted teaching: A guide to faculty-student teamwork* (pp. 69–76). Bolton, MA: Anker.

Zubizarreta, J. (1999). *Evaluating teaching through portfolios*. In P. Seldin & Associates, *Changing practices in evaluating teaching* (pp. 162–182). Bolton, MA: Anker.

Zubizarreta, J. (2004). *The learning portfolio: Reflective practice for improving student learning*. Bolton, MA: Anker.

Chapter 4

Electronic Learning Portfolios

THE ADVENT OF DIGITAL TECHNOLOGY has done much to alter the way in which learning is displayed, shared, and analyzed. The varied accounts of electronic portfolio applications in Part 2 of this volume provide compelling evidence of the increasing popularity of electronic portfolios as a powerful method of enhancing and assessing student learning. Cambridge (2001) and her team of assisting editors invite us "to read about the practices of individuals and institutions" invested in electronic portfolios, imagining, as we study the various cases and models in their volume, "what might be as we move at ever more accelerating rates into new possibilities" (p. viii) for using digital technology in portfolio development.

A number of diverse institutions use electronic portfolios to foster students' reflection and to assess and evaluate learning. The list includes colleges and universities as different as Albion College; Alverno College; Amsterdam, Utrecht, and Windesheim Faculties of Education (the Netherlands); City University of Hong Kong; Columbia College (Chicago); Dartmouth; FH JOANNEUM University of Applied Science (Austria); Indiana University; LaGuardia Community College; McGill University Faculty of Medicine (Canada); Messiah College; Miami Dade College; Newcastle University (United Kingdom); Oral Roberts University; Pennsylvania State University; Portland State University; Rose-Hulman Institute of Technology; Royal College of Ophthalmologists (United Kingdom); Spellman College; Stanford University; St. Olaf College; University of Florida; University of Melbourne (Australia); University of Otago (New Zealand); University of Virginia; Wake Forest University; and Washington State University, among others.

Also, professional organizations such as the Chartered Society of Physiotherapy in the United Kingdom (www.csp.org.uk; see the August 1, 2007, issue), American states such as Minnesota with its eFolio Minnesota public project (www.efoliominnesota.com), and a dizzying lineup of commercial vendors—such as Nuventive's iWebfolio (www.iwebfolio.com), Chalk & Wire's ePortfolio2 (www.chalkandwire.com), Sakai's Open Source Portfolio (http://osportfolio.org), Angel Learning's ePortfolio 2.1 (www.angellearning.com), and Epsilen's social-networking-powered ePortfolio (www.epsilen.com)—have also jumped into the electronic portfolio fray. Clearly, for students and faculty who are increasingly proficient in the ubiquitous technologies that have challenged and redefined traditional pedagogies, reshaping K–12 and higher education in our time, the electronic portfolio is an exciting and effective tool for improving, assessing, and evaluating learning.

Defining the Electronic Portfolio

What exactly is an electronic portfolio? Answers vary as considerably as they do in defining print portfolios because of the many purposes for which portfolios are developed and the multiple technologies available. Jafari and Kaufman (2006) provide an assortment of conceptual definitions from educators around the world, and the wide range of views is evident in their book. The same authors stay busy keeping the ePortConsortium Web site a dynamic repository of information about electronic portfolios, where countless links to online and print resources can potentially paralyze researchers because of the plethora of Internet sites dedicated to electronic portfolios for student learning, career preparation, program and institutional assessment, and, a more recent phenomenon, the swell of social-networking facilitated by "mashup" technologies in the evolution of the e-portfolio industry, as Waters (2008) reveals in his provocative commentary about new directions for electronic portfolio development. We can appreciate why even an enthusiastic advocate of electronic portfolios may be driven to ask the questions that Price (2006) poses in a challenging moment of self-reflection:

> Is it a medium? Is it a genre, or a set of genres? Is it a delivery system? Is it an assessment tool? Is it a means to reflection and learning? Is it a savvy career move? Is it a flashy new container for the work students already are doing? Is it a pain in the butt?

Still, definitions are useful, and Lorenzo and Ittelson (2005) articulate one concise meaning:

> What is an e-portfolio? An e-portfolio is a digitized collection of artifacts, including demonstrations, resources, and accomplishments that represent an individual, group, community, organization, or institution.

This collection can be [composed] of text-based, graphic, or multimedia elements archived on a Web site or on other electronic media such as CD-ROM or DVD.

An e-portfolio is more than a simple collection, however. . . . The benefits of an e-portfolio typically derive from the exchange of ideas and feedback between the author and those who view and interact with the e-portfolio. In addition, the author's personal reflection on the work inside an e-portfolio helps create a meaningful learning experience. (p. 2)

The former Alphabet Superhighway, a K–12 initiative of the U.S. Department of Education (a reminder that portfolios—even the electronic varieties—have enjoyed considerable attention in the grade schools as well as in higher education), posted the following definition, which is just as applicable to college-level portfolios:

Electronic portfolios are selective and purposeful collections of student work made available on the WWW. Portfolios focus on the students' reflections on their own work. They are records of learning, growth, and change. They provide meaningful documentation of students' abilities. Electronic portfolios provide information to students, parents, teachers, and members of the community about what students have learned or are able to do. They represent a learning history. ("Creating and Using Portfolios on the Alphabet Superhighway," n.d.)

Greenberg (2004) adds to the effort of defining the electronic portfolio, capturing the complexity of the task:

We are still working toward a common definition for electronic portfolios, or ePortfolios. Ideally, all work in an electronic portfolio not only is digital but also is available on the Internet. Yet even though materials may be visible on the Web, the ePortfolio is not simply a personal home page with links to examples of work. In addition, unlike a typical application program, such as word processing, an ePortfolio is a network application that provides the author with administrative functions for managing and organizing work (files) created with different applications and for controlling who can see the work and who can discuss the work (access). And unlike a course management system, in which instructors manage assignments and materials within the framework of a specific course, ePortfolios are controlled by the author (student), who manages his or her work across multiple courses throughout an academic career. Finally, the benefits of ePortfolio thinking can be realized only through communication services: the exchange of comments between the author and teachers, mentors, or coaches; the discussions and peer review with classmates, colleagues, or friends; the feedback for specific questions and concerns; and the personal reflection on work in progress or completed.

Definitions will vary across the spectrum of theorists and practitioners, but the common, central message among the varied voices is that electronic innovations enhance the virtue of portfolios in representing a rich, authentic, multilayered, living record of learning. With the advantages of digital technologies, electronic portfolios have enormous potential for conveying the breadth and depth of a student's learning history, allowing for a complex web of connections between deepening reflection and the full range of a student's abilities, achievements, and goals for improvement and application of learning.

Advantages of Electronic Portfolios

The former site credited to the U.S. Department of Education's Alphabet Superhighway provides a useful set of advantages to electronic portfolios, summarized in the following list:

- *Electronic portfolios foster active learning.*
- *Electronic portfolios motivate students.*
- *Electronic portfolios are instruments of feedback.*
- *Electronic portfolios are instruments of discussion on student performance.*
- *Electronic portfolios exhibit "benchmark" performance.*
- *Electronic portfolios are accessible.*
- *Electronic portfolios can store multiple media.*
- *Electronic portfolios are easy to upgrade.*
- *Electronic portfolios allow cross-referencing of student work. ("Creating and Using Portfolios on the Alphabet Superhighway," n.d.)*

Electronic media choices have introduced an array of strategies for archiving, organizing, and reflecting on information about a student's learning. Using hypertext links, for example, students can present and explore multiple layers of accessible documentary information in a way that reinforces the notion of learning as a shared, interactive process, inviting both the portfolio author and the audience progressively deeper into the constructed process of learning. Also, because Web portfolio projects often make much or all of the student's work publicly accessible online, the electronic portfolio heightens what Yancey (2001) calls the "social action" and "interactivity" (p. 20) of learning. Sometimes electronic portfolios are not posted as Web pages but presented instead on CD-ROM or DVD, or they may tap into more recent social-networking technologies, more fluid and constructivist Web 2.0 platforms, or other media that facilitate the shared dimension of learning in a way that is less cumbersome, more instant, more accessible, and more collaborative than hard-copy pages and folders.

Rogers and Williams (2001) succinctly state the advantages they found in implementing an electronic portfolio project at their institution, and I summarize their ideas and partially restate their words in the following list of positive features of a well-designed portfolio initiative:

- *The portfolio offers rich quality information about students in a breadth of outcome areas.*

- *The portfolio produces valid results and reflects the uniqueness of the institution.*

- *A thoughtful, strategically designed portfolio is minimally intrusive on the time of students and faculty.*

- *The portfolio engages students in reflection on their own education and helps them as they prepare for their careers or further education. (p. 1)*

Furthermore, Rogers and Williams (2001) reveal other advantages that carefully developed electronic portfolios have over more static paper models that often are reviewed only by the instructor and that lack the openly shared and continuously constructed qualities of their digital counterparts:

- Efficiency: *Portfolio systems can be very cumbersome to manage for both students and faculty. By developing an electronic system to access, store, view, and rate student material the amount of effort to manage the system is minimized. We were also able to design a system that integrates the student submission process, the rating process, the reporting process, and the curriculum mapping process into one module. When students enter the system they can easily access the list of student outcome objectives, see the rating rubrics, view on-line helps, or submit questions and comments.*

- Asynchronous access: *The RosE-Portfolio system is web-based and access is made through the local area network using the user's network username and password. This allows both student and raters to access the system from anywhere at anytime they have access to the web. . . . The system also allows for raters to rate at their convenience against preestablished rubrics. Because teams of raters are involved, the system also provides for inter-rater reliability testing.*

- Validation of process: *In designing the system requirements for the development of the software, it was found that the process of determining design requirements forced [us] to think through the purpose and scope of the system in ways that actually promoted the efficiency and validity of the process. That is, by having to clearly articulate what the features of the portfolio would be, it was necessary to think through what we wanted students to do, why we wanted them to do it, and what we were going to do with the information.*

- Adaptability: *One of the design constraints was that the system be developed to be adaptable to other forms of documentation and assessment. As the Institute-wide electronic portfolio system was developed, implemented, and improved it was adapted for use in individual classes. Building on the existing system, some faculty modified the portfolio structure for both student teams and individual student submissions for learning outcomes that were specific to the course, in some cases, moving to a paperless environment. Plans are also being made to prototype a system to be used for the faculty promotion, tenure, and retention process. The power of the electronic format and ease of adaptability serve to promote multiple uses of the system. (p. 2)*

Batson (2002) also highlights a number of advantages to electronic portfolio development, pointing out how portfolios today—rapidly going beyond rudimentary features of HTML-based Webfolios to more dynamic database-driven sites that are seamlessly interfaced with live social-networking capabilities—are particularly attractive to students weaned on MySpace, Facebook, cell phones, and text messaging. Faculty, too, benefit from electronic portfolio innovations that inspire new pedagogies and methods for demonstrating professional development and accomplishments. But the electronic portfolio is also useful for administrators looking for new ways of generating, gathering, archiving, and analyzing student learning information for assessment, evaluation, and accreditation purposes, including e-portfolios' potential for:

- *Creating a system of tracking student work over time, in a single course, with students and faculty reflecting on it*

- *Aggregating many students' work in a particular course to see how the students as a whole are progressing toward learning goals*

- *Assessing many courses in similar ways that are all part of one major and thus, by extension, assessing the entire program of study (Batson, 2002, p. 3)*

Undoubtedly, Batson's (2002) title is appropriate: electronic portfolios are booming in popularity and utility. Electronic portfolios have many advantages, and the dazzling array of design options and technical features can quickly distract us from the fundamentals of sound, meaningful, transformative portfolio development. In the rush to keep up with technology's influence on the learning portfolio, let's not forget that pedagogy should drive our decisions about portfolio development: learning should always be at the center.

The lesson is one that Fournier and Lane (2006) of the Catalyst Learning and Scholarly Technologies office at the University of Washington did not forget when they piloted a program to migrate a successful paper portfolio initiative in English courses to an electronic portfolio system. Some of their key findings in the process included the following:

- *Despite challenges of context (new teachers and little history of technology integration), e-portfolios proved easy to use by both TAs [teaching assistants] and students.*

- *TAs reported that the use of e-portfolios improved the portfolio process in the course, led to more efficient grading, and helped students consider the demands of a wider audience.*

- *E-portfolios helped students make strong connections to course learning outcomes and utilize evidence effectively.*

- *Students' experience with the portfolio process varied more by instructor than by format (paper versus electronic portfolios).*

- *Administrators expressed optimism about extending the use of e-portfolios to other courses. . . . (p. 2)*

The results of the study pointed to several positive features of an electronic format for portfolio development, but the researchers were careful to report that with an unswerving focus on student learning, the principal instructors and students involved in the project saw heartening but not overwhelming differences in students' reflections and outcomes when paper portfolios were compared with digital versions:

> *In winter, three pilot classes completed the e-portfolio and three completed the paper portfolio. Since students take English 131 only once, these sections allowed us to compare experiences of students completing the paper and electronic formats. Responses to the student survey at the end of the quarter revealed no significant differences between the two groups. Some students who completed e-portfolios remarked that they would have preferred completing a paper portfolio; at least one student reported the opposite. Survey responses collected from both winter and spring suggested that students' experience of English 131 and of the portfolio process differed*

more based on the instructor and specific assignment they received than on the paper or electronic format of the portfolio itself. (p. 6)

The instructors actually seemed more convinced and enthusiastic than the students in the project, adding a number of perceived benefits to the electronic portfolio. The takeaway message here is that technology may be a stimulating aid to learning, but ultimately, the medium matters less than the pedagogy—matters less, in other words, than the quality of teaching, feedback, mentoring, support, and opportunities for students to develop skills and habits of reflection and self-directed learning.

Disadvantages of Electronic Portfolios

The versatility of electronic portfolios in providing a high-tech means of collecting and storing information is intriguing but also problematic because of the often daunting amount of training necessary, the potentially confusing variety of hardware and software choices available, and the dizzying pace at which technology evolves. Springfield (2001), for example, mentions such barriers, commenting on problems encountered with numerous products. Barrett (2000a) reviews the advantages and limitations of common technologies for portfolio building. Lankes (1995) also points out various approaches to digitizing portfolios, referring to how some educators have had to develop customized templates for easier implementation of portfolios for assessment and career preparation.

Transferability of files from one type of computer program to another is an additional worry. Barrett (2000b) offers one solution in recommending the use of Adobe Acrobat PDF (portable document format) files as a useful medium for electronic portfolio development because of their user-friendly ability to cross many platforms and applications. Today, many vendors have emerged to provide a variety of alternatives, and a fair number of institutions have developed and launched their own in-house systems.

The National Education Association, taking into consideration the potential hurdles in moving from print to digital portfolio formats, issued the following cautions in a former Web site on portfolio assessment:

Bits and Bytes Advice

Data in digital form can easily be cross-referenced, overlaid, and analyzed. . . . If you want to take advantage of technological tools to create electronic portfolios, you should consider several factors, however, before you make a change from a traditional system:

- Access. *The hardware and software used to capture and store the student portfolios must be accessible to both teacher and students.*

If your computers, scanner, and printer are still down the hall in the Computer Lab, this may not be the time to initiate electronic portfolios.

- High-End Tools. *Depending on the subject matter, you'll want to be able to store multiple data sources (text, voice, video, image, etc.). The capacity to store more than a single file format will also give a more well-rounded representation of the student's work. Therefore, you will need access to at least one high-end workstation with scanner, OCR (optical character recognition) software, printer, and perhaps digital camera.*

- Space. *Graphics and photographic images take up a great deal more system storage than text does. Be sure that your school's system can support large files without compromising other applications. You may also want to develop a regular schedule of backing up files and archiving outdated material to magnetic tape or CD-ROM storage to avoid an unnecessary drain on your system or the loss of vital material.*

- Labor. *Accumulating information for an electronic portfolio is both labor intensive and time consuming. Although you may delegate this task to each student as part of his or her role in compiling a portfolio, always be careful to stay on top of the process.*

- Administration. *Before starting, determine how you will administer the electronic portfolios. You will want a database application that establishes an area for each student, stores various file formats, and allows for annotated comments appended to each item. You may also want a tool with security features and password protection, so that the privacy of portfolios cannot be compromised. You'll also want to make sure that the interface (ease of use, appearance, etc.) is "friendly" and appealing to both [you] and your students.*

- Hybrid Solutions. *More often than not, portfolios are the composite of evaluation techniques, including standardized testing, completed assignments, original works, teacher comments, student reflections, and peer reviews. You may not want—or be able—to capture all of these products into the electronic portfolio, so you should try to develop portfolio content on the basis of your identified goals and the needs of your students.*

The assessment portfolio—whether electronic or paper-based—is intended to document student learning and progress, as well as allow students to identify their own goals and accomplishments. Technology can be a powerful tool in your use of this instrument. ("Technology Briefs," n.d.)

Young (2002) reports on several responses to such issues. One is a consortium, called ePortConsortium, formed by the Indiana University–Purdue University Indianapolis and the University of California at Los Angeles to "develop e-portfolio software" that "will give students and advisers tools to build portfolios" (p. A32). The organization has grown considerably since Young's piece, and today it claims to be "an association of individuals from 67 countries and more than 800 higher educational and IT commercial institutions from around the world" (see www.eportconsortium.org). Another consortium is affiliated with the EDUCAUSE Learning Initiative (www.educause.edu/eli), and it consists of institutions from several states—including California, Massachusetts, Minnesota, and Washington—all attempting to make the process of developing electronic portfolios more cost and labor efficient with the positive outcome of enhanced student learning.

Fundamentals

The landscape of portfolio development has expanded astonishingly with the advent of multimedia, hypermedia, database structures, "mashup" applications, blogging and social networking, and more innovations in the digital world. Though the media have changed from print on paper to electronic hypertext and cyberspace, the fundamental process of learning portfolio development remains steadfast. Cambridge (2001) points out that "reflection is central to learning," and the reflective core of sound learning portfolios is what transforms mere accumulated "information" to meaningful "knowledge" (p. 3), an insight that I stress throughout this book. Yancey (2001) follows up with the assertion that "electronic portfolios are created through the same basic processes used for print portfolios: collection, selection, and reflection" (p. 20).

Villano (2006) lists twenty best-practice tips for helping us keep our eye on the central aim of all portfolio projects, especially when we contemplate tapping the resources and complexities of electronic portfolio development:

1. *The ePortfolio technology can be the architecture of the major itself, acting as the mechanism by which curricular objectives are supported and measured.*

2. *Collectively, ePortfolios can be mined to get a sense of overall program quality.*

3. *ePortfolios have become source material by which to gauge the value of the faculty-student interaction.*

4. *ePortfolios can boost students' ability to integrate learning and to make connections.*

5. *ePortfolios can help administrators/faculty evaluate the institution's capacity to deliver on curricular promises.*

6. *In order for ePortfolio efforts to succeed, schools must document the impact of the technology on students, faculty, and the institution.*

7. *Most ePortfolio efforts fall into three main categories: developmental, reflective, and representational.*

8. *The three main flavors of ePortfolio (above) may be mixed to achieve different learning, personal, or work-related outcomes.*

9. *At some schools, students can use the ePortfolio system to access personalized academic information and reports on academic history, take placement tests, and check on their placement recommendations.*

10. *ePortfolios offer better ways to collaborate on development of standards, criteria, and measurement.*

11. *Consider adopting ePortfolios gradually, in a handful of departments.*

12. *ePortfolios can allow students to participate in the campus housing lottery and submit evaluations of their resident advisers.*

13. *Students can customize their ePortfolios by adding RSS feeds of their interests from the web.*

14. *ePortfolios can be programmed to let students interface with the school's content management system.*

15. *Watch unchecked growth in ePortfolios: Adding applications can clutter ePortfolio systems, and organizing the apps after the fact can be challenging.*

16. *Some schools integrate ordinary ePortfolio sharing and assessment features with tools for community interaction such as asynchronous discussion. Individuals with common interests in particular areas can find each other and build connections across disciplines and groups.*

17. *Don't think only of institutional constituents creating ePortfolios: Each virtual community can have its own portfolio, welcoming newcomers into the fold.*

18. *Why not incorporate your students' learning records as a stan-dalone application your own faculty—and educators at other schools—can download for free and use at their convenience?*

19. *Why not use ePortfolios to evaluate student thinking on new ePortfolio-based (or other) curricula or courses your institution has debuted?*

20. *Think careers: ePortfolios are effectively used to help students articulate their own values and then relate them to career goals. (p. 5)*

In the interest of clarifying the deep purposes and value of creating electronic portfolios and keeping a premium on meaningful reflection and careful, strategic implementation, Yancey (2001) shares the following heuristic, further developed in her text, for effective "design and creation of student electronic portfolios":

- *What is/are the purpose/s?*

- *How familiar is the portfolio concept? Is the familiarity a plus or a minus?*

- *Who wants to create an electronic portfolio, and why?*

- *Why electronic? What about electronic is central to the model? And is sufficient infrastructure (resources, knowledge, commitment) available for the electronic portfolio?*

- *What processes are entailed? What resources are presumed?*

- *What faculty development component does the model assume or include?*

- *What skills will students need to develop?*

- *What curricular enhancement does the model assume or include?*

- *How will the portfolio be introduced?*

- *How will the portfolio be reviewed? (pp. 84–86)*

Having reflected carefully on the issues raised in the heuristic, one can then proceed to more detailed questions of implementation and use. Yancey (2001) follows with an expanded list of recommendations for setting up an electronic portfolio program. Here is a summary of her tips:

- *Think rhetorically. Who is creating the portfolio and why? Who is reading it and why?*

- *Consider how the electronic portfolio needs to be electronic. How will it be interactive? What relationships and connections does the digital form make possible?*

- *Consider how the portfolio will be interactive socially.*

- *Develop some key terms that you can associate with your model of an e-portfolio, and use them consistently.*

- *Be realistic about how long it will take to introduce the model and the skills that faculty and students will need.*

- *Be realistic about the difficulty that teachers may have in designing reflective texts, that students may experience in writing reflections, and that teachers may have in responding to and evaluating those reflections.*

- *Perhaps more than other innovative practices, the development of e-portfolios calls for a collaborative process of development. (pp. 86–87)*

Selected Resources

The amount of information on electronic portfolios available online is staggering. A simple query on a standard Internet search engine produces over a million sites, though not all are relevant to higher education; many are K–12 projects, student samples, commercial ventures, or simply inoperative links. Here are just a few that may prove useful, listed alphabetically:

- Albion College Digital Portfolio Project. Extensive information, a template, and student samples: www.albion.edu/digitalportfolio
- Alverno College Diagnostic Digital Portfolio. Password-protected information, but brief details are available: www.alverno.edu/academics/ddp.html
- American Association for Higher Education Portfolio Clearinghouse. Although this organization is now defunct, the site still has some useful information: http://ctl.du.edu/portfolioclearinghouse
- Barrett, Helen. Educational and entrepreneurial e-portfolio site with many links to information, guidelines, and resources: www.electronicportfolios.org
- California State University, Los Angeles, Webfolio Project. Information and student samples: www.calstatela.edu/academic/webfolio
- Spencer, Lisa. "Creating an Electronic Portfolio." Includes links to resources and rudimentary information on process and evaluation: http://cte.jhu.edu/techacademy/fellows/Spencer/webquest/lasindex.html
- Dartmouth College's Career Services Portfolio. Examples: www.dartmouth.edu/~csrc/students/portfolio

- EDUCAUSE Learning Initiative. Many useful links: www.educause. edu/E-Portfolios/5524
- Electronic Portfolio Action and Communication network: http:// eportfolio.merlot.org
- EPICS-2. Many useful British resources for portfolio development: www.eportfolios.ac.uk
- ePortConsortium. A rich compilation of print and online resources and links: www.eportconsortium.org
- Europortfolio. Reveals international interest in portfolios: www. europortfolio.org
- Florida State University's Career Portfolio. Helpful information on portfolios for career preparation: www.career.fsu.edu/portfolio
- GateWay Community College, Maricopa. E-portfolio information, rationale, and samples in disciplines: www.gwc.maricopa.edu/class/e-portfolio
- Inter/National Coalition for Electronic Portfolio Research. A global network of current information and connections: http://ncepr.org
- LaGuardia Community College ePortfolio. A strong model, with many valuable features: www.eportfolio.lagcc.cuny.edu
- Lankes, Anna Maria D. "Electronic Portfolios: A New Idea in Assessment." ERIC Document Reproduction Service No. ED390377: http:// eric.ed.gov
- Lone Star 2000 Project. Preservice teachers' and students' portfolios in CD-ROM format: www.thejournal.com (follow links to October 1996 issue of *T.H.E. Journal*)
- Pennsylvania State University. Various links to design guidelines, tips on evaluation, and blog tools: http://portfolio.psu.edu
- Reiss, Donna. Webfolio project with templates, resources, and student samples: www.wordsworth2.net/webfolio
- Seton Hall University. Samples of teacher education e-portfolios: http://education.shu.edu/portfolios
- St. Olaf College, Center for Integrative Studies. Valuable information, resources, and models: www.stolaf.edu/depts/cis/web_portfolios.htm
- University of Pennsylvania, College of Arts and Sciences e-portfolio. Information, guidelines, content and design strategies, and resources: www.vpul.upenn.edu/careerservices/college/elecport.html
- University of South Dakota, Technology Literacy Center e-portfolio. Offers guidelines, dos and don'ts, and common problems: www.usd. edu/tlc/eportfolio
- University of Virginia, Curry School of Education. Password required, but includes useful portfolio information with links to student samples: www.openportfolio.org

- University of Washington, Catalyst Learning and Scholarly Technologies. Resources and models: http://catalyst.washington.edu/web_tools/portfolio.html
- Virginia Wesleyan College's four-year PORTfolio program. E-portfolio information, brochure, and student samples: www.vwc.edu/academics/portfolio
- Wesleyan University's portfolios for advisement: https://wesep.wesleyan.edu/cgi-perl/session.cgi

One additional resource for helping us think of different ways to use the multifunctional virtues of digital technology in learning portfolio development is worth highlighting here. The digital video reflection projects employed as part of students' portfolios for teacher preparation at Wake Forest University highlight the core value of reflection in students' work and career readiness. The video reflections look both backward, at achievements measured against professional standards, and forward, at goals for improvement and anticipated applications of skills learned during rigorous curriculum and practicum experiences. Each video captures students' learning and personalities in unique ways, making their reflections meaningful, relevant, practical, creative, and enjoyable. Some examples of "DV Reflections" can be found at the following link: www.wfu.edu/~cunninac/dvreflections/dvreflections.html.

The Link to Learning

According to Cambridge (2001), technology, as it turns out, is "only one component of decision making about the use of electronic portfolios and . . . not the most crucial one" (p. 11). The real link to promoting learning with portfolios, regardless of the technologies pressed into service, is holding fast to the fundamentals. Discerning the foundational value of portfolios underneath the technology, Yancey (2001) puts it this way:

> [M]ore generally, portfolios bring with them three key characteristics:
>
> - *They function as a means of both review and planning.*
> - *They are social in nature.*
> - *They are grounded in reflection. (p. 19)*

The key elements of effective portfolio projects, then, as identified in Chapter 3, remain the most salient issues in portfolio development: reflection, evidence, and collaboration and mentoring.

Just as in teaching portfolios (Seldin, 2004), the three dimensions are the most strong determining factors in successful use of learning portfolios, whether the format is print or electronic. When all three components

are present in the process of constructing, reviewing, and revising the portfolio, student learning is richer, more lasting, and more transformative. We will then have realized the full, authentic value of the learning portfolio.

References

Barrett, H. (2000a). Create your own electronic portfolio: Using off-the-shelf software to showcase your own or student work. *Learning and Leading with Technology.* Retrieved October 2, 2008, from www.electronicportfolios.com/portfolios/iste2k.html

Barrett, H. (2000b). *Using Adobe Acrobat for electronic portfolio development.* Association for the Advancement of Computing in Education. Retrieved October 2, 2008, from www.electronicportfolios.com/portfolios/sitepaper2001.html

Batson, T. (2002, November 26). The electronic portfolio boom: What's it all about? *Campus Technology.* Retrieved October 2, 2008, from http://campustechnology.com/articles/39299_2

Cambridge, B. L. (Ed.). (2001). *Electronic portfolios: Emerging practices in student, faculty, and institutional learning.* Washington, DC: American Association for Higher Education.

"Creating and using portfolios on the Alphabet Superhighway." (n.d.). U.S. Department of Education. Original site unavailable but retrievable from http://web.archive.org/web/20041210095045/www.ash.udel.edu/ash/teacher/portfolio.html

Fournier, J., & Lane, C. (2006, November). *Transitioning from paper to electronic portfolios in beginning composition.* Catalyst Learning and Scholarly Technologies, University of Washington. Retrieved October 2, 2008, from http://catalyst.washington.edu/research_development/papers/2006/2006-eportfolio-report.pdf

Greenberg, G. (2004, July/August). The digital convergence: Extending the portfolio model. *EDUCAUSE Review, 39*(4), 28–37.

Jafari, A., & Kaufman, C. (2006). *Handbook of research on ePortfolios.* Hershey, PA: Idea Group Inc.

Lankes, A. M. D. (1995). *Electronic portfolios: A new idea in assessment.* Syracuse, NY: ERIC Clearinghouse on Information and Technology. (ERIC Document Reproduction Service No. ED390377)

Lorenzo, G., & Ittelson, J. C. (2005). *An overview of e-portfolios.* Retrieved October 2, 2008, from http://connect.educause.edu/Library/ELI/AnOverviewofEPortfolios/39335

Price, M. (2006, December 4). What is the purpose of an electronic portfolio? Is the answer the key to your successful implementation? *Campus Technology.* Retrieved October 2, 2008, from http://campustechnology.com/articles/41320

Rogers, G. M., & Williams, J. (2001). *Promise and pitfalls of electronic portfolios: Lessons learned from experience.* Accreditation Board for Engineering and Technology. Retrieved October 2, 2008, from www.abet.org/Linked%20 Documents-UPDATE/Assessment/Promise%20and%20Pitfalls%20of%20 Electronic%20Portfolios_2001.pdf

Seldin, P. (2004). *The teaching portfolio: A practical guide to improved performance and promotion/tenure decisions* (3rd ed.). Bolton, MA: Anker.

Springfield, E. (2001). A major redesign of the Kalamazoo portfolio. In B. L. Cambridge (Ed.), *Electronic portfolios: Emerging practices in student, faculty, and institutional learning* (pp. 53–59). Washington, DC: American Association for Higher Education.

"Technology briefs." (n.d.). National Education Association. Original site unavailable but retrievable from http://web.archive.org/web/20020803225931/www.nea.org/cet/BRIEFS/brief4.html

Villano, M. (2006, August 29). Electronic student assessment: The power of the portfolio. *Campus Technology.* Retrieved October 2, 2008, from www.campus technology.com/article.aspx?aid=41130

Waters, J. K. (2008, June 1). Unleashing the power of Web 2.0. *Campus Technology.* Retrieved October 2, 2008, from http://campustechnology.com/articles/63551_1

Yancey, K. B. (2001). Digitized student portfolios. In B. L. Cambridge (Ed.), *Electronic portfolios: Emerging practices in student, faculty, and institutional learning* (pp. 15–30). Washington, DC: American Association for Higher Education.

Young, J. R. (2002, March 8). "E-Portfolios" could give students a new sense of their accomplishments. *Chronicle of Higher Education, 48*(26), A31–A32.

Part Two

Models of Learning Portfolios

PART 2 PRESENTS a collection of models of different kinds of student learning portfolios. The variety of models suggests the many ways in which learning portfolios are adapted across purposes, disciplines, programs, and institutions. The diverse models of portfolio implementation offer both theoretical ideas and practical information, and readers are encouraged to consider what would work for them individually to improve student learning.

Chapter 5

Learning Portfolios in the Humanities Classroom

Promoting Intentional Learning by Helping Students Uncover What Is Meaningful to Them

Dorothe J. Bach
University of Virginia

> As a student of sociology, I find that I often critique—without interaction. I am proud that for one semester, I interacted with the people I would be critiquing.
>
> —Quynh Vu, political and social thought major, third year, 2007

> When I came to college, I expected to be taught, not to learn that I must teach myself, find meaning in the world myself, and experience the world for myself.
>
> —Hannah Trible, College of Arts and Sciences, undeclared, second year, 2006

AS TEACHERS, most of us have goals for student learning that go beyond the mastery of discipline-specific facts and principles. We want to help our students to become critical thinkers and adept writers, to make connections between different fields of knowledge, and to prepare for future careers. To these somewhat elusive yet practical objectives, many faculty add a number of holistic goals, such as helping students grow as individuals, become engaged citizens, and develop skills and enthusiasm for lifelong learning. But how do we incorporate these broader objectives into the fabric of our course? How do we translate what is essentially a shaping of attitudes and dispositions into assignments and classroom interactions? And finally, how do we assess that such learning has taken place?

As a humanities teacher, I have found learning portfolios to be an effective tool for advancing and assessing some of those hard-to-pin-down goals. When properly integrated into the overall design of a course, portfolios can be powerful in helping students recognize and appreciate what is meaningful to them, how to use what they have learned, and how to set goals for future learning. As Fink (2003) suggests in his volume on course design, I use portfolios in tandem with other reflective assignments as a final capstone. By asking my students to reflect regularly on their learning, I seek to remind them of the active role they play in shaping their education and in becoming "meaning-making beings" (Fink, 2003, p. 106). In the following pages, I describe how I use learning portfolios in a 300-level literature course to achieve such aims.

Reflective Practice by Design

My course Critical Approaches to Young Adult and Children's Literature is an elective, discussion-based seminar with an enrollment of twenty students. In part, because courses on topics having to do with children are often perceived as easy, I ask inquiring students to read carefully through the syllabus, course goals, and requirements, which can be found on the course's Web site (http://faculty.virginia.edu/doro). If, after reading, they are still interested, they e-mail me brief applications, stating their reasons for wanting to take this course and reflecting on what they would like to get out of their participation and what they believe they can contribute. I also ask them to react to the syllabus, course description, goals, and requirements.

The process has several purposes, aside from identifying students who are looking for an easy grade. It ensures that students actually read what I want them to know about the course, it encourages them to consider their own learning goals, and it helps them arrive at an informed decision about whether this course is for them. It also allows me to have a hand in the composition of the course (I aim for a diversity of majors, interests, and perspectives) and to get to know my students before the class starts. And finally, this reflective exercise sets the tone for the semester and produces a document that I will hand back at the end of the semester as students begin to compose their learning portfolios.

Although I assign the portfolio in lieu of a final exam, students reading through the course requirements will find the portfolio project on the top of the list. I consciously place it there because it provides another opportunity to communicate that I expect students to be active creators of their own learning experience. In the assignment I tell them that at the end of the course they will have to select as many as five pages from writings produced for this class, indicating the source (for example, reading journal, postings from the online discussion board, class notes, papers). At least 50 percent of this selection has to come from their own writing. Since one of my course goals is to convey that academic knowledge is not created in a vacuum but in discourse with others, I invite them to choose the remaining portion from the writing of classmates or critics we read in the course. The request allows me to communicate from the start that students' peers will be an important part of their learning and that they should carefully search their peers' online postings for illuminating ideas. Reading the assignment, students also learn that they will have to write a five- to seven-page introduction to this collection, explaining what it means to them and how it reflects the changes in their thinking about the course material.

Once the class begins, I make sure that students are provided with another opportunity to flex their reflective muscles and think about themselves as learners in a community of other learners. The first homework assignment asks students to complete Baxter Magolda's Measure of Epistemological Reflection (1999, pp. 283–289), a questionnaire that assesses students' intellectual development and helps them understand that we all have different ways of understanding the world. I use this questionnaire to initiate an in-class discussion on how the ways we know and learn may come into play in the classroom. Others have successfully used instruments such as the Myers-Briggs Type Indicator or personal strengths/weaknesses/interests inventories. The vehicle is not important; what matters is that students get a chance early on to think about their unique preferences, strengths, or weaknesses and how these might affect their learning in the course.

Throughout the semester, students continuously reflect on the content they study in one-minute papers, reading journals, and response papers. At the beginning or end of a class period, for example, I may ask students to write for a few minutes on a question related to the reading or the learning process, like the following:

- What was most significant, inspiring, puzzling, or annoying to you in today's reading? Why? How do you make sense of your reaction in light of what you know about yourself and the world?
- What do you take away from the discussion/lecture, and how might you use what you have learned?

At home students use journals (graded as pass or fail) to explore their own ideas concerning our readings, lectures, and discussion in more depth.

In my instructions I tell them that reading journals are a place to try out ideas without worrying too much about being evaluated. It is an invitation to experiment and ask, "How accurately can I explain my idea? Why is it significant?" The point of the journal is to help students develop a regular practice of figuring out what they think and make connections to other courses and areas of knowledge.

Connecting the Dots: The Reflective Essay

In the portfolio students use these introspective exercises together with their standard papers and their classmates' online postings as evidence for the argument they present in their reflective essay. To get them started, I provide a list of questions and let them choose two or three to guide their reflection. Examples include the following:

- How has your writing evolved? Which assignments were more comfortable and productive for you? Why? What have you learned from reading your peers' writing?
- Looking back at your responses to the Measure of Epistemological Reflection, how did your particular ways of knowing affect you during the semester? Did you notice any changes? If so, how would you describe them? What sense do you make of your observations?
- What major ideas, themes, and threads do you find in your writing and the writing you selected from others? How have you developed these ideas over the course of this semester? What does this development mean to you?
- How do your ideas connect to those you developed in other courses? How does this course fit into your overall undergraduate education?
- How do your insights connect to your life, personal values, and convictions? How might these connections affect your future learning?

One common concern about learning portfolios is that the assignment produces mandated confessionals and that it may encourage students to schmooze or hide behind shiny rhetoric. I add this warning as a safeguard: "As was the case for all previous projects, this is not the place for flattery or arguments you don't believe in. You will be evaluated for the depth of your critical and reflective thinking. You will receive an A for an essay demonstrating that you have not learned anything in this course if the argument is compellingly written and evidence based."

Over the years, I have succeeded in conveying my seriousness about this point. Students express frustrations about the course, and I have occasionally read portfolios that left me wondering whether I should change my occupation. Seriously, though, one student exceeded the page limit by five pages to explain in detail how this course failed her by consistently denying closure. She ends her reflections this way:

As I aged during the semester I began to long for something more conclusive and could no longer appreciate the new light shed on various topics. To reflect my sentiments about the course and its progression I think it only appropriate to omit a conclusion. Instead I will close with an open-ended question. Is it harmful to want a concise point or conclusion from a discussion?

Even the few students who focus on what did not work for them often demonstrate a level of reflection that accomplishes the assignment's goals. Most students, however, look for and write about things that were meaningful to them, and if they dwell on frustrations, they are usually able to recognize them as a learning opportunity in the course of the reflection.

As I do with other papers, I encourage my students to seek peer feedback before they hand in their portfolios, offer them models of successful portfolios written by former students, and share with them evaluation criteria such as these (adapted from McGregor, 1993; see Part 4 of this volume for a detailed rubric):

- Critical analysis of how your writing and thinking about the subject of the course have changed (or not changed)
- Evidence of your preparedness to take an active role as a participant in the discourse of our field of study, including accuracy of discipline-specific facts and principles
- Ability to connect the course material to other fields you have studied and to your personal interests in different areas of your life
- Depth and specificity of reflection
- Persuasiveness of your evidence-based argument
- Clear organization; engaging and comprehensible style; correct grammar and vocabulary

Samples of Authentic Self-Reflection

I have found that if I set the tone of reflective inquiry throughout the semester and clarify expectations, students will challenge themselves to produce meaningful, authentic self-reflection, which makes for an exceptionally rewarding reading experience. I am always surprised at how individual the responses are, how every student identifies a unique area of growth—most of the time, it's one that the student and I would never have suspected at the beginning of the course. The following excerpt from a reflective statement written by a third-year political and social thought major is a case in point:

My advisor guilted me into taking an English class. . . . "You don't want to be at a cocktail party and not be able to talk about Shakespeare or Wordsworth." I must have rolled my eyes because he followed that comment with, "Do you want to graduate from a liberal arts college, renowned for its English Department, saying that you have never taken an English class?" My elitist side took over.

When I rolled my eyes at my advisor's comment about Shakespeare and Wordsworth, I was displaying my Marxist and sociological leanings. I do not hold Shakespeare in high regard. I steered [away] from English classes because I held Marx's view that books and literature served to oppress or deceive the masses. I picked an English class in order to settle my elitist hankering. I chose this specific class to try to reinforce my Marxist thinking. I thought I would be learning . . . how books serve to socialize children, how books reinforce and legitimize the status quo. . . .

Most valuable to me and my experiment with this literature class is [knowing] that my beliefs in books were complicated. Before, I wanted to learn what books could do to a reader; I am starting to learn what readers can do to a book or a story. . . . This class has not made me a better writer or English critic, but it has helped me think of books and readers differently. My prior view of books was that they were artifacts, relics that academics can use to decipher the values in other cultures. I have never seen beauty in poems or literature, but rather messages of cultural norms. I have come to think of books now as a tool—both of larger societies, but also the marginalized. Books do not have meaning without actors. I can study a book all the day and postulate about the norms and values of society, but that is rarely the entire story. Books can only embody as much culture as a reader allows. I realized that books are only one side; the other side is the reaction and action of the reader.

The focus of learning portfolios depends on the question(s) on which students choose to reflect. In this excerpt a student analyzes her own writing and reflects on how the assignments have helped her develop a sense of purpose and have led her to take greater risks:

In reading over my contributions to our class's online discussion group, I am able to see how I have developed as a writer as well as a critical thinker throughout the course. In the beginning my writing style was formal and dispassionate, allowing me to easily adhere to any standards without taking too many risks in doing so. I have included an excerpt from my first reading response in my learning portfolio to show just how far I have come throughout the semester. Structurally, there is little to complain about in my first response. I address the topic from a creative approach, I include references to the book, and I make some general conclusions based on what I have written.

However, any strength in my early writing stops there. I was in no way attached to what I was writing and simply wished to finish up the assignment in order to turn it in. Compared to my later post on the "Child_Lit" listserv [an Internet discussion forum created by Rutgers University for authors and scholars of children's literature], I can see my honest interest in and knowledge of the topic shine through. This was confirmed when I received several replies to my original thread. The posters were not simply making bland comments about my ideas or ignoring what I had said. Rather, they were searching for more, asking questions, finding articles, and offering up their own reflections on the topic. It was incredibly exciting as well as validating to hear what others had to say and to see that I could spark a conversation not only in class or in the class forum but also in a far larger and public domain.

Among my students' contemplations, I often find broader reflections about the limits of education and discipline-specific knowledge sometimes mixed in with a compassionate exploration about what it means to grow and be human:

When I came to college, I expected to be taught, not to learn that I must teach myself, find meaning in the world myself, and experience the world for myself. I didn't have enough confidence in my own abilities to find that charge appropriate or safe. In college and in this class, however, I have learned that we all must traverse our lives alone to the best of our abilities. It is the charge that God gives humans, the responsibility and burden of free will. Anthropology charges forward and demands that we question what we think we know, and, as I have discussed, that can be quite unsettling. Literature provides an opportunity for humans to commiserate about the difficulty of being human, and it is more sensitive to our feelings of rupture and brokenness.

Other moving pieces include those of students (often fourth-years) who (re)discover their own voice through personal reflection. In her learning portfolio, an English major who seemed disenchanted throughout the semester gives me a glimpse into how she struggled to recover her love for literature:

> *Reflecting on this semester and completing this essay had been, per-haps, one of the most honest and personal things I have done in a long time. For too long, I have been caught up in the typically disaffected nature of academia. . . . I tend to read literature with a certain disregard for the ways it truly affects me, at least for class. Writing in a journal, posting responses online, class exercises—all of these have both forced and allowed me to more fully consider the literature that we have read, in ways that I rarely have time for. I have begun connecting themes and ideas of different works, and I have begun to think critically of books in ways that I never did before.*

Some students chose to write about a text or discussion that was partic-ularly meaningful to them. Reflecting on her experience reading Carolivia Herron's *Nappy Hair* and bell hooks's *Happy to Be Nappy*, as well as on the controversy sparked by the first book, a student majoring in psychology writes:

> *Reading the two books brought back so many memories for me of being a child very uncomfortable in her skin. Memories of longing to be White, longing for straight, blonde hair, and longing for acceptance came rush-ing in. Why were parents [who threatened a teacher for using Herron's book] in such an uproar? Did they realize that these two books were dealing with some of the most important issues that a Black child faces? After reading these two books and having Ms. S. [a guest lecturer from the education school] come in to speak more about minority children's literature, I realized that I was very interested. It actually encouraged me to look into reading more of the genre, as well as talking to others with younger minority children.*
>
> *One day, while visiting, I began to tell [an acquaintance] about our class and what we were reading. Being African-American and having a daughter slightly younger than [me], she said that when her daughter was younger, it seemed that the genre was just beginning to take off. She went home and brought me back a stack of books that she had shared with her child. I asked her if she thought the books were helpful in exposing her child to positive role models as well as encouraging her to be proud of herself as a Black female. She said that they absolutely were. Thus, I can't help but think about how important such literature is for minority chil-dren, and how it has evolved. I believe that from taking this class, a new interest has been whetted, and that I will continue to explore the area.*

To anyone unfamiliar with this particular student, the last sentence may seem like an attempt to win the teacher over. I can quote it here because I have since received an e-mail from this student in which she describes how she followed through with her plan after graduating from the university. Two years after taking my class she writes:

I am here in L. teaching 8th grade science through Teach for America. Wow, it is so hard. I never could have imagined just how difficult it would be, but I am glad that I am here. There is such a need, and even though I often feel like I am failing, every now and then I see a glint of hope as a child improves by even just a little. More than anything, I think that this experience has really shown me what a state of disrepair our American education system is in, and I think that I am going to apply for a PhD in education. My passion really is education, but I don't think I am cut out to be a great teacher. My patience level is a little too small.:)

Also, I thought you would like to know that I have cut my hair, and it is now completely natural! So, yes, I have an afro!:) Whenever anyone asks me what made me decide to do it, I say, "Well, it all started with this book called Nappy Hair *that I read in a children's literature class . . . . Honestly, I have to say that reading that book in your class was such a monumental point in my decision to cut my hair . . . . I just kept thinking to myself that I wished someone had said that to me as a child—that I was beautiful and that included all of me, even my nappy hair ! . . .*

Even now, though I LOVE my crazy, nappy fro, I still can get very self-conscious. Especially now that I teach 8th graders. Middle schoolers are not known to be kind, and they very often say things like, "Miss B., why is your hair like that?! You need a perm!". . . Though I don't put much value on a 13-year-old's comments, it's hard not to let your insecurities sneak in. Still, I know that I made the right decision . . . . How can I claim to be an independent woman who accepts herself, and yet smother my hair in chemicals only to better fit in? Furthermore, how can we tell our society's girls that it's okay for them to be themselves, but only if they fit the mold?! . . .

I hope that I am reaching my students on both an academic level and a personal level. Especially the girls in my class. I really want them to see a strong Black woman who is not afraid to be herself. I try to be that person, but I don't know how well I succeed.

A regular practice of reflection can encourage students' self-awareness and renew their commitment to their education. Rather than thoughtlessly going through the motions, they begin to see how what they learn connects to their own ambitions and aspirations. By asking students to construct a narrative about their own learning, we give them permission to articulate what's meaningful to them and to formulate their own learning goals in life. In the process, I find that many students develop an appreciation for the practice of reflection. In end-of-semester evaluations I read comments such as "The writing assignments really forced me to sit down and sort through my brain" or "I found unity and connections between my writings that I didn't even think were there. I understood my ideas so much better and saw a clear development. In short, I was proud of what I accomplished and the portfolio helped me to see that."

References

Baxter Magolda, M. B. (1999). *Creating context for learning and self-authorship: Constructive-developmental pedagogy*. Nashville, TN: Vanderbilt University Press.

Fink, L. D. (2003). *Creating significant learning experiences in college classrooms: An integrated approach to designing college courses*. San Francisco: Jossey-Bass.

McGregor, J. (Ed.). (1993). *New directions for teaching and learning: No. 56. Learning self-evaluation: Fostering reflective learning*. San Francisco: Jossey-Bass.

Chapter 6

Getting Started with Portfolios

A Vision for Implementing Reflection to Enhance Student Learning

Stephanie Burrell, Laurence Miners, Kathryn Nantz, and Roben Torosyan

Fairfield University

ANY INSTITUTION THAT'S getting started with portfolios should ask how such a system of reflection and writing may fit its unique purposes. At Fairfield University, a Jesuit university of five thousand students and 250 full-time faculty, we have been both flexible and planning oriented about designing and redesigning learning portfolio initiatives. Because our mission and the Ignatian paradigm emphasize reflecting on experience and putting learning into action, the learning portfolio is a natural tool for our institution's goals.

When Tom Regan, the provincial superior of the New England Jesuits and a former professor and associate dean at Fairfield University, described the paradigm at our 2007 commencement, he highlighted five big questions for student reflection:

1. *Out of what particular* context *did you come to Fairfield University?*

2. *How did you* experience *the learning process once you got here?*

3. *How did the process of* reflection *assist you in becoming more aware of what you were learning so that you could understand it better?*

4. *How did you move your newly acquired knowledge into* action?

5. *What process of* evaluation *will you use throughout your lives to determine whether or not your Jesuit education here at Fairfield was successful? (Regan, 2007, pp. 2–3)*

More than a five-step process, however, the Jesuit paradigm endorses particular values—a set of attitudes and convictions that can guide the portfolio process. With our emphasis on the formation of men and women of service to others, students can ask themselves, "What will be my contribution to others in the community?" To serve any such "other," we need to understand diverse backgrounds and ways of thinking and make the most of such differences. In particular, students can reflect on how to create a more just society where they question the assumption that socioeconomic privilege should remain as it is. By caring for the whole person, we mean to integrate intellect and affect, thinking and feeling, as well as a wholeness of body, mind, and spirit.

Putting student learning at the center of our work, we turn to learners themselves—and not simply to a course, program, or institutional assessment—as owners of the process of reflection on learning. Nationally, an emphasis on "integrative learning" has arisen, "asking students to 'go meta' with their learning in order to identify, assess, and strategize about next directions" (Huber & Hutchings, 2004, p. 8).

"But," write Huber and Hutchings (2004), "students are unlikely to develop such habits of reflection and intentionality if *faculty* do not do the same" (p. 8). At our institution, as at any mission-oriented organization, we need to ensure that our people and structures across campus interconnect and align. Stepping back for such a strategic overview involves thinking about not only student and faculty development but organizational development. To this end, we consider the following:

- *Curriculum:* how portfolio reflection can focus on integrating learning across the core curriculum and within a concentration
- *Faculty:* how faculty can experiment with portfolio methods
- *Administrators:* how administrators can model reflection on their own learning
- *Students:* how students can help design the ways their learning is assessed
- *Assessment:* how portfolios can guide assessment of both individual student outcomes and program outcomes

What follows is not a statement of policy but an exploration of potential directions to pursue, at Fairfield or elsewhere.

Core Curriculum Unmasked to Enhance Student Learning

Fairfield University's undergraduate core curriculum composes fully half of each student's four-year program. This large core reflects our Jesuit roots and traditions, and though we have reviewed and reconsidered it often over the past thirty years, each time the faculty renews the commitment to delivering it.

The core's organization is based on the principle that exposing students to disciplinary breadth is a fundamentally important aspect of a liberal education. Areas of the twenty-course core include English, history, the natural sciences, mathematics, the social sciences, the visual and performing arts, and modern languages. Most students are required to take five common courses; they choose the remaining fifteen from menus of options. The idea is not just to provide common content or broad content coverage but to introduce students to the diversity of disciplinary approaches to questions. For example, an economist and a historian both have an interest in understanding the Great Depression, but the economist might look for causes in the Federal Reserve's monetary policies, while the historian focuses on the post-WWI Treaty of Versailles and the isolationist mood it created in the United States. Though such approaches are in no way mutually exclusive, they reflect different lenses through which the two disciplines view the world.

Although the institution remains committed to the notion of disciplinary breadth and the importance of exposing students to diverse ways of constructing knowledge, we seem to have lost the importance of turning back to a "core of the core," a common *mission* for core learning that the university articulates in its mission statement. Focus groups indicate students tend to see the core as a checklist rather than a set of experiences that, when integrated, will help them make a difference in the world. Also, focus groups indicate that students tend not to understand the purpose of courses outside their own areas of study. As one student stated:

> *I was taking core classes because I had to, to get them out of the way. I wasn't sure what I was doing. It would be very powerful to be educated about what the core is, why you have to take it. Freshman year, you come in and you're just told this is what you have to take, and it's overwhelming.*

The core of the core is that integrative opportunity for students to make connections between their core courses and between their core courses and other courses in their curriculum. As such, this purpose needs to be made less mysterious to students. We need to be more transparent about the goals and objectives of the set of courses that make up the core. Without specific structures, students may not see how core courses fit together to create an intellectual experience and how they themselves might start to make the connections that we believe are so important.

How might a learning portfolio project provide such a structure for students to return to the core of the core? How might such work make the goals of our core curriculum more transparent to students? Our conversations have led us to two important points. First, students need to practice looking at their own work through a variety of lenses to think about how their own writing and thinking for particular course assignments can lead them to the kinds of connections that are important. They need prompting to take the opportunity to bring individual assignments for particular courses back to the core of the core. For example, a portfolio assignment might ask students to reflect on how work they did for two (or more) of their core courses has helped them take some sort of action in the world. A student might take knowledge from his or her politics and history courses, knit together connections, and then decide to apply this newly integrated perspective to work on a political campaign. This sort of reflection leading to action is important for students to recognize.

Second, students need to reflect on their own development as learners and, in some cases, as teachers. For instance, a learning portfolio assignment might ask students to select from several courses work of which they are most proud and to discuss why they believe that it represents significant learning on their part. Or they might reflect on how their work as a peer writing tutor relates to their own learning as well as provides a service to students. Such intentional attention to their own journey through core courses establishes a relationship between those core courses and the institution's mission. The core curriculum is, in fact, one of the most important delivery mechanisms for our institutional mission—namely, educating men and women to serve others. The learning portfolio provides an opportunity for students to assess their intellectual progress and for faculty to assess student progress and construct learning experiences that help achieve core goals.

Faculty: Innovation Aimed at Integration

Several portfolio initiatives are already under way at Fairfield University. The most extensive and organized effort has been in the School of Nursing. While additional nursing faculty members are using portfolios in individual courses, one faculty member has been using e-portfolios for three years and has students in sophomore-, junior-, and senior-level classes participating. In total, about 350 nursing students have been involved, at some level, in the project. The school's goal is to enable students to establish a foundation for reflective moments in the consideration of their career. In addition, it hopes that the portfolios will facilitate communication with advisers, provide a structure for collecting works, help the students create exciting résumés, and remain useful for students in their nursing careers. A recent survey of nursing students indicated that, as a result of the portfolio initiative, more than half the students gained an appreciation of their accomplishments, reported enhanced identification of goals, and appreciated reflecting on what they learned. They also indicated that the e-portfolio had helped them organize their résumés and enhance their interactions with course instructors. However, 70 percent of the nursing students still preferred paper résumés to electronic portfolios, and fewer than half the students envisioned sending their e-portfolio to a prospective employer or using it as part of a graduate school application. The school hopes that as additional faculty members come on board and as the software improves, acceptance of the e-portfolio initiative will become more widespread. (We are grateful to Professor Suzanne Campbell for sharing detailed information with us about her use of e-portfolios with her students.)

For the past few years, Fairfield's University College, which coordinates the university's study-abroad programs, has asked students to keep portfolios of their experiences. In particular, students studying in Australia have been creating e-portfolios to record and reflect on their international internship experiences. Additional work needs to be done with these portfolios when students return to campus to assist students in incorporating study abroad with their overall college experience.

Students in Fairfield's premed program have been creating nonelectronic portfolios to bring together their work in natural science classes and other medicine-related disciplines. This portfolio system is still being developed, and the university is considering several e-portfolio software alternatives.

In the Department of Visual and Performing Arts, studio-art students are evaluated by the content and form of their visual pieces. In addition, students submit one to two papers per semester, and they are asked to participate in group and individual critiques. While each class is structured differently, all students are evaluated on how well their visual assignments summarize their understanding of a particular medium, theme, and/or working methodology. At the end of the term, faculty members review each student's entire body of work. (We are grateful to Professor Suzanne Chamlin for providing us with information about the studio-art program.)

While individual departments and schools have been committed to developing and using portfolios, the larger task that remains, from a university-wide perspective, is to explore how portfolios can aid in the integration of core learning. Our intent is to begin small. A pilot group of ten to twelve faculty members needs to begin the initiative. Ideally, these faculty members will be from different departments and teach courses that include students at various stages of study. A common (though by no means identical) approach should be used in formulating and assessing portfolios. As the program expands, students could be asked to take one course per year that includes a portfolio. The strategy would enable students to evaluate their own learning over time and encourage them to think more deeply about themselves as lifelong learners. Over time, we could also expect that portfolios would be part of a certain number of core and major-field courses. Such application of portfolios would facilitate the horizontal and vertical integration the university hopes to achieve both across core courses and between the core and the major.

In a related part of the university's strategic plan, five faculty learning communities (FLCs) have been formed to support faculty as they explore new ways to integrate their teaching (see Cox, 2004, for an introduction to the FLC model). Several of these yearlong communities are considering incorporating portfolios into their courses, and we expect that there may be enough interest next year to form a separate learning community centered on the development and use of portfolios. Each of the thirty faculty members participating will write a report that explains their work in the community. We hope, through this process, to encourage faculty members to explore using teaching portfolios and thus establish a practice of reflecting on their own work. Such modeling will be important as we introduce portfolios to students.

Administrative Leadership and Support

Fairfield University is in the process of updating its course management system (CMS), and during the fall 2007 semester, the university's Educational Technology Committee, at the request of the administration, reviewed several CMSs. While the primary objective of the exercise was to identify the preferred CMS for the university, the committee was also asked to consider the compatibility between a CMS and electronic portfolio software.

One of the key components of the university's strategic plan is the desire to instill in learners a lifelong reflective practice. Portfolios are viewed as an integral piece in accomplishing our goal. The CMS review process offers an example of administration and faculty cooperation in fostering an integrated approach to learning.

The e-portfolio initiatives already under way on campus have been hosted by the Connecticut Distance Learning Consortium. A staff person from the university's technology support division has provided hands-on, one-on-one support for faculty using the e-portfolio software.

While faculty acceptance is the most important part of implementing a portfolio initiative, administrative leaders can give support in terms of reward and recognition for the use of reflective practice. Administrative financial support has also been important for bringing national experts to Fairfield's campus and sending faculty leaders to conferences. Implementing a culture of reflective practice will take time. Faculty members and administrative leaders alike can model reflection themselves by being open to feedback from colleagues, showing how they learn from *their* experiences.

To foster the creation of a community-wide culture of reflective learning, the administration should also support programming and initiatives that attempt to bridge the gap between academics and student affairs. Such integration of living and learning is an important part of the university's strategic plan and recognizes the need to include students in the planning process.

Involving Students

When we create and assess portfolios, we cannot involve only the students themselves; we must also create *involving* students—that is, people who involve others in creating community and even in changing the world. Students who involve others may seek out other perspectives on new learning or on their own work, or they may enlist others in student organizations, campus events, community service, or activist interventions to rectify injustices.

In exploring portfolio processes, we have formed small focus groups of Fairfield University students to solicit input. Themes voiced by students include the following:

- Before demanding reflection, orient students to what is expected.
- To motivate interest, make the process fun, interesting, and useful or relevant to job and graduate school applications, for instance.
- Set the goals of the portfolio and require it for a program (not simply one course), but then give students lots of freedom to be creative about how they reach those goals.

One student said, skeptically, "Regular reflection would only be practiced by my friends who are motivated and committed to their education. If it becomes a norm, however, I can easily see students changing their habits for the better."

Such student concerns about expectations, relevance, choice, and peer cultural norms can be addressed by providing clear criteria for portfolio evaluation. As Myles Horton described the essential task: "You only learn from the experience you learn from" (Newman, 2006, p. 240); but the question becomes how to guide learning from experience without inviting students to game the system by generating good confessions or conversion stories.

To elicit such authentic reflection, one prompt in a modern philosophy course asks the following of students:

> *Reflect on your own assumptions, strengths, and areas to improve. Show, for example, how your own thinking changed or deepened, or how that was a struggle and what you take away from the change or struggle to change. Avoid a "mandated confessional" (Brookfield, 1995, p. 13); examine honestly any tension or difference you felt with course goals or methods, for instance; just be sure to clarify what you learn from your self-analysis.*

Criteria for evaluating the responses to such a prompt, as well as to portfolios in general, include the following:

- Avoids making several superficial reflections. Instead, develops a few fully. Expands and explains reflections by giving examples of what the student takes away from the change or struggle to change. Likewise, avoids amassing lots of details; instead, selects a well-chosen few and clarifies their point.
- Avoids a static view of learning as perfect or final by instead focusing on a learning edge where the student questions assumptions.

Perhaps the first criterion would better read, "Avoids making superficial reflections or else examines why the student honestly struggles to do so," and the second could read likewise, " . . . where the student questions assumptions or honestly struggles to do so." The point for faculty is to experiment with redesigning portfolio instructions and criteria, at least from time to time, to continuously improve how well we reach intended learning outcomes.

Assessment: Avoiding Putting the Cart Before the Horse

As with any new initiative, a plan to assess the effectiveness of the program must be developed before the initiative is put into place. Unfortunately, what usually occurs, in our experience, is that such a conversation takes place at the end of the process and sounds like this: "How do we know if this process worked? Was it useful or helpful to students? Did students learn what we wanted them to learn?" On one hand, we acknowledge how such questions are difficult to answer before beginning a program; however, our goal is to reverse the trend by asking such questions up front and developing an assessment plan that will help us meet the goals of the learning portfolio initiative. A few pointers about assessment are shared next along with an account of where our team is in the process of developing a plan for implementation. We offer the tips as guidelines for effectively launching a portfolio initiative.

First, determine the overarching goals and objectives of the learning portfolio initiative, and use them as the driving force when developing an assessment plan. Stassen, Doherty, and Poe (2004) suggest using the following questions as a guide: "What do you want students to know?" "What do you want students to be able to do?" and "What do you want students to care about or value?" This process works best if outcomes are connected to the mission of the university and to the student learning goals of the departments using learning portfolios. In our case, our goal is tied to the college's strategic plan and core integration initiative discussed earlier in this chapter. We believe the learning portfolio initiative can help the university and departmental programs determine how well we are achieving the goals and objectives of the strategic plan and the educational outcomes set forth for disciplines individually and collectively; we believe, too, that the initiative can create a process for assessing our general education program that is "meaningful, manageable, and sustainable" (Allen, 2006, p. 157).

The overarching student learning goal for the learning portfolio initiative at Fairfield University is "to help students reflect on and understand the 'wholeness' of their Fairfield education" (Learning and Integrity, p. 12). Examples of measurable objectives for this goal include students' ability to describe their learning process, demonstrate self-assessment skills, apply the methods of reflective writing, and create a junior-level project demonstrating integration of the core. Such goals and objectives reflect what Zubizarreta (2004) proposes are the "core aims of portfolio development":

- *Engage students in a process of inquiry into what they have learned.*

- *Provide students with a model for demonstrating the outcomes of learning.*

- *Establish a reflective learning environment that helps students go beyond accumulation of knowledge to analysis of how, when, and why they have learned.*

- *Promote thinking about what lies ahead for improvement and future learning. (p. 28)*

At Fairfield, we are now determining student learning outcomes for the learning portfolio initiative and hope to move beyond this stage soon.

Second, determine how to collect evidence that shows how well and why students are meeting the learning outcomes developed for the program (Walvoord, 2004). We believe that assessment is truly about improving courses, programs, and such to increase student learning. For that reason, formative assessment is our top priority. A combination of direct and indirect measures can be used to assess student learning. An example of a direct measure would be the junior-level project mentioned as a goal. An online survey, similar to the one administered at LaGuardia Community College, is an example of an indirect measure we plan to consider. The survey will allow us to examine students' attitudes toward learning portfolios, the impact of learning portfolios on their learning process, and the usefulness of the program during several stages of the assessment cycle.

A preassessment was done to bring student voices into the process early on and give students the opportunity to share their opinions of learning portfolios before we implement the initiative. Results from the questionnaire used to glean this data will guide our decision making throughout this process. Sample questions from the survey include the following: (1) In what ways would a learning portfolio be useful to you during your time at Fairfield? Why or why not? (2) What are the biggest challenges you see for yourself in using a portfolio? (3) In your opinion what is the best way to get students at Fairfield excited about using portfolios? We have collected information from just a few students at this point and plan to invite more students to complete the questionnaire in the near future.

Third, use the data collected to improve student learning and the portfolio system you select for the initiative. If results show that students want more choice in selecting which assignments will be included in their portfolio, or that the program is not user friendly because of particular students' learning disabilities, or that students have difficulty applying the methods of reflective writing, or that students of color are less likely to engage in portfolio development—take action right away and close the loop to improve results for the next assessment cycle. We have not reached this stage in our process but plan to use our own advice once we get there!

The fourth and final suggestion is to make the final assessment report accessible to everyone. It should include the results from the data analysis, how what was learned from the evaluation will be addressed, and a timeline for implementing changes. Such careful implementation will help all involved with the initiative believe that their voices count and that leaders of the process "walk the talk."

References

Allen, M. J. (2006). *Assessing general education programs*. Bolton, MA: Anker.

Brookfield, S. D. (1995). *Becoming a critically reflective teacher*. San Francisco: Jossey-Bass.

Cox, M. D. (2004). Introduction to faculty learning communities. In M. D. Cox & L. Richlin (Eds.), *New directions for teaching and learning: No. 97. Building faculty learning communities* (pp. 5–23). San Francisco: Jossey-Bass.

Huber, M. T., & Hutchings, P. (2004). *Integrative learning: Mapping the terrain*. Retrieved October 2, 2008, from www.carnegiefoundation.org/Integrative Learning/mapping-terrain.pdf

Learning and integrity: A strategic vision for Fairfield University. (2005). Fairfield, CT: Fairfield University.

Newman, M. (2006). *Teaching defiance: Stories and strategies for activist educators*. San Francisco: Jossey-Bass.

Regan, T. (2007). *Commencement address, Fairfield University, May 20, 2007*. Retrieved October 2, 2008, from www.fairfield.edu/pr_index.html?id=2107

Stassen, M. L. A., Doherty, K., & Poe, M. (2004). *Program-based review and assessment: Tools and techniques for program improvement*. Amherst: University of Massachusetts.

Walvoord, B. E. (2004). *Assessment clear and simple*. San Francisco: Jossey-Bass.

Zubizarreta, J. (2004). *The learning portfolio: Reflective practice for improving student learning*. Bolton, MA: Anker.

Chapter 7

The Oral Health E-portfolio

A Three-Year Project

Russell Butson, Jennifer Marie Cook, and Rosemary Kardos
University of Otago, New Zealand

THE THREE-YEAR ORAL HEALTH E-PORTFOLIO PROJECT is aimed at introducing bachelor of oral health (BOH) students working to qualify as dental hygienists and dental therapists to the use of a personal e-portfolio for advancing their academic and professional development. The e-portfolio also assists staff in meeting the professional development requirements for their annual practicing certificates (APCs). It enables BOH students to collect evidence of their achievements and personal reflections throughout their three years of undergraduate study, culminating in registration and an APC. The project focuses on developing a structure where users store and select information that is then displayed or published as high-quality evidence of accomplishments.

The Health Practitioners Competence Assurance Act (HPCAA) was passed by the New Zealand Parliament in 2003 and came fully into force on September 18, 2004. The act repealed eleven occupational statutes governing thirteen professions, including dentistry, and it provides a regulatory framework for health practitioners. It was created with the principal purpose of protecting the health and safety of the public by providing mechanisms to ensure that health practitioners are competent and fit to practice their professions (Ministry of Health, 2006).

The legislation resulted in the constitution of the combined Dental Council of New Zealand (DCNZ). The DCNZ is a self-regulatory body for the dental professions. The minister of health appoints members of the council. There are fourteen members: eleven professionals (five dentists, two dental therapists, one dental hygienist, two clinical dental technicians, and one person involved in teaching dentistry) and three lay members (DCNZ, 2007b). The DCNZ ensures that undergraduate and postgraduate programs in dentistry, leading to registration, meet acceptable national and international standards. The BOH degree is a program for education and training accredited by the DCNZ and the Australian Dental Council, and it allows its graduates to register as dental hygienists and dental therapists. The council sets clinical, cultural, and ethical standards for dental professionals; authorizes certification; and deals with practitioners whose fitness to practice or competence has been called into question (DCNZ, 2007c).

The DCNZ has defined some twenty scopes of dental practice. A scope of practice defines what a registered practitioner is permitted to do. Practice outside of a registered scope is illegal and has significant penalties. To be registered in a scope, applicants are required to be fit for registration, competent to practice within the scope, and have fulfilled a prescribed qualification for that scope of practice. Practitioners may be registered in one or more scopes of practice (DCNZ, 2007a).

All dental professionals are required to hold an APC issued by the DCNZ. The DCNZ's Dental Hygienist Board and Dental Therapist Board are responsible for ensuring the continuing professional competence and fitness to practice of all registered dental hygienists and dental therapists practicing in New Zealand. The recertification program for dental hygienists and dental therapists operates on a two-year cycle and is designed to assist them in maintaining their competence to practice through engagement in Continuing Professional Development (CPD) activities, maintaining contact with their peers, and meeting defined professional standards.

Compliance monitoring was phased in during 2007 with a random selection of 10 percent of all registered dental hygienists and dental therapists. They are required to provide evidence of competency (within a ten-day time period) in the form of a professional portfolio.

The DCNZ's requirement that all dental practitioners maintain a professional portfolio offered a rationale for developing and introducing e-portfolios into the faculty of dentistry. This was an opportunity to engage students and teaching staff to support learning and to train students in the development and maintenance of a portfolio. The ultimate goal was to create an application to facilitate portfolio preparation by busy practitioners within the dental hygiene and dental therapy scopes of practice.

The BOH Degree and the Positioning of the Oral Health E-portfolio

The BOH curriculum (University of Otago, 2007a) has a multidimensional structure of interconnecting and overlapping themes that have been isolated and individually identified to clarify their importance: ethics and jurisprudence, communication, teamwork and collegiality, intraprofessional and collaborative learning, research and self-directed learning, public health, reflective practice, clinical skills, and integration of knowledge. It also has a strong focus on health promotion and cultural knowledge that underpins best practice in the provision of oral health care. The person who emerges as a BOH graduate is both a teacher and a healer who will be able to promote health and provide care as a dental hygienist or dental therapist (University of Otago, 2007b).

The oral health e-portfolio system has been constructed as a Web-based environment that allows users to capture and manipulate information to organize and map out their academic and professional goals, experiences, and achievements.

To date, three portfolios have been created within the oral health e-portfolio system. The environment has been designed to allow a number of specific portfolios to coexist within the single system. This is important when creating communities of users who wish to review peers' portfolios. All users of the system may be invited to be part of a social network of reviewers, either singularly or as groups.

The three portfolios currently within the oral health e-portfolio are the following:

1. The BOH portfolio (for oral health undergraduate students)

2. The dental hygiene professional portfolio

3. The dental therapy professional portfolio

These portfolios are part of a much larger architecture that encompasses the progression from undergraduate to practicing professional as a lifelong learning career.

The professional portfolio has been created in accordance with the requirements of the DCNZ. Similarly, the BOH portfolio could meet DCNZ requirements, but it is more comprehensive; it provides a means for integrating the learning identified in the curriculum. Students capture material from relevant events during their educational experiences and then organize these in a manner suitable for inclusion in their portfolios. By the completion of the three-year course, students should be capable and confident in capturing, organizing, and presenting a significant body of evidence showcasing their achievements.

The successful use of the e-portfolio system depends on students' discovering the relevance of the curriculum, their response to the curriculum, and their understanding of the importance of being able to document and present evidence of their proficiency. A paramount principle of the project is that the course is not perceived as a succession of assignments but rather recognized as a complex and holistic underpinning to a career in oral health.

The Individual Portfolios

As previously mentioned, three portfolios have been developed—one for oral health undergraduates and two for practicing professionals—and both the BOH and the professional portfolios are entities within a larger architecture. The BOH portfolio has been designed to offer students a personal digital working environment that enables them to commence building a body of material from which they can capture evidence of their achievements; monitor their progress; and organize, evaluate, and publish relevant material. The decision to introduce professional portfolios for staff was seen as a logical progression from the BOH portfolio. It was considered advantageous to develop and introduce an e-portfolio system suitable for both staff and student use.

Several differences exist between our project and other e-portfolio initiatives, primarily in the complexity of the design but also because both student and staff involvement in the trial was voluntary.

The design of the e-portfolio system is comprehensive and functionally complex; however, it employs straightforward processes for the user. The application has been structured into three stages of data refinement, as shown in Figure 7.1. Each stage allows users to further refine their material and evidence in order to display and share the highest-quality material in their final output.

As further illustrated in Figure 7.2, the three stages of data refinement are the following:

- The data repository
- An area for selection, organization, and filtration
- The display section for filtered material

The file repository "My Files" allows users to input, store, and archive pieces of information within predefined forms. Many of these forms allow for multiple sources of data and detailed input by users. For instance, a form for an activity collects the standard title, date, place, and time information. The form then requires the student to describe the activity, to reflect on the experience, and to relate it to his or her professional plan, describing a future course of action. Forms also allow reviewers, who have been selected by the user, to post comments.

The next stage requires the user to choose particular forms from the data repository and add them to specific presentation templates. These have been developed to meet DCNZ requirements. Finally, material is displayed on an aesthetically pleasing, multiple-menu Web site that can be viewed via a Web address. It can also be saved to disk or simply printed.

FIGURE 7.1

The Three Stages of Refinement

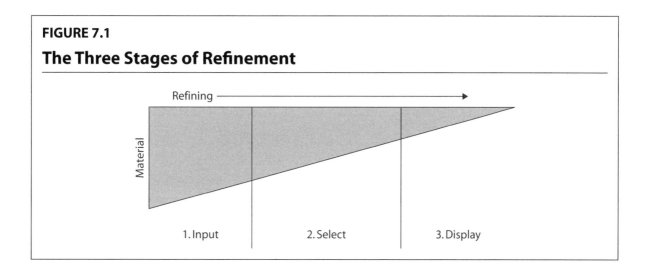

FIGURE 7.2

The Three-Stage Process of Refining Material for Display Within the Oral Health E-portfolio

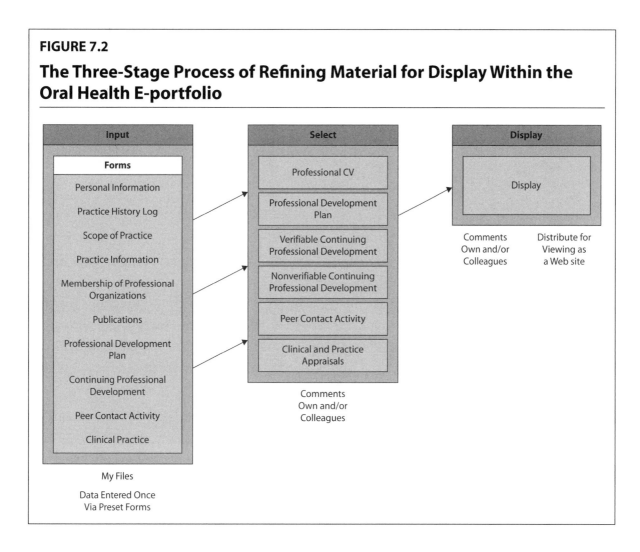

The Professional Portfolios

For staff, the oral health e-portfolio offered a straightforward, convenient alternative to paper-based approaches to meeting the DCNZ's requirements for the APC. As previously mentioned, the two initial professional portfolios have been designed for dental hygienists and dental therapists.

Each professional portfolio contains a series of templates and forms, based on DCNZ requirements. The DCNZ requires records of verifiable continuing professional development (CPD) activities, nonverifiable CPD activities, a professional development plan, a professional CV, and interactive peer contact activities. Self-assessment of personal performance and clinical and practice appraisals are also required. Digital forms and templates have been created in line with the DCNZ requirements and supported by a series of additional templates that allow users to develop their professional portfolios beyond the DCNZ's minimum requirements. The additions were conceived through discussions with registered dental hygienists and dental therapists. For example, a CV form was developed within the professional portfolio that is informative and relevant to dental professionals. It was agreed that the CV would contain a section where dental hygienists and dental therapists could indicate their registration in additional scopes of practice and any conditions that may limit their practice.

The BOH Portfolio

The BOH portfolio focuses on reinforcing the merits of situating students at the center of their learning experiences and observing how they manage and control their own records and information to make sense of and map out their academic and professional goals, experiences, and outcomes. The oral health e-portfolio offers a progressive structure that facilitates the capturing, organizing, and publishing of proficiencies from students' learning experiences. It is an environment within which the student's accumulating activities can be consolidated into meaningful output. We proposed that the requirements for an APC would drive the students' need to know how to capture, organize, reflect on, and present their evidence.

Project Year One: Experiences

The initial trial phase took place during the February–June 2007 semester. During that time, the project team met with students on a number of occasions. The project team held an introductory session, followed by a series of professional development sessions, focus groups, and workshops on various topics.

Voluntary Participation, Preliminary Exposure, and Support

The first phase of the project involved collaborating with students and creating the BOH portfolio. Students were informed of the project and invited to participate. Students were told clearly that no aspect of their participation in the project would contribute to their final grade. In particular, students were told the following:

- Participation in the initial trial was voluntary and did not replace or supersede the traditional teaching and learning processes offered within the faculty of dentistry.
- While the juxtaposition of the trial project and the BOH curriculum was important, the two processes remained firmly separate.
- There was no assessment involved and no contribution to their final grade.

Feedback from students and staff was encouraged at an early stage to develop the software applications further and to inform future deployment of the applications.

While inputting data into the e-portfolio is straightforward, we recognized that data collection could be challenging for students. Students were introduced to a range of digital tools that would allow them to capture, organize, reflect, share, collaborate, and publish. A number of such resources were Web 2.0 tools, but we also introduced applications commonly used in professional practice: information management, social networking, and electronic calendars. Drop-in sessions were offered to support and observe the students' use of software applications. The sessions also offered a safe environment to discuss the importance of students' assuming control of their learning and how to go about the process. Our intention was to encourage students to use digital resources to help take control of their learning.

An important element in maintaining a professional portfolio is self-reflection. Reflective writing is a new and daunting concept for many first-year BOH students. A workshop on reflective writing was held for the students. They were introduced to a technique for reflective thinking and writing to help them write reflectively about their learning experiences, including clinical and professional practice. The workshop was informative, and students who attended the session reported, during a focus group, that while they found the task challenging, it had inspired them to consider their experiences more methodically.

Research Design and Methodology

The project embraces design-based research (DBR) as a suitable method for addressing complex problems in real contexts in collaboration with practitioners. The DBR approach supported our view that we needed to identify the problems before building solutions. As a framework, DBR allowed us to tackle theoretical questions about the nature of what we were trying to achieve. Also, by integrating known and hypothetical design principles, DBR helped us determine relevant solutions to changing requirements. We believed that we should adopt an approach that would support a participatory model of development while upholding a rigorous and reflective inquiry aimed at testing and refining (Bell, 2004). DBR was the only model we were able to find that met such demands.

Our Expectations

We wanted to work with students and engage them in a more self-directed approach to their learning (Candy, 1991). By giving students such a space, we anticipated that they would be inclined to the behaviors illustrated in the self-directed paradigm of Table 7.1 rather than those in the instructional paradigm.

We were confident that students would see the relevance of linking their educational experiences to career development. We anticipated students would take responsibility for understanding, structuring, and organizing their learning, enabling them to present their work in a professional manner.

Our aim was for students to become empowered not only to create records but also to manage, collaborate on, reflect on, evaluate, and quantify their experiences. As a result, we anticipated that students should have a greater understanding about the importance of their academic and professional education and learning. Students should develop a new awareness of themselves not as students but as emerging professionals capable of providing evidence of their competence and fitness for practice. Furthermore, we predicted that student participation would result in a greater degree of engagement (McMahon & Portelli, 2004), improved work/study habits, a higher quality of work, and most importantly, a deeper understanding of and control over their learning.

TABLE 7.1

Comparison of Two Educational Paradigms

	Instructional Paradigm	Self-Directed Paradigm
Knowledge	Transfer from faculty to students	Jointly constructed by students and faculty
Students	Passive vessel to be filled by faculty's knowledge	Active constructor, discoverer, transformer of own knowledge
Faculty Purpose	Classify and sort students	Develop students' competencies and talents
Relationships	Impersonal relationships between students and between faculty and students	Personal transactions between students and between faculty and students
Context	Competitive and individualistic	Collaborative learning, involving teams and faculty
Assumptions	Any expert can teach	Teaching as complex activity that requires considerable training

Source: Adapted from Barr and Tagg (1995).

Our Findings

By the end of the February–June 2007 semester, we observed a general reluctance in BOH students to try new things, particularly those associated with information technology. Students were encouraged to explore the oral health e-portfolio independently, through the use of an online user guide.

Student Response to the Oral Health E-portfolio Project

Although students were generally supportive, the degree of commitment to and engagement with the oral health e-portfolio project was low. A weekly drop-in period was offered to support students in using technology and to answer questions concerning the purpose and use of the e-portfolio. Students were invited to attend weekly focus groups aimed at exploring their approach to learning, their readiness to integrate technology into their learning, and their perceptions and expectations of the project. The drop-in and focus groups were both poorly supported, with only 15 percent of students participating. Self-exploration of the oral health e-portfolio system did not drive students, nor did it capture their imagination. The project team interpreted the result as an unwillingness to move away from the teacher-centered instructional paradigm (Table 7.1). Students saw no relative advantage in adopting a self-organizing approach and often cited lack of time as their primary reason (Rogers, 1995).

Assumptions and Misconceptions

Clearly, some of our early assumptions were off target: we had assumed that students would be eager to be involved in the project and that they would be regular and proficient users of computer technology. Instead, we made the following discoveries:

- While students saw the importance of a portfolio for their professional career, they didn't believe they had the time to work on it while studying.
- Generally, students were focused only on work that was a course requirement. The e-portfolio project was voluntary and therefore a low priority.
- Students were not as tech savvy as the project team had expected. We found a very high level of inexperienced users of a wide variety of applications. Most students printed off all material and worked exclusively with hard copies.
- Students felt the portfolio was associated with postdegree practice and was therefore not relevant to their current stage.

Both formal and informal discussions with students revealed a reliance on compliance behaviors rather than behaviors allied with self-directedness: achievement was seen as being determined by contact activities (that is, attending classes) rather than by noncontact study (that is, engaging with content). We also observed students' unease with capturing and organizing material in digital form. We found this to be particularly pertinent, given the degree of computer literacy required to engage in and maintain the related processes associated with compiling a comprehensive e-portfolio.

Conclusion

The requirement for health practitioners to collect evidence for certification under the HPCAA 2003 created an opportunity to use industry requirements to inform practices for emerging professionals. The concept of an e-portfolio seems to be a logical approach to meeting such a requirement. Individuals have access to and control over capturing, storing, sharing, and publishing evidence of their professional abilities and experiences. The initial phase of the project was to design and construct a comprehensive e-portfolio architecture for DCNZ certification requirements. Student and staff feedback was considered valuable, although it was not an integral part of the initial phase.

A Web-based portfolio system has been created and will be tested and evaluated further by staff and students in coming years. We hope, in the second part of the project, to be able to illustrate working processes that allow users to capture, organize, collaborate on, share, and publish details of their experience and their professional skills and attributes effortlessly. While our primary interest has been to work with students, we believe further development of the application could also provide other health professionals with a superior solution to generating professional portfolios that meet the requirements of their own professional councils and boards.

The second phase focuses on the student and professional staff's use of the portfolio and varying approaches to gathering evidence. Staff and student involvement in this stage will be crucial. Given the difficulties experienced in engaging students to date, we will need to explore other approaches to achieve a higher participation rate. The primary focus of the second phase is to increase our understanding of the students' perceptions, needs, and approaches to learning in order to design approaches that will help them take control of and be more engaged with their learning.

Trials are under way to introduce students to a private online social network. We anticipate social interactions online will act as a catalyst for engaging students in other, more meaningful online activities. We hope such an environment will act as a platform on which to engage students in exploring their learning practices and in seeing the relevance of a professional portfolio in their future careers.

References

Barr, R. B., & Tagg, J. (1995, November/December). From teaching to learning—A new paradigm for undergraduate education. *Change, 27*(6), 12–25.

Bell, P. (2004). On the theoretical breadth of design-based research in education. *Educational Psychologist, 39*(4), 243–253.

Candy, P. C. (1991). *Self-direction for lifelong learning: A comprehensive guide to theory and practice.* San Francisco: Jossey-Bass.

Dental Council of New Zealand. (2007a). *The dental council.* Retrieved October 2, 2008, from www.dcnz.org.nz/dcAboutCouncil

Dental Council of New Zealand. (2007b). *Registration—Overview.* Retrieved October 2, 2008, from www.dcnz.org.nz/dcRegistrationOverview

Dental Council of New Zealand. (2007c). *Roles and functions.* Retrieved October 2, 2008, from www.dcnz.org.nz/dcAboutRoles

McMahon, B., & Portelli, J. (2004). Engagement for what? Beyond popular discourses of student engagement. *Leadership and Policy in Schools, 3*(1), 59–76.

Ministry of Health. (2006). *Health Practitioners Competence Assurance Act 2003.* Retrieved October 2, 2008, from www.moh.govt.nz/hpca

Rogers, E. (1995). *Diffusion of innovations.* New York: Free Press.

University of Otago. (2007a). *Bachelor of oral health (BOH).* Retrieved October 2, 2008, from www.otago.ac.nz/courses/qualifications/boh.html

University of Otago. (2007b). *Dental students get their teeth into new oral health degree.* Retrieved October 2, 2008, from www.otago.ac.nz/news/news/2007/23–02–07 _press_release.html

Chapter 8

EPAC

Building a Community of Practice Around E-portfolios

Helen L. Chen
Stanford University

John C. Ittelson
California State University–Monterey Bay

ELECTRONIC LEARNING PORTFOLIOS, or e-portfolios, are more than just a technology: they imply a process of planning, keeping track of, making sense of, and sharing evidence of learning and performance. Consequently, the e-portfolio audience is wide ranging and heterogeneous, including individuals and organizations interested in the design of e-portfolio tools—such as commercial vendors, open source systems, and homegrown solutions tailored to specific institutional needs—as well as the faculty, the students, and others who use e-portfolios for a pedagogical approach in the classroom, a means to showcase one's experiences to prospective employers, or a method for gathering data for institutional assessment and accreditation.

The common interest in e-portfolios, broadly defined, was the motivation behind the formation of the EPAC community of practice (EPAC originally stood for Electronic Portfolio Action Committee and then evolved to Electronic Portfolio Action and Communication, but it's more commonly known by its acronym). At its inception in fall 2001, EPAC was composed of individuals and organizations that were involved in the creation of tools or systems to enhance the development of electronic portfolios in higher education. Today, the membership is predominantly focused on the use of e-portfolios in teaching, learning, and assessment rather than on tool development, and it includes primary and secondary educators as well as those involved in lifelong learning initiatives.

This chapter provides a brief overview of the evolution of the EPAC community of practice as a model for identifying future directions and areas of exploration to support the use of e-portfolios in higher education and beyond.

A Brief History of EPAC

EPAC began as a consortium of individuals, institutions, and organizations, including California State University–Monterey Bay, the Carnegie Foundation for the Advancement of Teaching, Indiana University–Purdue University Indianapolis, the Massachusetts Institute of Technology, Northwestern University, Stanford University, the University of Washington, and others. Early conversations focused primarily on the technological aspects of e-portfolio tools and took place at face-to-face conferences and via e-mail, phone, and videoconferencing. The distributed meetings often required a great deal of logistical planning to schedule rooms and the use of audio bridges and early multipoint IP videoconferencing. Most of these virtual meetings were essentially a series of one-way communications where the individual work of each campus was presented and then followed by questions. These presentations were useful in raising awareness of the range of ongoing projects and defining the space and interests of those involved with work related to e-portfolios.

EPAC's early face-to-face meetings took place at various learning technology conferences, including the annual meetings for EDUCAUSE and the National Learning Infrastructure Initiative (NLII, now the EDUCAUSE Learning Initiative). NLII was instrumental in supporting the beginnings of the EPAC community through the work of NLII fellow John C. Ittelson of California State University–Monterey Bay (CSUMB). One of the first major undertakings of the group was to plan and hold a NLII focus session on e-portfolios at Northwestern University on October 25, 2002. This interactive working session explored issues relating to teaching and learning in higher education, institutional planning and implementation, uses of e-portfolios, and functional specifications for e-portfolio systems. The work completed during the focus session included a revised set of scenarios describing the potential consequential uses of e-portfolios, a set of functional requirements corresponding to e-portfolio system uses, a draft rubric for evaluating e-portfolio systems, and a list of pedagogical and implementation issues that informed the agenda for the e-portfolio summit held by the American Association for Higher Education (AAHE) in November 2002.

On the day before the focus session, sponsored by CSUMB and the university's Ready2Net series, John C. Ittelson organized a live satellite broadcast on the same theme as the session. The program, titled "Teaching, Learning and Assessment with ePortfolios," explored the following questions:

- Why would an institution implement an e-portfolio program?
- How are teaching and learning transformed through the use of e-portfolios? What pedagogical changes are possible and/or required?
- What is the impact of implementing e-portfolios on the institutional infrastructure (that is, network, hardware, software, administrative systems)?
- How do e-portfolios influence how courses are managed? How schools track student progress? How teachers and students interact?
- What is the value of e-portfolios to their users and developers? What are their trials and tribulations?

Hosted by Kenneth Green, founder and director of the Campus Computing Project, and Helen L. Chen of Stanford University, the experts participating in the focus session were also featured in the Ready2Net program. The educators on the Ready2Net program eventually became active volunteers and founding members of EPAC (see http://ready2net.csumb.edu to access an archive of the webcast and view the list of presenters).

From 2003 to 2004, NLII fellow Darren Cambridge, currently of George Mason University, included EPAC as a pilot group in the EDUCAUSE Virtual Community of Practice (VCOP) initiative. Support provided by the organization included facilitator training at the EDUCAUSE annual conference, weekly conference calls, and NLII staff support. The technology used by the community at that time offered tools that encouraged distributed work, including an audio bridge, and interactive multimedia that facilitated webcasts, narrated presentations, and videoconferencing.

In early 2004, EPAC was able to expand its activities through joint support from NLII and AAHE. At this point, Helen L. Chen officially joined John C. Ittelson and Darren Cambridge as a facilitator and coordinator for the EPAC community. Unlike the short-term and conference-specific common interest groups offered only during face-to-face meetings, AAHE provided an online space for community participants to share and collectively generate resources; to collaborate, coordinate work, and provide feedback and encouragement through chats, e-mail lists, and threaded discussions; to keep members updated on upcoming events through a shared schedule; and to get to know others interested in a common practice. In-person meetings at the annual conferences of EDUCAUSE, NLII, and AAHE consistently offered opportunities for EPAC members to put names with faces (and voices) and to enhance the community's efforts by providing concentrated time for planning collective work ("AAHE Launches Communities of Practice," 2004).

AAHE's support of EPAC ended in June 2005 when the organization disbanded, but continued expansion of the EPAC community paralleled a corresponding growth in interest in e-portfolios both nationally and internationally. In fall 2003, the first international conference on e-portfolios was held in France by the European Institute for E-Learning (or EIfEL; www.eife-l.org), which administers the Europortfolio consortium (www.europortfolio.org). The Inter/National Coalition for Electronic Portfolio Research (http://ncepr.org) was established in spring 2004 with the selection of ten institutions composing its first cohort. Since then, the coalition has worked with over forty campuses and now also addresses how e-portfolios can support student learning and educational outcomes in a UK and European context.

Although EPAC's formal face-to-face meetings are less frequent, synchronous and asynchronous virtual activities have expanded in the form of webcasts and online chats to discuss case studies, pedagogical approaches, assessment techniques, and best practices. In addition, the exchange of resources, the tracking of international and national conferences, requests for proposals and collaboration opportunities, and active exploration and evaluation of tools and practices to support activities, reflective thinking, and community building related to e-portfolios are ongoing. EPAC has continued to flourish through partnerships with the Inter/National Coalition for Electronic Portfolio Research, MERLOT (Multimedia Educational Resource for Learning and Online Teaching; www.merlot.org), and the higher education community of the Apple Learning Interchange (http://edcommunity.apple.com/ali).

Sustaining the EPAC Community

The EPAC community has been largely maintained by promoting the following three components: organizing and holding online events, planning and executing face-to-face meetings, and keeping an up-to-date Web space. As shown in Figure 8.1, the integration of these activities over time creates an iterative "rhythm" and "sense of place" that sets expectations for the opportunities for how one might participate in the community (Cambridge, Kaplan, & Suter, 2005, p. 2).

In general, EPAC's experiences with the EDUCAUSE VCOP initiative have shown the following:

- Coordination of both face-to-face and online events can multiply their individual effectiveness.

FIGURE 8.1

Recognizing the Components Composing the Iterative "Rhythm" of a Community

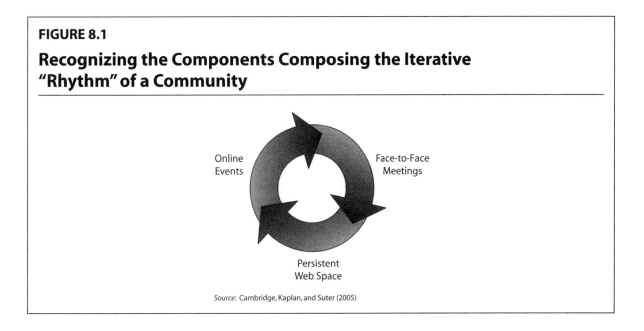

Online Events

Face-to-Face Meetings

Persistent Web Space

Source: Cambridge, Kaplan, and Suter (2005)

- A VCOP can serve as a virtual place for bridging collaborative projects and networking.
- The diversity of participants, interests, and backgrounds, particularly with a topic such as e-portfolios, can increase both the challenges and the opportunities for building a community of practice.

One of the unique features of the EPAC community of practice is how the Web space was initially conceived. The EPAC facilitators had conceptualized the Web space as an e-portfolio for the community itself, consisting of a collection of artifacts representing the various experiences of the community—including, for example, transcripts of online chats, conference materials, syllabi, curricular materials, and links to e-portfolio tools. EPAC members would then offer their varied perspectives on these artifacts. The e-portfolio concept was a useful model to frame the community's work, especially when harvesting insights from various talks and meetings so that they could stand alone and would make sense to a community member who did not participate in the event. The growth and sustainability phases of community work are where the EPAC community is currently focusing its efforts.

Future Directions

On one hand, evaluating the success of the EPAC community and its efforts could be simply defined by the number of members as well as the range and kinds of initiatives and opportunities offered. However, we use the guiding questions developed by Cambridge et al. (2005) to assess the quality of the design, development, and support of the EPAC community of practice in relation to community activities. Drawing on actual examples of products and processes, we provide some additional insights into how EPAC will continue to evolve and some directions for future exploration.

Stage 1: Establish a foundation through building relationships of trust, mutual respect, reciprocity, and commitment necessary for strong communities *Key questions:* How regularly are members interacting? To what extent do interactions have continuity and depth? Are members opportunistic about chances to interact in other settings (conferences, etc.)? Are members taking on new leadership roles? How much and what kind of reciprocity is occurring? To what extent is a shared understanding of the community's domain and approach to practice beginning to emerge?

EPAC was built on a strong foundation of relationships between individuals who possess a common interest in e-portfolio tools and technologies. These personal relationships were advanced regularly through face-to-face meetings at conferences as well as through virtual meetings and interactions. The depth and quality of the relationships most notably manifest in cross-institutional collaborations for conference presentations (including the annual meetings of the American Educational Research Association, the Assessment Institute at Indiana University–Purdue University Indianapolis, the Association of American Colleges and Universities, EIfEL's annual international e-portfolio conference, Campus Technology, the National Educational Computing Conference, Professional and Organizational Development Network in Higher Education, and Sakai, among others) and workshops (including Clemson Portfolio Institutes, Summer Institute at Wallenberg Hall at Stanford). Evidence of reciprocity and trust in EPAC relationships is also seen in the letters of support written for grant proposals; joint contributions to journal articles, edited collections, and books; and invitations to give talks as part of, for example, a teaching-and-learning speaker series or an e-portfolio day on various campuses.

Stage 2: Learn and develop a shared practice, based on an existing body of knowledge *Key questions:* How rich and accessible are the community's knowledge representations for existing practice? To what extent does community design support deeper learning for community members?

The most regular collaborative learning activities of the EPAC community have been the online chats and webcasts. The discussion topics for these events are often proposed by community members and cover a range of issues and questions:

- How can learning communities support and promote e-portfolio use and vice versa?
- How does the e-portfolio relate to an institution's educational process/philosophy?
- Who are today's students—digital natives or digital immigrants?
- The reflection fad: Is "reflection" simply an excuse for lack of rigor?
- What role can e-portfolios play in facilitating and supporting integrative learning?
- What are the implications of social software and other emerging technologies for the design and adoption of e-portfolios?
- Are e-portfolios a valid alternative to standardized tests? Are standardized tests a valid alternative to e-portfolios?

Transcripts and recordings of each of these events are archived and accessible for later use.

What has been most striking about the online chats via text messaging are the intense involvement of the participants and the high quality of the conversation. The discussion are often chaotic, with lots of ideas and comments flying back and forth, and chat participants are encouraged to share Web sites, references, key resources, and experiences, which are later summarized for the community. While the number of EPAC members who can feasibly contribute to such a discussion is limited, those who do get involved are often quite satisfied with the experience and regularly participate in similar activities.

Stage 3: Take action as a community to carry out tasks and projects *Key questions:* Are collaborative efforts beginning to emerge naturally? Are there community structures to support volunteering for projects and working with others? Are members recognized and rewarded for their contributions?

One example of a collaborative effort occurred in spring 2002 when a subset of EPAC members created a set of scenarios attempting to describe how e-portfolios could be used to provide a special focus on a range of learning environments and activities. One of the deliverables resulting from the analysis of these cases was a set of guiding questions developed by learning designer Cynthia Mazow of Stanford University, with input from other EPAC members. The questions describe the range of activities, applications, and learning contexts in which e-portfolios can be used. The set of questions not only represents new knowledge being created in the domain of e-portfolios by the community but also reiterates the important role that EPAC plays in facilitating and organizing interested members for such an initiative by providing online spaces (such as a wiki), tools (such as the EPAC Listserv), and facilitator support to publicize the efforts:

Learning Context

- What is the purpose(s) of using the portfolio (evaluation, assessment, promote student learning, promote student ownership/responsibility for learning)?

- At what level in the institution is the portfolio used (institutional, program, course, activity, individual)?

- What are the intended learning outcomes?

Participant Information and Interaction

- Who are the participants in the portfolio process?

  - What are the various roles of the participants?

  - Who is the owner of the portfolio?

  - Who are all the other users?

  - How do participants interact?

- What is the motivation for using portfolios for all participants?

- What are the participants' goals?

Portfolio Contents

- Who determines what goes into the portfolio?

- How is what goes into the portfolio determined?

- What are the contents of the portfolio?

  - What is the nature of the contents (collection of artifacts, selection of artifacts, showcase works, completed works, stages of incomplete work)?

  - What do the contents represent? How?

  - What is the physical form of the contents?

- Why are the contents important?

- Who creates the contents? How?

- How are the contents organized? What is the significance of the organization? Who organizes the contents?

- Who uses the contents? Why? How?

- How do the contents affect future learning, behavior, activities?

Portfolio Activities

- How long does the owner maintain/use the portfolio?

- What is the duration of the portfolio process?

- How often and by whom are portfolios viewed/accessed/reviewed?

Reflection

- What role does reflection play in the portfolio process?

- What is reflection?

  - What aspect of the owner is the object of reflection?

  - When does reflection occur? How often does it occur?

  - What prompts reflection?

  - What is the process of reflection?

  - What is the medium of reflection (conversation, writing, organization)?

  - What is the product of reflection (writing, images, audio)?

  - How are reflections used?

- How is reflection taught and supported?

- What is the desired quality of reflection (superficial, deep personal meaning)?

- What is the desired learning outcome from reflection?

- Is reflection represented in the portfolio process and/or product? How?

Scaffolding

- Are participants familiar with any part of the portfolio process?

- What support is offered students during the portfolio activities?

Change over Time

- How do the various components of the environment change over time? How do the participants, portfolio, and relationships between the participants change?

- Value

- How does using portfolios benefit all participants?

    - How are portfolios used to achieve learning outcomes?

    - How are portfolios used to achieve programmatic/institutional/course goals? (Mazow, 2002)

Stage 4: Create knowledge in the domain *Key questions:* How open is the community to new ideas and leadership? To what extent is the community influential in its domain? Are community members being invited, as community members, to present on leading-edge ideas?

EPAC is a community that continues to grow as newcomers to e-portfolios join the group and access and revisit the products and resources EPAC has contributed to this domain over time, such as the EDUCAUSE-sponsored series of foundational white papers on e-portfolios (Lorenzo & Ittelson, 2005a, 2005b, 2005c). Recognizing the community's need for an objective approach to evaluating the range of e-portfolio tools available, EPAC partnered with EduTools and the Western Cooperative for Educational Telecommunications to review seven e-portfolio products on behalf of seven partner institutions or systems of institutions, including California State University–Monterey Bay, the Connecticut Distance Learning Consortium, Minnesota State Colleges and Universities, Portland Community College and Southwestern Oregon Community College, New Jersey Edge (Seton Hall University, Fairleigh Dickinson University, Montclair State University), Texas State Technical College–Waco, and the University System of Georgia. A set of sixty-nine electronic portfolio features were identified and defined, and the feature set and reviews were eventually made available for public use (EduTools, 2006).

E-portfolios are increasingly recognized by faculty, departments, and institutions as an effective record of student work and as a tool to assess learning outcomes and improve learning. Exploration of such issues is most obviously seen in the joint work on integrative learning by the Association of American Colleges and Universities and the Carnegie Foundation for the Advancement of Teaching (www.carnegiefoundation.org/files/elibrary/integrativelearning/index.htm) and the Valid Assessment of Learning in Undergraduate Education and Rising to the Challenge initiatives, for which several EPAC members serve on the advisory board (see www.aacu.org/value and www.aacu.org/Rising_Challenge for more information).

Interest in the implications of social software tools and virtual learning environments has also sparked new relationships and collaborations around developing, for example, a next-generation e-portfolio in an environment such as Second Life. Through collaborative in-person and virtual discussions and serendipitous formations of individual projects around defining feature sets, creating and analyzing use cases, and more, a shared practice and understanding of e-portfolios and how they are defined, implemented, and sustained continue to emerge. The EPAC community and leadership are flexible enough to accommodate all these efforts, yet the more established relationships with organizations such as MERLOT are necessary to ensure reliable infrastructure support for EPAC's Listserv and greater exposure and promotion of the community to a broader audience interested in teaching and learning issues. EPAC's expanded Web presence on the MERLOT ePortfolio Portal (http://eportfolio.merlot.org) offers free widespread access to EPAC resources, practices, and tools. EPAC members are also invited to join MERLOT and to contribute learning materials and assignments related to e-portfolios, submit their resources for evaluation, and access ideas from other community members to help improve online and classroom learning using e-portfolios.

Conclusion

EPAC follows a model of practice defined by Wenger (1998) as "a kind of community created over time by sustained pursuit of a shared enterprise" (p. 45). Community members regularly come together to discuss the practices they have in common, which results in integration and coherence characterized by what Wenger summarizes as mutual engagement, a joint enterprise, and a shared repertoire (p. 73).

In summary, EPAC aims to bring together diverse individuals, programs, organizations, companies, and institutions around common issues of interest related to e-portfolios. By engaging in the creation, implementation, and evaluation of electronic portfolio pedagogy, methods, and tools in higher education and beyond, the EPAC community of practice provides a critical bridge between those who design, administer, and use e-portfolios for teaching, learning, and assessment. The knowledge that is created by EPAC members is expressed, documented, and shared both in the activities in which members participate as well as in the growing collection of artifacts and reflections in the EPAC e-portfolio collection, representing the evolution and insights of the community over time.

References

AAHE launches communities of practice. (2004, January). *AAHE News.*

Cambridge, D., Kaplan, S., & Suter, V. (2005). *Community of practice design guide.* Retrieved December 15, 2007, from www.educause.edu/ir/library/pdf/NLI0531.pdf

EduTools. (2006). *EduTools ePortfolio review.* Retrieved December 15, 2007, from http://eportfolio.edutools.info

Lorenzo, G., & Ittelson, J. C. (2005a). *Demonstrating and assessing student learning with e-portfolios.* Retrieved October 2, 2008, from http://connect.educause.edu/Library/ELI/DemonstratingandAssessing/39337

Lorenzo, G., & Ittelson, J. C. (2005b). *An overview of e-portfolios.* Retrieved October 2, 2008, from http://connect.educause.edu/Library/ELI/AnOverviewofEPortfolios/39335

Lorenzo, G., & Ittelson, J. C. (2005c). *An overview of institutional e-portfolios.* Retrieved October 2, 2008, from http://connect.educause.edu/Library/ELI/AnOverviewofInstitutional/39336

Mazow, C. (2002). *Portfolio use questions.* Unpublished manuscript.

Wenger, E. (1998). *Communities of practice: Learning, meaning, and identity.* Cambridge: Cambridge University Press.

Wenger, E., McDermott, R., & Snyder, W. M. (2002). *Cultivating communities of practice.* Boston: Harvard Business School Press.

Chapter 9

Encouraging a Reflective Disposition
Scaffolding Critical Thought Through Portfolio Development

Ann C. Cunningham
Wake Forest University

DESPITE A PERVASIVE and disheartening view that anyone can teach, I believe that the preparation of future teachers is a serious proposition, and my commitment to this endeavor comes from the belief that teaching is a valuable, honorable, and rewarding profession. The challenges associated with teaching in a twenty-first-century classroom have only served to increase my commitment and double my efforts to ensure that my students, future teachers, are prepared to face these challenges and rise above them. Mainstream media and personal experience are where most Americans gain their knowledge about schools and contemporary public education. Unfortunately, scattered and disconnected reports and anecdotes fail to articulate fully the complicated mélange of social problems, academic standards, accountability movements, inclusion concerns, immigration issues, technology challenges, learner differences, political pressures, and hosts of other regional and local issues that contribute to the complexities that a public school classroom teacher navigates daily. The love of children, the desire to contribute to the creation of a better future, and a passion for a particular body of information are not enough to bolster many teachers through the challenges of modern classrooms or to ensure a successful and rewarding teaching career. In many states the conundrum is evidenced by critical shortages of teachers and expensive recruitment efforts. Teachers entering classrooms must be prepared to address the challenges they will face so that they can do the good work they set out to accomplish when they chose to enter the profession.

Research supports the importance of a solid base of content knowledge, awareness of a variety of teaching and assessment approaches, and an understanding of learning theory and diverse learner needs for all teachers (Darling-Hammond, 2000; Stronge, 2002). Nationally accredited teacher education programs must demonstrate their provision of coursework addressing these topics as well as their teacher candidates' successful completion of supervised field experiences and teaching internships that provide opportunities for the development of knowledge and skills. However, one of the most vital teaching qualities identified by John Dewey in the 1920s and mentioned repeatedly in research on teacher preparation ever since typically is not isolated in a specific course, measured with a standardized test, or listed on an academic transcript. The key to high-quality and effective teaching lies in a teacher's ability to reflect on practice, and with the increased complexities of contemporary classrooms, meaningful reflection cannot be a simple iteration of events and actions contemplated solely from the teacher's perspective. Reflection must be analytical, evaluative, and inclusive of content, pedagogy, learning theory, standards, accountability, and individual learner needs. Reflection is not just a skill; it's a disposition that develops over time and through experience. It can be coaxed, practiced, and expressed in a variety of ways, but it must be regarded as a necessary component of teacher preparation.

Context

Wake Forest University is a small university in the southeast United States, offering teaching preparation programs to undergraduates seeking elementary and secondary licensure and graduate students with baccalaureate degrees who earn a master's degree while pursuing initial licensure. Undergraduates are admitted through a selective process conducted by general admissions, but they must meet education department expectations before being admitted to a professional teaching program. Graduates are admitted to the Master Teacher Fellows program through a highly selective process; in fact, the program accepts no more than twenty-eight fellows each year into secondary mathematics, science, English, social studies, and K–12 foreign language initial licensure programs. All programs have state and national accreditation endorsements through the North Carolina Department of Public Instruction and the National Council for Accreditation of Teacher Education.

In addition to size and selectivity, another important feature that directly affects the teacher preparation programs is the university's commitment to ubiquitous technology. This commitment is actualized through a laptop initiative that provides new laptops and printers to all undergraduates during their freshman and junior years, a generous standard load of software installed on the laptop with access to high-end specialized software through a key-server, two-year-old laptops to all graduate students, and a fully wireless campus with access to remote server space for publishing Web sites, file sharing, and storage. University faculty receive the same resources and are given a choice about the type of laptop they receive every other year. Technical support can be accessed via phone, e-mail, or face-to-face. Most classrooms are furnished with equipment for supporting faculty technology integration, and all departments are able to submit yearly budget requests for specialized technology. In addition, each department is provided with a full- or part-time technology staff member whose responsibility is to support faculty technology integration needs for teaching and research.

Such an environment has an effect on the education department faculty and the teacher preparation programs. In 1998, a new faculty position was created for an assistant professor of instructional design, and a search was conducted for a candidate possessing knowledge in the field of educational technology, as well as extensive experience in teaching, learning, and assessment. The deliberate and strategic decision aligned with the vision that department leaders be nurtured for marshaling the university's technology resources. The alignment complemented the burgeoning field of educational technology driven by contemporary theories of pedagogy-based technology integration. Subsequent faculty searches for appointments of methodology professors have included expectations for a demonstration of appropriate integration of technology in teaching, learning, and research. Intentional efforts to build a faculty that contributes to the refinement and perpetuation of a vision for teacher preparation that includes appropriate use of technology have been sustained since the late 1990s.

In the years following the initial push for technology integration on campus and in the education department, faculty collaboration and a focus on the acquisition of software and hardware to support a shared vision have resulted in several technology initiatives that enhance teacher candidate experiences with meaningful and relevant technology integration. One of the hallmarks of the teacher preparation programs is the integration of technology to support electronic portfolio creation as a means for demonstrating professional growth in content and pedagogy. A vital part of the electronic portfolio process is a commitment to developing a reflective disposition throughout each phase of the professional teacher preparation programs. This chapter provides a snapshot of the electronic portfolio development process with an emphasis on how faculty collaborate to scaffold the development of a reflective disposition in all teacher candidates.

Portfolio Development Processes: Portfolio Design

The faculty in the education department believe that developing a reflective disposition begins upon entrance to the professional teacher preparation program, and this belief is inherent in the design of programs and coursework. The two major areas of teacher preparation, elementary and secondary, approach the portfolio development process in a similar fashion, although the course content, sequence, and field experiences are substantially different. All undergraduate candidates apply for admission to the program at the beginning of their junior year. Table 9.1 outlines the course sequences required before and during the professional preparation program for undergraduate candidates. Graduate-level teacher candidates are admitted during the summer and follow a course sequence similar to the secondary undergraduates. That program sequence is delineated in Table 9.2.

Notable in the course sequences is the deliberate alignment of the technology and methods courses. The intentional alignment promotes faculty collaboration and development of projects and assignments that influence meaningful content-specific technology integration. The development of technology pedagogical content knowledge (TPCK) as a field of study is rela-

TABLE 9.1

Professional Education Course Sequences for Undergraduate Elementary Program

Semester	Sophomore (spring) or Junior (fall)	Junior (spring)	Senior (fall)	Senior (spring)
Course Requirements	Educational Foundations Educational Psychology Field Experience One	Children's Literature Technology in Education Field Experience Two Methodology courses by content area: • Social Studies • Science • Reading	Elementary School Curriculum Methodology courses by content area: • Language Arts • Mathematics • Arts and Movement Student Teaching	Special Needs

TABLE 9.2

Professional Education Course Sequences for Undergraduate and Graduate Secondary Programs

Undergraduate				
Semester	**Sophomore (spring) or Junior (fall)**	**Junior (spring)**	**Senior (fall)**	**Senior (spring)**
Course Requirements	Educational Foundations Field Experience One	Educational Psychology	Technology in Education Methodology courses by content area: • English • Foreign Language • Mathematics • Science • Social Studies	Student Teaching Seminars: • Special Needs • Diversity • Classroom Management • Student Teaching

Graduate				
Semester	**Summer**	**Fall**	**Spring**	**Summer**
Course Requirements	Psychology of Diverse Learners Sociology of Diverse Learners Research and Statistics	Technology in Education Descriptive Research Methodology courses by content area: • English • Foreign Language • Mathematics • Science • Social Studies Teaching Rounds	Student Teaching Seminars: • Special Needs • Diversity • Classroom Management • Student Teaching	Professional Development Seminar Educational Leadership

tively new, although the concept is not novel. The purpose of defining this field of study is to help teachers "design and implement more meaningful applications of technology that are clearly directed at improving learning and teaching" (Thompson, 2007). *The Handbook of Technological Pedagogical Content*

Knowledge for Teaching and Teacher Educators (2007), a publication edited by the technology and innovations committee of the American Association of Colleges for Teacher Education (AACTE), defines TPCK and includes specific descriptions of how the concept can be integrated through all content areas and levels of teacher education. The publication validates and articulates more fully a vision that the Wake Forest University Department of Education pursues for the teacher preparation programs, and the electronic portfolios created by teacher candidates demonstrate how the skills and dispositions associated with meaningful and appropriate content-specific technology integration can be encouraged with scaffolding that begins with thoughtful and deliberate program design.

Electronic Portfolio Development

All candidates are encouraged to save papers and products created during coursework, but the first formal selection and publication of their products occurs during the semester they are enrolled in the required Technology in Education course. At a time when many teacher preparation programs have chosen proficiency skill testing or integrating technology in other courses, Wake Forest views the technology course as a vital opportunity for candidates to learn a wide range of software and hardware that is then integrated in courses throughout the programs. Such spiraling of technology skills and experiences guarantees that candidates experience a breadth of professional uses for technology and understand the value of the tools for a variety of teacher-related tasks. The technology course is a general survey of how common hardware and software tools can be integrated into content area instruction to support teaching, learning, and professional development. Course topics include contemporary issues relating to educational technology such as Universal Design for Learning, digital equity, safe and ethical use of technology, and national technology performance expectations, including the National Educational Technology Standards for Students (NETS*S) and Teachers (NETS*T) and the 21st-Century Skills (International Society for Technology in Education, 2000, 2002; Partnership for 21st-Century Skills, 2004). In an effort to ensure that the technology tools models can be integrated effectively into future instructional practice, the theoretical foundation of all course assignments and activities is based on situated cognition and is implemented through an authentic task approach (Brown, Collins, & Duguid, 1989). This approach permits teacher candidates to develop products that are meaningful and relevant to their content area, increasing motivation and engagement with the assignments. Focusing on content while teaching valuable technology skills yields several positive outcomes: candidates develop technology problem-solving and troubleshooting skills while engaged in meaningful and satisfying tasks they are likely to encounter in their own classrooms; candidates focus on content-specific applications of technology, promoting retention and the transfer of skills and integration ideas; candidates develop products that are included in their electronic portfolios, increasing pride in craftsmanship as these work products are shared with an unlimited Internet audience. Table 9.3 outlines the course assignments, technologies used, and alignment with the NETS*T.

Because the course projects integrate technology tools that are appropriate for a range of teacher- and student-related activities, each product is submitted with a reflection that requires the candidate to think beyond the product developed to the value of the tools used in the creation of the product for future professional or instructional uses. Candidates are required to make connections to the NETS*T for all examples of teacher technology integration ideas, and for all examples of student-centered integration activities, candidates are required to consider the value of the integration idea in terms of learning theory as well as state curriculum and technology competencies. The rationale behind this approach to reflective thought is to encourage candidates to move beyond iterations of technology use and content coverage to a deeper analysis and evaluation of the value of the technology for their own grade and content-specific instruction. Table 9.4 presents three columns: a teacher candidate's reflections on the newsletter assignment, the first assignment of the course, are shown in the center; the reflections are deconstructed in the right column to highlight how the candidate addresses the various NETS*T expectations and standards articulated in the left column.

Such expectations are challenging and represent the nascent stage of the disposition of a thoughtful and analytical reflective educator. The instructor scaffolds the reflection requirement through written expectations (see "Reflections in Technology Portfolios" in Part 4 of this volume), through full-class discussion and brainstorming activities, and through individual meetings and opportunities for revision of the assignment. Teachers must learn to integrate technology appropriately with a meaningful and relevant instructional purpose. Requiring teacher candidates to consider multiple options for technology use in the classroom and then to reflect on their technology integration ideas through the lens of learning theory and standards fosters the development of a metacognitive approach

TABLE 9.3

Course Assignments, Technologies Used, and Alignment with the NETS*T

Project	Technologies	NETS*T Alignment	NETS*T Standards[*]
			I. Technology Operations and Concepts
Standards Newsletter	Word processing Desktop publishing Photo editing WWW research	I. A, B II. A III. A IV. B V. B, C, D VI. A, B, D, E	A. Teachers demonstrate introductory knowledge, skills, and understanding of concepts related to technology (as described in the ISTE National Educational Technology Standards for Students). B. Teachers demonstrate continual growth in technology knowledge and skills to stay abreast of current and emerging technologies.
			II. Planning and Designing Learning Environments and Experiences
Digital Video Anchor	Digital video-editing software Camcorder Tripod Microphone	I. A II. B III. C V. A, D VI. B	A. Teachers design developmentally appropriate learning opportunities that apply technology-enhanced instructional strategies to support the diverse needs of learners. B. Teachers apply current research on teaching and learning with technology when planning learning environments and experiences.
Multimedia Assessment Instrument	Multimedia development software Digital images, video, and audio Spreadsheet WWW research	I. A, B IV. A, B, C V. B, C, D VI. B	C. Teachers identify and locate technology resources and evaluate them for accuracy and suitability. D. Teachers plan for the management of technology resources within the context of learning activities. E. Teachers plan strategies to manage student learning in a technology-enhanced environment.
			III. Teaching, Learning, and the Curriculum
Virtual Travel Plan (elementary)	Database Spreadsheet Web design software Word processing (mail merge) Others as selected by students	I. A, B II. A, B, C, D, E III. A, B, C IV. A, C V. B, C, D VI. A, B, C, D, E	A. Teachers facilitate technology-enhanced experiences that address content standards and student technology standards. B. Teachers use technology to support learner-centered strategies that address the diverse needs of students. C. Teachers apply technology to develop students' higher-order skills and creativity.

Project	Tools	Standards	
Field Trip Plan (secondary)	Database Spreadsheet Word processing (mail merge) Desktop publishing (mail merge) WWW research	I. A, B IV. B V. C, D	D. Teachers manage student learning activities in a technology-enhanced environment.

IV. Assessment and Evaluation

A. Teachers apply technology in assessing student learning of subject matter using a variety of assessment techniques.

B. Teachers use technology resources to collect and analyze data, interpret results, and communicate findings to improve instructional practice and maximize student learning.

C. Teachers apply multiple methods of evaluation to determine students' appropriate use of technology resources for learning, communication, and productivity.

Project	Tools	Standards	
Web Site	Web design software Photo editing Networking File sharing Adobe Acrobat	I. A, B II. C V. A, C, D VI. A, E	

V. Productivity and Professional Practice

A. Teachers use technology resources to engage in ongoing professional development and lifelong learning.

B. Teachers continually evaluate and reflect on professional practice to make informed decisions regarding the use of technology in support of student learning.

C. Teachers apply technology to increase productivity.

D. Teachers use technology to communicate and collaborate with peers, parents, and the larger community in order to nurture student learning.

Project	Tools	Standards	
Instructional Design Project (software/hardware tools vary by project)	Minimum of: Word processing Multimedia development software Web design software	I. A, B II. A, B, C, D, E III. A, B, C IV. A, C V. A, B, C VI. A, B, C, D, E	

VI. Social, Ethical, Legal, and Human Issues

A. Teachers model and teach legal and ethical practice related to technology use.

B. Teachers apply technology resources to enable and empower learners with diverse backgrounds, characteristics, and abilities.

C. Teachers identify and use technology resources that affirm diversity.

D. Teachers promote safe and healthy use of technology resources.

E. Teachers facilitate equitable access to technology resources for all students.

TABLE 9.4

Deconstructed Student Reflection on Newsletter Assignment

Standards	Reflection	Learning Theory
	Even before the first day of Educational Technology class, I knew that I would be expected to create a newsletter using Microsoft Publisher because I had heard past education students talk about their own newsletters. Though I did not know the specific information that my newsletter would contain, I was already excited about the prospect of playing around with Microsoft Publisher and formatting my newsletter in a visually appealing way. Now as I reflect on my experience creating my newsletter, I realize that my initial attitude toward the project highlights one of the benefits of using desktop publishing and word processing in the classroom—it makes some *students excited and can engage students who may not enjoy more traditional means of presenting their knowledge.* Though I could have easily written a paper about how I would *connect curriculum and technology standards* in my future classroom, it was more fun to express my thoughts on the topic in newsletter form.	Motivation and engagement Traditional vs. alternative assessment Diverse learner needs Universal Design for Learning
Student standards NETS*T (II and III)	The value of using desktop publishing and word processing in the classroom, however, goes beyond making a means of assessment more "fun" for students and can have a significant impact on student success. Desktop publishing and word processing tools make it easier for me as a teacher to *support the diverse needs of learners.* (II, III) One of the three fundamental principles of *Universal Design for Learning (UDL)* is that teachers should provide multiple representations of content in order to best help a diverse group of students successfully learn that content. Tools such as Microsoft Word and Microsoft Publisher make it easier for me to do this by providing a means of *organizing and representing content visually.* For example, if I were teaching a lesson on *6 causes of the American Civil War* I could use Microsoft Word to create an outline of those causes. This would be helpful for a variety of students, including students *who are not auditory learners or who have trouble picking out key points from a lecture or discussion,* as well as students who *have physical difficulties taking written notes.*	Visual representation of content Nontraditional learners Students with special cognitive and physical needs Universal Design for Learning Alternative assessment Project-based learning

		Annotations
State Standard Course of Study for Secondary Social Studies NETS*T (IV)	Word processing and desktop publishing can be useful not only for instructional design, but also for *planning assessment and evaluation. (IV)* By using these tools to provide *multiple means for students to express their knowledge* (another principle of UDL), I can give more students a chance to succeed. For example, to assess student learning on the *American Civil War* I could *provide students with two possible options:* create a newspaper dated April 10, 1865, looking back on key turning points in the war or write a paper highlighting these same turning points.	School-home learning connection
State Standard Course of Study for Secondary Social Studies NETS*T (V)	These technological tools can also help me become a more *productive and professional teacher. (V)* Creating documents such as newsletters, class calendars, and daily lecture notes may take some time in my first few years of teaching, but as I continue to teach I can reuse most of these documents. It may take some more work at the beginning, but in the long run it will be more productive and efficient. Newsletters and calendars will also help me to keep parents *informed about what we are doing in the classroom so that they can best know how to nurture student learning at home.*	Meaningful and relevant instruction
State Standard Course of Study for Computer Skills 21st-Century Skills	Finally, it is important for students to know how to use these tools themselves. (III, VI) In the world today, *word processing and desktop publishing skills are a vital component of many jobs.* By encouraging students to improve these skills, I can empower them to *increase their ability to succeed in their future lives.*	
	Creating this newsletter has reinforced my belief that word processing and desktop publishing tools provide effective and relatively easy ways to increase both student learning and my own professional success. I will continue to make use of them!	

to technology-enhanced instructional design that promotes meaningful future integration.

The disposition of reflective practice is developed throughout each candidate's preparation experiences, since written reflections are required as course assignments and as portfolio artifacts. Faculty determine the time and purpose of written reflections for their own courses but confer with program area colleagues to identify key experiences where formal written reflections are necessary and relevant. In many instances, the expectations of the National Council for Accreditation of Teacher Education (NCATE) are significant to the institutional report and enter into the decision-making processes regarding formal reflection assignments as demonstrations of candidate growth and measurement in terms of the department's conceptual framework. However, the skills and dispositions outlined in the conceptual framework are determined by the faculty and have been seriously deliberated and identified as key characteristics of a teacher leader. The spiraling of the reflective process through all programs provides an opportunity for a variety of meaningful opportunities for reflective thought and communicates the integral nature of practice and reflection. The emphasis and seriousness with which faculty communicate expectations for reflection help candidates recognize the value of such exercises in terms of present or future practice. Reflections are excellent evidence of professional growth and are an integral part of the portfolio development process.

The portfolios that best represent the department's commitment to high-quality teaching and its emphasis on the development of technology skills and dispositions are the Web-based technology and teaching portfolios. The products represented in these portfolios reflect departmental values as exemplified through the skills and dispositions of its conceptual framework, projects of significant meaning and value selected by the teacher candidates, and the development of technology skills appropriate for a professional educator as outlined by the North Carolina Department of Public Instruction (NCDPI) and the International Society for Technology in Education NETS*T. At a time when many teacher preparation programs are choosing commercial online products to support the development and storage of electronic portfolios because of ease of use and delivery of data (which can be aggregated and disaggregated for accreditation and program analysis), our small department has opted to remain with Web development tools that facilitate the candidates' ability to customize their portfolios and exercise a measure of control over the design while still meeting program requirements for the final product. The locus of control provided with this option increases engagement, motivation, and confidence for developing competence with online publishing skills and professional Web-editing tools. The choice to use a tool that is not specifically for portfolio development supports departmental values for fostering meaningful, relevant, and transferable technology skills while providing a resource for candidates to showcase their growth as a technology-proficient educator.

The Web-Based Portfolio Development Process

The key factor in successfully developing Web-based portfolio products is involving faculty stakeholders in the final product. And not all faculty need to understand the technicalities of Web site development to support candidates through the portfolio process. However, faculty without the technical skills must be comfortable with the process in two important ways: they must value the final product and feel that they contribute to decisions about the portfolio's content, and they must trust that their students are competent and independent users of the technology tools that enable the creation of the portfolio. In many cases, the value of digital portfolios is driven by the need for accreditation documentation and the ease of archiving and retrieving valuable materials for accreditation visits. Regardless of the motivations, faculty concordance is a crucial part of the success of any summative electronic portfolio endeavor that spans the preparation program.

Content and Structure

Determining the general structure and content of an online portfolio is best done before introducing the task to the teacher candidates, and agreement on such aspects of the portfolio depends on the collaborative efforts of the faculty, who can provide a variety of perspectives that improve the content's quality. One method for engaging individuals who are not totally comfortable with Web development is to provide them with tangible materials that make the abstract product more comprehensible. Visualizing a Web site structure is an exercise in the abstract that can be facilitated by the representation of levels, pages, and links with a graphic organizer. Figures 9.1 and 9.2 represent the structure and content of the online portfolio for teacher candidates in the secondary and elementary programs. Note that in Figure 9.1 additional pages can easily be designated for specific secondary content areas within the structure of the Web site. The flexibility provides content area advisers an opportunity to customize the sites before development of the portfolio begins and removes them from the technical aspects of portfolio development while keeping them engaged with the content requirements.

FIGURE 9.1

Structure and Content of the Online Portfolio, Example 1

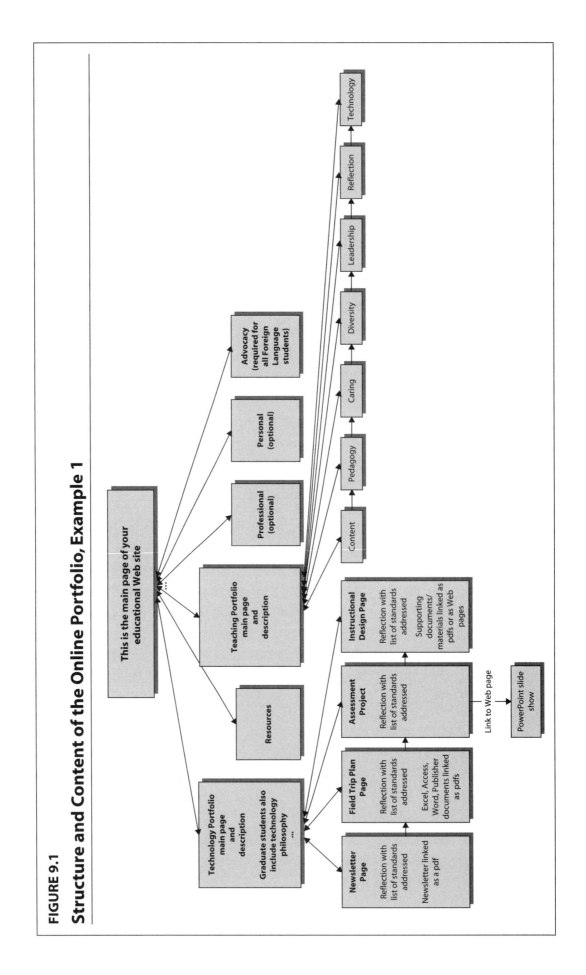

FIGURE 9.2

Structure and Content of the Online Portfolio, Example 2

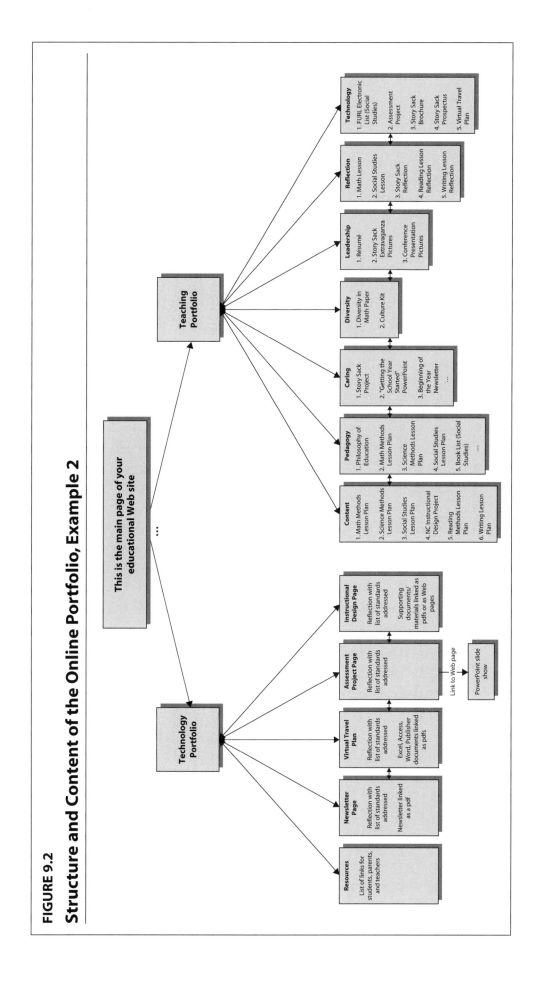

The graphic organizer is helpful for communicating the final appearance of a Web site to faculty or students who are not comfortable with the concept of Web editing. It increases faculty engagement in decision making about content and structure while scaffolding the overall conceptualization as well as the page and link construction process for students during portfolio development. As each new program cycle begins, the graphic organizer can be revisited, revised, and updated with minimal effort. Determining the content and structure before developing the site makes the process smoother and more understandable to teacher candidates while keeping faculty engaged and aware of the portfolio development process.

One Web Site, Two Portfolios

The alignment of the technology and methods courses facilitates the initial stages of portfolio development and provides a foundation that ensures successful completion of the Web-based portfolios. Communication both to faculty and to students about the portfolio development process is critical to guaranteeing that candidates understand the meaning and value of their work and how what they do in one semester affects assignments throughout their programs. The Web-based portfolios have at least two major sections with different goals, audiences, and purposes. These sections are the technology portfolio, which is subjected to external evaluation by local teachers to meet state requirements for initial licensure, and the teaching portfolio, which is a program requirement used to demonstrate growth in the skills and dispositions outlined in the department's conceptual framework. Each section is linked from the main page of the Web site but is separated through the navigation structure.

The decision to organize the sites in this manner reflects the different goals of each section of the portfolio and facilitates the evaluation procedures required for each section. The technology portfolio evaluations must be conducted by an external group during the early part of the spring semester in order to meet expectations outlined by NCDPI and to ensure timely licensing of program graduates. The evaluators for this section focus on the quality of the products to assess the technology skill levels of novice teachers and not on the development of their teaching skills, although the candidates' thoughtfulness regarding use of software and hardware in the classroom (revealed in their reflections) is considered during the assessment of the products. The technology portfolio demonstrates ability by showcasing sample products and reflections on the use and value of technology tools for students and teachers. One other particularly unique dimension of students' technology portfolios is the addition of video reflections uploaded to their portfolio Web sites. The videos showcase students' creativity and ability to reflect meaningfully in a technology-rich portfolio environment. For more information about the online video reflections, check the "Technology Projects" link at www.wfu.edu/~cunninac.

The purpose of the teaching portfolios is to demonstrate growth as a novice teacher. These summative products are evaluated by the content area advisers, and evidence of success in this portfolio is included in the data system that is ultimately reported to NCATE. The portfolio contains a page for each disposition of the conceptual framework, and evidence is collected in an effort to demonstrate the candidate's growth in each disposition. Unlike the technology portfolio, candidates choose many of the products they want to include in the teaching portfolio and write a global reflection that articulates their growth in each disposition. Because the teaching portfolio is a collection of evidence that demonstrates growth over time and the deadline for submission falls at the end of the student teaching internship, a time when candidates should be focused on teaching rather than on portfolio creation, the faculty have determined that communication of the teaching portfolio expectations should occur early in the candidates' professional programs. Also, moving from hard copy to Web-based publication of the teaching portfolio inspired faculty to create the structure for housing both Web-based portfolios at the same time to scaffold the ongoing nature of developmental portfolio creation. The result is that the structure of the Web site that houses both portfolios is created during the fall semester, when candidates are enrolled in the technology and methods courses, enabling faculty to articulate the goals, purposes, and content of both portfolios most efficiently.

The design of the technology course and the timing of software introduction are planned to make sure that instruction relevant to portfolio creation is ongoing throughout the fall semester. Introduction to the portfolio requirements coincides with the onset of Web-editing instruction, where the authentic task is the creation of a professional Web site to demonstrate growth and showcase products that represent a teacher leader's skills and dispositions. Candidates are taught how to create and link Web pages by creating the pages of their Web sites. Web-editing skills are taught within the context of the creation of their own Web sites, and content publication occurs when students have had enough time to gather and create products to post on their sites. For example, the concepts of formatting text and creating absolute links are taught within the context of publishing content-specific annotated Web sites to the resources page on the Web site. The conversion of a newsletter created in Microsoft Publisher to a PDF format for linking to the portfolio occurs after candidates have completed and revised that assignment. Instruction that produces evidence for the technology portfolio happens throughout the semester. Once each product is created, evaluated, and revised, it is then published on the Web site under the instructor's guidance.

The assessment project, a PowerPoint-based formative or summative assessment tool that fits into the candidate's instructional design project, is published online using the Web page creation feature in PowerPoint. Because the project is published differently from a PDF document, the instructor walks the class through the publication strategy when the product is completed. The final publication occurs long after the initial development of the Web site. Such a spiraling instructional method for teaching Web editing facilitates the creation of the online portfolios while scaffolding the development of new and valuable skills that ensure students have the ability to work on their Web sites independently. Additionally, the skills learned from creating the technology portfolio are directly applicable to the teaching portfolio, allowing students to work simultaneously on both the technology and the teaching portfolios. The support of content area advisers and the technology instructor increases the probability of successful completion of both portfolios.

The collaborative method scaffolds the successful completion of both major portfolio assignments by ensuring that candidates possess the skills, awareness, and understanding requisite to the challenges. One important affective outcome is that a positive experience with developing online portfolios is likely to have an impact on the way candidates contemplate use of technology tools in the future. The increase of confidence developed by consistent use of technology skills over time improves the chances of experimentation with new or different tools and reduces anxiety associated with Web-based publication in other environments.

In addition to delivering content-rich and pedagogically sound instruction, the faculty also want graduates to feel comfortable using the tools associated with the professional educator now and in the future. Teachers in twenty-first-century classrooms need to be prepared to evaluate and use effectively the new and interactive tools of the future, including tools that capitalize on the skills of a new generation of students already comfortable using Internet tools to research, communicate, publish, and engage in learning. Designing teacher preparation programs that weave content, pedagogy, and technology together seamlessly and that scaffold the development of a reflective disposition throughout course experiences and portfolio development is an approach that has proved successful for our department.

References

American Association of Colleges for Teacher Education, Technology and Innovations Committee. (2007). *The handbook of technological pedagogical content knowledge for teaching and teacher educators.* Mahwah, NJ: Lawrence Erlbaum Associates.

Brown, J. S, Collins, A., & Duguid, P. (1989). Situated cognition and the culture of learning. *Educational Researcher, 18*(1), 32–42.

Darling-Hammond, L. (2000). How teacher education matters. *Journal of Teacher Education, 51*(3), 166–173.

International Society for Technology in Education. (2000). *National educational technology standards for students.* Eugene, OR: International Society for Technology in Education.

International Society for Technology in Education. (2002). *National educational technology standards for teachers.* Eugene, OR: International Society for Technology in Education.

Partnership for 21st-Century Skills. (2004). *21st-century standards.* Retrieved October 2, 2008, from www.21stcenturyskills.org/index.php?option=com_content&task=view&id=351&Itemid=120

Stronge, J. H. (2002). *Qualities of effective teachers.* Alexandria, VA: Association of Supervision and Curriculum Development.

Thompson, A. D. (2007). TPCK: A new direction for technology in teacher education programs. *Journal of Computing in Teacher Education, 23*(3), 78.

Chapter 10

A Journey Involving Integrating an E-portfolio into a Course Management System

Marilyn Drury
University of Northern Iowa

COURSE MANAGEMENT SYSTEMS (CMSs) have become common in higher education institutions over the past ten years. More faculty have adopted the use of such systems to facilitate and complement various elements of the courses they teach. Many students have come to expect the use of such systems to help them access course materials, to facilitate discussion groups and chats, and to assist them in submitting course assignments and materials in a secure environment. During this same time frame, most campuses have found increased interest in moving from paper-based portfolios required by many programs of study to electronic portfolios.

Electronic portfolios, or e-portfolios, were introduced in the early 1990s. Many educators view them as enabling the creation of a more learner-centered and outcome-oriented learning culture because e-portfolios facilitate the collection of digital objects or artifacts, allowing students to demonstrate their efforts, abilities, and progress toward particular goals. Once a student has entered artifacts into an e-portfolio, the artifacts can be used for a variety of purposes, such as assessment, reflection, evidence of having met standards, or career purposes, depending on the student's needs at the time. Many items a student may wish to incorporate into an e-portfolio are the same as those submitted into a CMS.

After gathering data from surveys sent to our faculty and students over the past several years, our institution reviewed various vendors' e-portfolio products. There are many e-portfolio products available as separate stand-alone products. Those integrating e-portfolio software with CMSs are less common. It seemed a logical choice to pursue the adoption of an e-portfolio that integrated with our supported CMS. Students would need to place their digital artifacts into the system only once and could then use such artifacts within the CMS, as required for a course, or they could incorporate selected artifacts into their learning e-portfolio, their career e-portfolio, or other e-portfolios they owned.

Pilot Efforts

In the spring 2007 semester, six invited faculty interested in using e-portfolios began a pilot effort on our campus. Representing the efforts in terms of an ongoing pilot allows for the testing of various uses and purposes of e-portfolios, the review of the interest of various colleges within our institution, the evaluation of the value and costs associated with the implementation and support of the product, and the time frame necessary for evaluating the vendor support of and road map for the product.

Using the e-portfolio tool is as simple as clicking on the tab labeled "Portfolios" within the CMS environment. Since students are comfortable with the CMS and familiar with the menus and general terminology, using the e-portfolio tool is fairly easy for them.

The six pilot faculty were from various colleges and programs within our institution and had previously expressed interest in piloting the uses of e-portfolios. With our institution's focus on a liberal arts core, the faculty were interested in using e-portfolios to assess and allow for student reflections related to the philosophies and core competencies surrounding liberal arts education. The educational technology staff worked closely with the faculty, encouraging them to assess how they might incorporate and integrate e-portfolios while emphasizing liberal arts core learning into their curriculum, activities, and student outcomes assessment strategies, both programmatically and at the individual course level. While each faculty member in the original pilot group had specific purposes he or she was hoping the e-portfolio would facilitate, the pilot group also shared several similar purposes, including reflecting on learning, presenting evidence of mastery of goals, and exploring the integration of liberal arts core competencies.

The faculty felt that having the e-portfolio integrated with the CMS was an advantage. They liked having their course and the portfolio available in the same log-in space, requiring only one log-in. They also liked the single submission and central storage of items that could be used for both the CMS and the e-portfolio. Students responded positively toward the single submission as well, with one stating, "I felt like I was more able to focus on the work, not how I was going to submit it."

Reflective Learning

All faculty shared the goal that students would be able to easily submit assignments for the course into the CMS for grading purposes and into the e-portfolio for reflective purposes. Using the e-portfolio as a learning portfolio provides a structure that facilitates reflection on the learning process, fostering the formation of habits and the development of skills and abilities that are necessary for critical reflection (Zubizarreta, 2004). Shulman (1998) discusses reflection as one of the key elements of the learning portfolio.

Faculty from the English department and writing programs wanted the students to reflect on their own writing, on peers' writing, and on peers' comments about their own writing examples. Zeichner and Wray (2001) found very positive benefits from using e-portfolios related to experiences involving mentoring, collaboration, and feedback given by faculty, peers, and others throughout the creation and development of artifacts representing an individual's work. Here is an excerpt from one student's reflection on her writing process throughout the semester (the professor and peers in the course could then comment on her reflection):

My general fictional strategy starts with inspiration. If an idea for a story strikes me, I jot a few notes about it in my notebook. When I have time to write, I find an idea that seems to be strongest at that moment and run with it. . . .

I have discovered a visual technique for writing this semester. I used to think through the entire story for days or months before writing. This semester, I started being less organized (on purpose). I . . . allow myself to envision only the opening scene. . . . Once I actually sit down to write, I picture the story like it is a movie in my imagination. This is a strategy I developed between my first and second stories of the semester.

Another strategy I have changed is the time I allow myself to write. . . . For the first story and in the past, I only wrote when I had a lot of free time and knew I could complete the story and its revision. . . . This caused my stories to fall off at the end. For . . . story 2, I wrote for about three hours before I ran out of steam. I stopped and continued writing on another day. This change in strategy has caused two of my stories to be a little late but I feel it is worth the result. For the future, I know the extra time makes all of the difference. This long break allows my mind to refresh and fill with new ideas.

This semester has taught me a lot about writing. I feel that I have been able to take a lot of small things from past teaching and study and combine them into one cohesive strategy. Some of these improvements are in the areas of characterization, imagery, dialogue and flow.

These stories reflect this overall strategy because the difference between my first story and second one is very representative. My first story felt rough and unfinished. My second and third stories were revised half as much before submission but feel stronger and cleaner. They are more complete stories. They were fun to write and were not work to write.

The theater faculty wanted students to reflect verbally on a play that they had directed and was captured on video. Students were to watch the play and reflect on each scene with audio comments regarding their directing techniques. The faculty hoped to add their own evaluative audio comments to the students' audio reflections, with the e-portfolio housing the audio/video clips.

The education faculty took a metacognitive approach by asking the students to reflect on a series of guiding questions throughout the semester to help them internalize the course material and go beyond simply reading the material. Examples of the questions related to the content area of higher education organizational theory include:

- What is academic advising?
- What are reasons for doing academic advising? (justifications and uses)
- What does well-done academic advising look like? (criteria)
- What are some challenges to doing academic advising well? (challenges)
- What are some tools, strategies, and resources for conducting academic advising activities? (resources)
- What thoughts, questions, confusions, future activities, and goals do I want to capture while they are fresh in my mind? (questions)

The students were asked to submit in their e-portfolios a final project: a learning analysis that provided reflections on their concepts regarding the course content at the beginning of the semester and how they added to these concepts or changed their views throughout the semester.

Mastery of Goals

The communications studies faculty focused on providing students with a template of departmental goals or desired student outcomes once students were at the point of concluding their studies in this major field. Students were asked to provide an artifact offering evidence of their learning and mastery of each goal. In addition, they needed to reflect on why they chose the particular artifact to represent their learning outcome for the goal.

Other faculty involved in the pilot intend to include programmatic or departmental goals in the e-portfolio in the next year. One of the lessons we have learned thus far in our pilot is that programs or departments should have well-defined, articulated goals or student outcomes before using e-portfolios. Such a careful structure of goals and outcomes can then be provided for assessment and reflection purposes.

Liberal Arts Core Competencies Integration

The University of Northern Iowa is a comprehensive university focused on liberal arts learning. Besides focusing on programmatic or departmental goals integration, faculty should work on integrating the liberal arts core competencies into students' e-portfolio work. Such core competencies can provide yet another framework for the e-portfolio that reflects overall general education learning outcomes. Many of these outcomes overlap with programmatic or departmental outcomes, allowing the student to demonstrate various intersections of learning outcomes. The intersections and interconnections assist students in seeing beyond partial disciplinary perspectives to the wholeness and integration of their educational experience in the liberal arts core.

The core competencies at our institution are as follows: development of *critical-thinking* skills; effective use of *quantitative* data by applying relevant math and statistical methods; effective *communication* skills; the ability to access, analyze, and manage *information*; and development of *interpersonal* skills. E-portfolios provide an excellent means for capturing artifacts at the beginning of a student's education and again at various milestones throughout the student's education, reflecting interdisciplinary learning growth related to each core competency in the liberal arts area. As was observed in our pilot, students do not naturally reflect on their conceptual learning process and must be exposed to activities early in their education that help them learn the importance of how to think critically.

Authentic Assessment

Technology tools and various uses of the Internet that have emerged in the past decade offer students and teachers a variety of technologies, enabling simulation, visualization, collaboration, and experimentation. Used in an effective manner, such tools and technologies can provide students with additional authentic learning experiences. Just as there is a great difference between doing and listening, there is a great difference between learning about jet engines and learning to be an engineer. Students often express the desire to focus on real-world applications, solving problems related to real-life situations, and participating in role-playing exercises and simulations that apply to real experiences or situations unavailable to them in a typical educational environment (Lombardi, 2007). In other words, authentic learning activities and strategies are often more meaningful to students.

Course management systems provide an excellent way for faculty to provide access to links and materials within a secure environment. Using an integrated CMS/e-portfolio provides a convenient way for items captured in the CMS environment to be used as artifacts that offer evidence of outcome achievement. The CMS/e-portfolio also provides a method for collaboration, one of the elements of authentic learning. Discussions and chats facilitated through the CMS can be placed into the e-portfolio with all members of the discussion, except the e-portfolio owner, remaining anonymous to those guests viewing the individual's e-portfolio. Figures 10.1 and 10.2 are examples of Ed Tech's discussion thread from the CMS, included as an artifact in his e-portfolio.

FIGURE 10.1

Discussion Thread 1

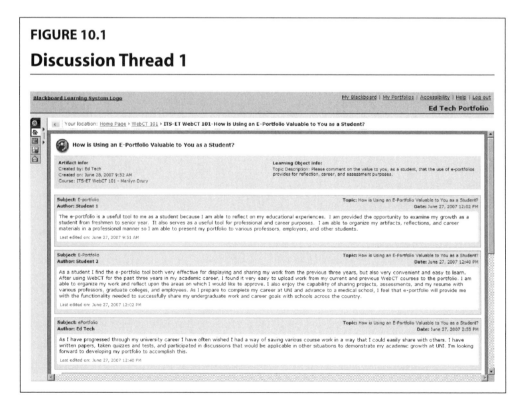

FIGURE 10.2

Discussion Thread 2

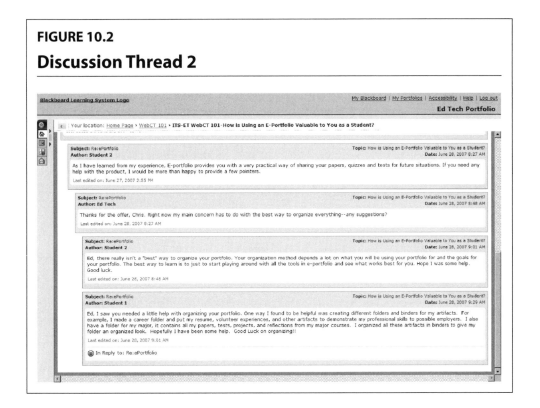

Other collaborative examples might include video and audio of a work session involving several participants. Audio tracks reflecting on the work or discussions provide tone and inflection that cannot otherwise be captured in text reflections.

As we move forward, we hope that authentic learning becomes a primary focus for those using e-portfolios. Whether we include simulations, audio, video, or other artifacts, we must understand that such items can be used effectively to reflect students' outcomes via their e-portfolios. During the pilot, the theater students involved began this process. They discovered, as do many, that properly capturing and including artifacts take time and planning. Students (with guidance from the faculty) should realize that investing the needed time to present and to reflect on artifacts properly is very important; they are not only fulfilling a requirement for an immediate course but also creating an opportunity to select artifacts in their e-portfolio for career or other purposes in the future.

Moving Forward: Reflections on Our Learning

Our goal is to make the use of e-portfolios as simple and seamless as possible for our students and faculty. We will be refining a series of workshops for students on using e-portfolios and offering those early in each semester.

Our goal is to have students understand the potential expansiveness of their e-portfolios while recognizing their strong ownership of the process and resulting product. We also want students to comprehend the reasons for and scope of e-portfolio use. In recent semesters, few students were familiar with e-portfolios, even though a large percentage were familiar with paper-based portfolios. Some students saw the vision of the potential of e-portfolios immediately, while other students struggled with the vision; they seemed to understand only the immediate purpose for a particular course or assignment. Faculty must work with students so that learners understand the big picture of what e-portfolios can do and how the tie to the CMS and the single submission of artifacts, rather than multiple submissions in multiple places, can help with organization and ease of use. Students must understand that e-portfolios can also be used for career purposes, professional purposes, and even nonindividual purposes. (Concerning nonindividual purposes, departments or institutions often use an e-portfolio for presenting information about themselves.)

Ideally, the use of e-portfolios begins as students enter an institution. Our institution is considering offering a first-year experience. Many institutions currently offer such a course or program as a method of helping new students develop academic skills, adjust to college life, become aware of campus resources and facilities, and develop learning communities. Working within structured learning communities would be an ideal way to initially expose students to the concepts of reflection, to documenting their learning progress over the next four to five years, and to thinking about personal learning outcomes they hope to achieve. Reflection is a skill that must be developed, and we cannot simply expect students to be reflective or reflexive without coaching.

We have begun developing specific examples of e-portfolios that will incorporate many best practices of e-portfolio use. Each will be thematically based on the different colleges, their purposes, and their content areas. Our hope is to use the examples so students and faculty can visually understand possible organizational methods and functional purposes of e-portfolios as portrayed in the examples. We also intend to tie in samples of liberal arts core integration and learning into each college example.

We are working closely with the academic assessment staff as consultations occur with departments about student outcomes assessment strategies and planning. E-portfolios provide a valuable tool for departments to present goals and expected outcomes, measurement methodologies for those outcomes, and possible examples of artifacts that provide evidence of meeting those outcomes. Many departments are considering the construction of templates or rubrics that will allow for clear, concise communications regarding expectations, measurements, and results. Common electronic templates are valuable (Bauer & Dunn, 2003; Wilhelm et al., 2006) because they provide a common interface, clearly delineating elements related to goals, outcomes, and assessment. These templates and rubrics will be valuable not only to the departments but also to the students, who can include them in their e-portfolio for multiple purposes.

Establishing a collaborative working environment with the career services area of campus is also very important. Of course, e-portfolios are serving many career functions for new graduates as well as those who continue to develop their portfolio over the course of their professional work. Employers are becoming more familiar with e-portfolios and often review those of the final candidates for a position. With the e-portfolio tool we use, students are able to invite guests to view a portfolio, give them a fixed period of time for the viewing, and track when and if the faculty member, peer, potential employer, or other invited guests did actually review it. Tools such as these allow for security, and they also provide valuable information to the e-portfolio owner.

Finally, several policy issues loom in the future. Students have raised questions regarding the continued use of their e-portfolio after leaving the university. How long will they continue to have access to it if they choose not to take it with them? Why would they want to take it with them and keep placing it in new environments? Can the university provide lifetime access to e-portfolios just as many do with e-mail? Some institutions provide access for free. Others require that students join the alumni association, which then gives them access.

During our pilot, other issues arose regarding appropriate material to place into the e-portfolio. If the student is the owner of the e-portfolio, should he or she be allowed to put anything he or she wants in it and expect the university to provide the storage? Would a snippet of a play that contains nudity be appropriate? Would a section of a writing sample that contains offensive material be acceptable?

Another question that arose was whether the e-portfolio should primarily serve the purposes of the faculty or the purposes of the students. All of these, plus other issues and questions, have caused interesting and informative discussions. Various models and policies exist at other institutions that can be used as beginning guidelines for those getting started with e-portfolios.

We walk this journey one mile at a time, and miles and miles lie ahead of us. We are anxious to see what the next year holds for us and what expressions of creativity students will incorporate into their e-portfolios. Our journey is an exciting one and well worth it!

References

Bauer, W. I., & Dunn, R. E. (2003, Fall). Digital reflection: The electronic portfolio in music teacher education [Electronic version]. *Journal of Music Teacher Education, 13*(1), 7–20.

Lombardi, M. (2007, May). *Authentic learning for the 21st century: An overview* (ELI Paper 1: 2007 EDUCAUSE Learning Initiative). Retrieved October 2, 2008, from http://net.educause.edu/ir/library/pdf/ELI3009.pdf

Shulman, L. (1998). Teacher portfolios: A theoretical activity. In N. Lyons (Ed.), *With portfolio in hand: Validating the new teacher professionalism* (pp. 23–37). New York: Teachers College Press.

Wilhelm, L., Puckett, K., Beisser, S., Wishart, W., Merideth, E., & Sivakumaran, T. (2006). Lessons learned from the implementation of electronic portfolios at three universities [Electronic version]. *TechTrends, 50*(4), 62–71.

Zeichner, K., & Wray, S. (2001). The teaching portfolio in US teacher education programs: What we know and what we need to know [Electronic version]. *Teaching and Teacher Education, 17*(5), 613–621.

Zubizarreta, J. (2004). *The learning portfolio: Reflective practice for improving student learning.* Bolton, MA: Anker.

Chapter 11

The E-portfolio and Liberal Arts Education at Agnes Scott College

Emily Hauck, Olivia White Lopez, and Shannon Yarbrough
Agnes Scott College

THE FOLLOWING INTERVIEW-STYLE essay by Agnes Scott College students is a reflection of their experiences in creating a film explaining the meaning and value of a liberal arts education. The film was the centerpiece and creative outcome of a video-based e-portfolio program at the college, encouraging reflection, collaboration, and hands-on, active learning.

As junior and senior art students at Agnes Scott College, all of us have been exposed to the electronic learning portfolio campaign on campus. In many courses we are taught the value of reflective learning as well as the technological skills that come as a bonus in the process of creating a reflective Web site about our work. As we stumbled through the creation of our first e-portfolios, each of us went through a process of reflection on our learning.

After completing an introductory design class, our professor, Nell Ruby, invited each of us to join a small group of student designers called Dana Design. Members of the campus community, including both faculty and staff, come to us to create solutions for their graphic design needs on campus. The needs include department and group identities, posters and programs for events, the cultural events brochure, and the annual writers' festival magazine, to name a few. The relationship between Dana Design and the Agnes Scott community is inherently symbiotic; the community gives us opportunities to learn how to communicate graphically, and we in return produce designs that are inspired by the inside perspective on campus life that we have as students.

In the spring of 2007, the assistant dean of the college and director of academic advising, Jennifer Cannady, approached the Dana Design team to create a short film on the meaning and value of a liberal arts education at Agnes Scott. The mission of the film was to introduce viewers (first-years and their families) to the concept of a liberal arts education and impart important information concerning degree requirements, specific requirements, and academic advising. In creating the orientation video, we strove not only to inform but also to connect with the incoming class in a way that former presentation panels never quite managed to do; the video needed to be engaging, exciting, and relatively short. We were given special funding and free housing to allow us to work and live together over the summer. The project was a unique opportunity for the three of us to work independently as a group—managing our own schedules, meetings, and work responsibilities.

Making the orientation video involved several stages that can be roughly categorized as planning, filming, and editing. Planning encompassed research, scriptwriting, storyboarding, and presenting and revising ideas. While filming, we learned how to operate the equipment, frame shots, and conduct interviews. Each of us was at one time or another a camerawoman, actress, or interviewer. We learned how to communicate effectively through both visual and verbal means, on film and with each other, giving us a more holistic learning experience. We used Final Cut Pro to edit. We learned how to add transitions, manipulate sound, insert captions and other text, and make fast-action sequences and freeze-frames. We also used GarageBand to create a music track for a portion of the video. Finally, we learned to create multiple variations of the video to optimize performance for different formats, such as projection in an auditorium or on a personal computer.

Though the project was not intended to be a practice in reflective learning, that is exactly what it has become as the center of our e-portfolios. We not only learned what a liberal arts education is but also connected what we were doing to the goals of such an education and experienced again the insights that reflective learning brings. In the remainder of this essay, we use an interview format to expound on these insights, thus continuing our creative and reflective process.

First Thoughts on Defining a Liberal Arts Education

Shannon: In the first meeting we had about the video, Jennifer Cannady, assistant dean of the college and director of academic advising, mentioned incredulously that students come to Agnes Scott without even knowing what a liberal arts education is. It wasn't until she made this statement that I realized that I was one of those students. I started to worry that I was not qualified for the job, but when Emily, Olivia, and I met to discuss our new ideas, we clearly discovered that none of us was quite sure of the meaning of the day's message. I do not remember any of us actually admitting that we didn't yet understand what we were supposed to explain, but we all decided that instead of writing up a definition, we could have a montage sequence in the beginning of the film in which the president, faculty, staff, and students would give us their own definitions. We figured that people would give us an array of explanations and we would end on the one that sounded the most correct.

Emily: Before embarking on the project, I honestly do not remember hearing the phrase "liberal arts education," much less thinking critically about it. I started to butt heads with the concept while writing the script, but due to the decision to make a montage of people defining what a liberal arts education means to them, it was still easy to relegate what I read from the course catalog and on the Web site to the realm of definitions and answers, rather than engaging with the meaning. It really was not until I began interviewing people and hearing multiple perspectives that my own perspective began to develop.

Olivia: Funny enough, I never really thought too much about what a liberal arts education meant until I had to make a video describing the concept. The making of the film was really a series of *Oh, that's what that means!* moments for me. What I did know is that it was supposed to be a general type of education—one encompassing a wide range of subject matter (thus forcing us to take a number of undesirable distribution courses). However, what I did not yet grasp was the real amount of thought and theory behind this type of education. It was almost a surprise when I realized that the connections I had been making between various courses and subject areas were really the *point* of my liberal arts education.

We met early on to discuss the film with various administrative officials, and Shannon, Emily, and I later held several meetings to discuss and reflect on what the term *liberal arts* meant and how we would go about conveying that to fellow students. These meetings were only the beginning of my enlightenment on the subject because the term's meaning would become increasingly nuanced for me with each person we interviewed.

Interviewing

Shannon: While our initial decision to create a montage of definitions may have been an attempt to avoid defining a liberal arts education ourselves, it was no easy way out. To catch students before they left for the summer break, we decided to interview people during a luncheon right after commencement. I am pretty sure our randomly chosen interviewees were just as surprised to realize that they were not sure how to explain the education they had just completed as I was in that first meeting. That we had not actually prepared many other questions besides "What's your definition of a liberal arts education?" enhanced the confusion. To get cohesive responses, we all had to figure out how to be more specific on the spot. We began asking questions leading to more concrete responses: "What connections did you discover between seemingly unrelated classes?" and "Did you take any required classes that made you change your mind about that field of study?" Such questions yielded some insightful responses about the impact that a liberal arts education has on one's development of diverse interests.

Emily: When I began to interview people and hear them speak firsthand about liberal learning, my perception really began to develop. I learned to distinguish between a liberal education and a liberal arts education. I finally understood the liberal arts education that I was three-fourths of the way through for what it was: an unsurpassed opportunity for me to guide my own educational pursuits, explore all disciplines, and discover likes and dislikes I wouldn't have otherwise encountered; a process geared toward personal growth and development; a catalyst for learning new ways of analyzing and synthesizing information, thinking critically, and presenting an argument effectively; an emphasis on the expansion of skill sets rather than a hard-and-fast decision to lock into a specific educational track; and perhaps most importantly, an engaging instructional experience that reveres and promotes knee-deep, hands-on learning rather than the simple memorization and regurgitation of textbook definitions.

Shannon: When I later sat down to edit the footage that we collected from other interviews, I realized that there was not any one correct definition of a liberal arts education. I was surprised to find, however, that there also was not much discrepancy between the answers. The president and members of both the faculty and the staff differentiated a "liberal education" from a "liberal arts education," and the students defined the latter term based on their experiences at Agnes Scott. One student even stated, "Liberal arts learning is Agnes Scott." Because this unexpected and simple statement nailed the purpose of the video, we decided to use it to end the montage.

Olivia: Ultimately, my personal definition of a liberal arts education has come to be that of pursuing knowledge in a wide array of diverse subject matters and drawing connections between them. Doing this allows us to gain a better, more complete understanding of our studies and research interests and widens our perspectives to include even seemingly unrelated topics or impossible viewpoints.

Consequently, I no longer see my required math course as "coincidentally" related to my studies in anthropology and art, but inherently and necessarily so. A liberal arts education gives me the ability to see my world—a vision certainly distorted by my personal interests—through the eyes of another (a mathematician, even!). And really, I will never be able to grasp the complete picture fully (or maintain it for very long, anyway), but what I have gained is the understanding that I can see or understand only a portion of a given situation or subject at any time and that I must work hard to inform myself of other influences, outcomes, and possibilities in relation to the matter at hand.

Shannon: Even after we wrote the script and explained its content, the impact of what we created did not hit me until the middle of the process when I left to do a study-abroad program in Avignon, France. Another women's liberal arts institution sponsored the program, but I recognized cultural differences in instruction soon after I started my classes. In one course about French culture, the professor discouraged us from continuing class discussion beyond the questions posed at the end of the chapters in the textbook. When the program director asked how our classes were going, another student and I asked whether we could start bringing our own questions about the chapters to the class to spark a deeper level of conversation than what the textbook encouraged. She laughed and said that our request was both "Socratic" and "very American," and she went on to explain that in France the professor is the authority. At that moment, I understood how the process of creating the liberal learning video was in itself a contributing component of my liberal arts education. We were the authorities over our project, experiencing a learning-by-doing approach to education. In attempting to explain the countless connections between the classic fields of study, we were reflecting on and thus reexperiencing those connections ourselves. We were not only learning how to educate others but also learning how to enhance our own learning processes.

Emily: I really feel that as a result of reflecting on the process of creating our film, all three of us have seen that the benefits of the project go far beyond résumé building. Each of us has enriched her personal definition of a liberal arts education and has unexpectedly begun to examine the meaning and value of her studies. The process has continued to enrich our experiences in our current courses—across all disciplines. Furthermore, we have become aware of the ways in which we as individuals and as a group process information, approach and work through problems, overcome difficulties, and adapt to unfamiliar technology and situations.

Previous Preparation

Olivia: I do not think I could have even begun to conceive of creating an orientation film had I not taken the introductory design course in the fall of 2006. We were highly encouraged to take risks and explore new and different (to us, anyway) design media and media productions (including e-portfolios, print materials, and more), and it was because of such an open, collaborative, and challenging atmosphere that I ventured into creating my first short film. Working with a small digital camera, I began to record the everyday events and small moments that were happening all around me, mostly without paying them much attention. I began to see greater meaning in perhaps trivial occurrences, and at the same time, I began to learn how to communicate my thoughts, ideas, and emotions effectively through the medium of film. On the more technical side, I also became familiar with iMovie's editing software, which undoubtedly helped me later tackle the task of learning Final Cut Pro for the orientation film.

Essentially, the course taught me how to communicate through design. I do not think I could have taken on the challenge of working collaboratively on a film targeted for an audience of four hundred to five hundred people without having had such an experience.

Shannon: In addition to the technological skills I learned in the introductory design class, I also gained confidence in my decision-making skills. Our professor encouraged us to design and direct our own projects, and I learned not to ask for her approval every step of the way. Because we worked on the orientation film without a supervisor, our newfound self-confidence proved invaluable in the film-making process.

Building my e-portfolio also prepared me for this project in a somewhat unexpected way. The main part of that process that I remember is how difficult it was—I had a big vision for what I wanted my Web site to be but very few technological skills with which to work. I went into the video project understanding the concept of a learning curve; I knew that I would run into unexpected challenges, but I was ready to learn and appreciate the struggle.

One component of my motivation was just being at and loving Agnes Scott. My desire to explain the value of the education that Agnes Scott and other liberal arts institutions offer helped me overcome the frustrations I encountered along the way.

Emily: My initial experience with the introductory design course at Agnes Scott, combined with a semester of Dana Design, really paved the way for me to be able to take on the project. In both experiences I took on new technologies and struggled with the learning curve to produce high-quality results. For example, I was completely unfamiliar with Dreamweaver before I began the process of producing my e-portfolio, and I was equally ignorant of Adobe InDesign when working on the writers' festival magazine.

As a result of such experiences, I entered the project expecting to be confused, frustrated, and stressed at some point or another, but I was confident that through hard work and problem solving, the process of learning by doing would overcome any difficulties that arose.

Reflection and Empowerment

Shannon: Dean Diedrick's touching introduction to our film at a recent first-year orientation verbalized our discoveries. He mentioned that our achievement as students in making the movie was representative of what Agnes Scott is all about: students helping students and learning through doing. Instead of hearing a professor explain a liberal arts education through diagrams on a PowerPoint presentation, the first-years witnessed this type of education in action. Liberal arts institutions, as Agnes Scott says, empower students to find their own voices and then use their voices to empower others.

Emily: The development of my views of a liberal arts education and what it means to me, my future, and who I am did not even become clear to me until I began the process of reflection. As a part of the project, we wrote reflections on the entire three-month journey (including other Dana Design projects we worked on during the time). In fact, this very essay for this volume has allowed me to step back and view the project objectively. While writing, I have realized how the project has changed me. The process has been ongoing, and we have shown the video at orientation events, to friends and family, and as a part of a presentation on our work open to the campus. Each time I have presented the video and spoken about the process, my understanding of my learning has become more refined through reflection.

As a result of my experiences in the production of the video, I treasure my liberal arts education at Agnes Scott all the more. I have gained invaluable experience in thinking critically, overcoming obstacles, and collaborating with others through the process of reflective learning. I know that much of what I have learned as a participant in our project will continue to serve me throughout my life. Such empowerment is an extremely satisfying feeling.

Conclusion

The ongoing process of reflection has enriched our perspective on the value and outcomes of our unique film-based e-portfolio development experience. It has also deepened our continued studies as part of a liberal arts education. From the initial reflections to screenings and presentations, and from discussing the project on our e-portfolios to writing this essay, each step in the reflective process informs the next. The continual act of reflection adds to our recognition of and appreciation for the results of our particular project, but the process itself and the ways in which our revelations affect our learning will inform future endeavors, making the e-portfolio's emphasis on reflection and collaboration a powerful component of an outstanding liberal arts education.

Chapter 12

The Lebow College of Business My LIFEfolio

An E-portfolio Program

Frank Linnehan
Drexel University

> Unfortunately, students today seem to have a very short
> half-life of knowledge.
>
> —Dr. M. Gombola, chair of the finance department

EVEN LONG JOURNEYS begin with a single step. Dr. Gombola's statement, made during one of the many faculty discussions focusing on a major revision of the entire undergraduate curriculum, was the beginning of one such journey for the LeBow College of Business. The first leg of this journey culminated in the development and introduction of our My LIFEfolio program, which uses electronic portfolios to integrate the academic and experiential components of a student's learning across the curriculum. The program was designed in conjunction with LeBow's new undergraduate curriculum, which was introduced and implemented in fall 2006. This chapter will describe why we thought it was important to create the program, a description of the student portfolios, and our experiences during the first year.

Why E-portfolios?

While other institutions have successfully used electronic portfolios for learning assessment (often to satisfy accreditation requirements), our primary objective for using electronic portfolios was student focused—that is, to provide (1) evidence of the connectivity of learning across the curriculum, (2) opportunities to reflect on what students learn, and (3) a place to retain and show evidence of student accomplishments. When designing the program, we operated under the assumption that student motivation would be the key to the program's sustainability and effectiveness. To maximize this motivation, we had to convince students that building and maintaining portfolios would help them succeed at LeBow and in their professional careers.

Achieving the goal of connecting learning across our undergraduate curriculum is made more difficult given our educational mission, which closely integrates academics with career preparation. The majority of our students are enrolled in a five-year program that includes three six-month co-op jobs. Since students rotate between class and their co-op assignments, they are always either preparing for their next assignment or making the transition back to the classroom and campus life. Such a schedule makes it very difficult for them to see connections between the various lessons they learn as they progress through their coursework. The long lines of students waiting to sell their textbooks back to the bookstore or to the resale merchants on campus also provide further evidence to us of the disconnection of learning across our curriculum.

Despite such challenges, we wanted to develop a way to integrate learning across the curriculum. In our discussions, we believed that methods to integrate the curriculum employed by smaller teaching-oriented colleges and universities, such as team teaching or connecting courses across terms or years, wouldn't work in our environment. We eventually came to the conclusion that one way to accomplish our goal was to take advantage of the students' familiarization with and continual reliance on technology. A Web-based portfolio system seemed to be an ideal way to help us meet our objective. Our timing was also opportunistic, as we were progressing through the arduous process of revising the entire undergraduate curriculum. Additionally, a technology-based solution to the challenge fit into the institution's history because Drexel was one of the first universities to require its students to have access to a personal computer and was one of the first to have an entirely wireless campus.

Since the goal of the program was connectivity of learning, a benefit in developing the portfolio system was that the project induced interested faculty to talk with colleagues within their departments, across departments within the college, and across colleges and schools within the university. We as a faculty began to see disconnections that were not apparent to us before. For example, we discovered that economics department faculty used different approaches to teach the core microeconomics class. Some of the faculty had become so frustrated with students' lack of quantitative skills that they taught the class using as little math as possible, while others continued to struggle with students' poor math knowledge and skills.

Another benefit was the discussion we began with the math department faculty about their courses; the conversations informed our approaches to teaching courses such as operations management, finance, and economics, and we became very familiar with the content of the required math courses. The collaboration reduced the temptation to point fingers at the math department when students came to business courses unprepared.

While such conversations among faculty were extremely beneficial, the most important questions for the portfolio committee concerned the content of the electronic portfolios because we wanted to ensure that the portfolios would be used by students across the entire curriculum.

The Program

The number of electronic portfolios that should be created and the materials that should be included in the portfolios were critical decisions that had to be made in the early stages of the program development. To make such decisions, we had to ask fundamental questions about the education we were offering our students, similar to questions raised in developing a learning assessment program. The three questions we needed to answer were as follows: (1) What do we want students to learn? (2) What evidence should students retain of their learning? (3) How do we induce students to reflect on what they've learned?

After much discussion in our committee, we decided that the program would include four electronic portfolios: (1) writing, (2) quantitative reasoning, (3) career, and (4) business (the student's field of concentration). We determined that there would be minimum requirements for each portfolio but that we would encourage students to be creative and add more than the required content. We also decided that the program would not be optional and that certain courses across our curriculum would include graded portfolio assignments that the students would upload and ultimately use as the focus of their learning reflections.

The Writing Portfolio

This portfolio consists of assignments from coursework in English and communication (both taught by faculty in the College of Arts and Sciences) and in business. The English department in our College of Arts and Sciences worked with us to develop the format of the portfolio. With the department's help, a common writing rubric was created and incorporated into the portfolio design (Appendix A). The rubric's criteria (for example, audience, organization, evidence) are used as elements of the portfolio.

When students upload a sample of their writing to their writing portfolios, they link the work to one of the elements in the rubric. As an example, a well-organized memo the student may have written while on a co-op job may be uploaded to the portfolio and linked to the organization criterion, showing evidence of the student's writing skills.

These messages are reinforced by the description of the portfolio:

The minimum requirements of each LeBow College of Business writing portfolio will include the LeBow writing rubric and assignments from:

- *English 101–103 courses*

- *Business 101 and 102*

- *Writing-intensive business courses*

For a portfolio to showcase your writing, we strongly recommend that it include (but not be limited to) the following:

- *Other writing assignments you complete in any of your courses; this may include research papers, reports, business plans, case analyses, essays, lab reports, take-home exams, personal journals, expository writing, persuasive arguments, etc.*

- *Comments or feedback from instructors or peers on your writing*

- *Writing completed for an employer*

- *Personal documents*

- *Use of multimedia in your communication*

Your portfolio should also include a reflective narrative or essay in which you discuss your strengths as a writer, your progress, and other aspects of your writing. Here, you will tell the story of your writing over your time at LeBow either from a personal perspective or from a business or employer perspective, which may be useful in your job search.

For those students interested in showcasing their writing skills, we also strongly recommend that you take the Literature of Business course, which will include a complete review, reflection, and completion of your portfolio. It is also strongly recommended that you consider becoming a writing instructor.

The Quantitative Reasoning Portfolio

The quantitative reasoning portfolio is created while the student is taking the required math courses during the first year of the curriculum. As we developed the plan for the portfolio, business faculty in the departments of decision sciences, economics, and finance wrote math problems related to their disciplines, which the math department faculty reviewed and used in their courses. The answers to the problems, in such areas as compound interest and the time value of money, are uploaded by the students into their portfolios during their math courses. The process allows the students to reference their work when they take the core business courses that require knowledge of such concepts. Similar to the writing portfolio, links are used in the portfolio to organize the student's work.

We describe the quantitative reasoning portfolio to the students as follows:

> *The purpose of the portfolio is twofold. First, it will act as a resource for you as you take your core and upper-level business courses, and second, it can help you demonstrate evidence of your mastery of topics in mathematics. This latter objective is met by uploading your work to your portfolio and including links to these files under the appropriate math concept or topic.*

> *The minimum requirements of each LeBow College of Business quantitative reasoning portfolio will include material from the following:*
>
> - *Math 101 and 102 (this will include problem solutions, teaching notes, and assignments)*
>
> - *An introductory reflection on the use of math in business, which will be completed in Math 102*
>
> - *Assignments completed in Math 101 and 102 that will be referred to in core business courses in economics, finance, operations management, statistics, and accounting*
>
> - *Assignment files from core business courses and your reflections on these assignments*

The Career Portfolio

Consistent with the university's mission, which focuses on career-integrated education, the career portfolio consists of work from across the entire curriculum. It begins with a student reflection on a personality and career interest assessment completed in the first year. It also includes the student's initial résumé created during a course that introduces him or her to co-op. As students progress through their six-month co-op work experiences, they are required to reflect on these experiences, revise their résumé, and upload and link their performance evaluations from co-op employers to their portfolios. As part of the development of the portfolio program, we also created a one-credit course that is taken after the final co-op experience. In this class students write a career plan and present their portfolios to faculty and co-op advisers in preparation for the transition into their professional careers.

The portfolio is described as follows:

Similar to your other electronic portfolios, your career portfolio can serve multiple purposes. First, it is an opportunity to showcase your experience, skills, and knowledge to a prospective employer as you search for co-op jobs and you begin your job search for your first position after graduation. It can also be used as a repository of information that may be useful to you in your job search, containing information about personal resources, contact information to build your job search network, and projects you have successfully completed, which can be used to demonstrate your expertise in an area of interest to an employer. The portfolio can also be used to help in your career development and planning.

The career planning process begins with a look inward to help you identify your strengths, interests, and development needs. It includes personal reflections on your work and educational experiences, as well as thoughts about your future. It also includes the development of a formal career plan, which is based on your assessments, interests, strengths, and goals. This plan is a living document that we encourage you to continue to modify and update throughout your professional career. The elements of the career portfolio have been selected to follow these career development steps.

The minimum requirements of each LeBow College of Business career portfolio include:

- *Your résumé created in COOP 101*

- *Personal assessments completed in UNIV 101*

- *Performance evaluation data from your co-op jobs*

- *Personal reflections on your co-op experiences (these are a series of questions about your on-the-job experiences and your evaluation of these experiences)*

- *A career plan created and presented after your last co-op*

In the second term of UNIV 101, which will be taken after your last co-op job, you will present your career portfolio and create the career plan. The presentation will focus on (1) the awareness of your skills and knowledge relevant to a professional career, (2) communicating these skills and knowledge to others, and (3) your career plan.

The Business Portfolio

Each of our academic departments has developed strategies for the use of portfolios in their disciplines. Similar to the other three portfolios, information collection and learning reflection are the critical components of the business portfolios (which are still under development). For example, the finance department is considering using podcasts that can be uploaded by the students into their portfolios. The podcasts will explain key concepts in finance to which students may refer as they progress to their upper-level courses. Students in the entrepreneurship concentration will be required to document and save ideas for new businesses and perhaps keep a record of their experiences with entrepreneurs. Each concentration will have the students finalize their portfolios in the discipline's capstone class.

Implementation

Rather than introduce My LIFEfolio to all our undergraduate students at once, we decided to launch it to first-year students only during the 2006–2007 academic year and to each subsequent incoming class. The plan gives us the opportunity to modify and improve the program, based on our experiences each year. Before its introduction, we also conducted a pilot test of the software with a small number of students who were asked to create portfolios and give us feedback on the system.

When the program was introduced, communication material focused on connectivity across the portfolios (and, thus, the curriculum). This meant encouraging the students not only to identify connections within a discipline (using concepts learned in the introductory courses for success in advanced courses) but to connect materials and learning across disciplines and extend the connections to their work experiences. We recommended, for example, that a case analysis completed for an accounting class be linked to the writing portfolio to demonstrate skill in technical writing. Critical to this effort was the development of a complete description of each portfolio's contents (Appendix B), showing the student an overview of the first few years of the program and, coincidently, of his or her coursework during that time.

Securing the buy-in and ownership of the program from faculty who were not part of the initial design was also an important consideration in our implementation plans. The LeBow College of Business has over a hundred full-time faculty members, and we knew it would be challenging to gain commitment from every faculty member. Although most faculty members reacted favorably to the program as it was being developed, we understood that its universal acceptance will take time. Hence, we identified three key contact points that span the five-year curriculum: (1) our introductory business courses that are taken in the first year, (2) our core courses required of all business students (usually taken during the second through fourth years), and (3) the discipline-based capstone classes taken in the final year. We then focused our implementation plans on key faculty members who teach at each of these stages in the curriculum. These faculty members agreed to embed portfolio assignments in their courses, with the ultimate goal of institutionalizing the assignments in all sections of that course, regardless of the instructor. The assignments would constitute the minimum content of the portfolios and would create a linkage across the entire curriculum, without requiring all faculty members to use portfolios in their courses.

We focused the implementation of the program in the first two terms and then expanded it on a selective basis to the core business courses with faculty who agreed to work with us. For example, an economics professor agreed to incorporate My LIFEfolio into his microeconomics course by using assignments students had uploaded into their quantitative reasoning portfolios from a calculus course in the previous term. The pilot was a success, as evidenced by one student's reflection on the experience:

> I had taken an economics course in high school, but it was mainly conceptual. I had also taken three years of calculus. Not once did I see a connection between these two subjects. My experience in this calculus-based section of microeconomics has shown me otherwise. I would never have thought to pull up previous math assignments and to find a correlation between what we had done and what we were currently learning in economics.
>
> In Math 102, we focused greatly on derivatives, optimization, and marginal revenue, cost, and profit. However, in math, these things only applied to meaningless problems. I mean, who honestly believes they will use calculus after being through with math courses? Yet, in Econ 201, these same concepts kept making an appearance. However, instead of having no real meaning, economics brought practical uses to these basic calculus concepts. I now understand why the margin is the first derivative and why a person might use this in situations other than becoming a math teacher.
>
> [My portfolio] serves as a showcase of how different courses such as these relate. It allows you to see a progression from concept to concept, to access past assignments and to relate them to current ones. Hopefully, the assignments from Econ 201 will relate to later courses, just as Math

101 and 102 related to Econ 201. I feel this proves that introductory courses are actually relevant, and serve a greater purpose than merely offering useless information.

As we continue to implement the program, we plan to build on successes such as these to help gain additional faculty commitment. Maximizing faculty use, along with our course-embedded portfolio assignments, will help ensure student commitment and use as well.

After the first few terms of the program, we realized the importance of developing a mechanism to track students' progress as they created and enhanced their portfolios. To this end, we asked an academic adviser to be the point person for all portfolio inquiries. Students are required to give this adviser access to their portfolios so that she may monitor the students' progress, read their reflections, ensure assignments are linked to the portfolios correctly, and identify future training needs as we introduce the program to our new students.

Conclusion

After one year, we know the journey to integrate electronic portfolios into our undergraduate curriculum fully is just beginning. A number of decisions still need to be made as the program matures. Our guiding principle in making such decisions will continue to focus on the goal of enhancing opportunities for students to reflect on what they have learned, further distancing them from the "checklist" or "learn and purge" mentality toward education we have observed all too often in the past.

Appendix A: LeBow College of Business Writing Rubric

Gross Mistakes (binary)	This reader did not find gross mistakes that would immediately cast suspicion on the effort/expertise of the document's creator.		This reader found gross mistakes that would immediately make an average reader suspicious or feel negative about the document.	
Ethics (binary)	This reader thinks the document is presented in an ethically sound way, using solid evidence.		This document shows ethical lapses that could undermine its entire purpose and message.	
	Excellent	**Good**	**Fair**	**Poor**
Purpose/Main Point	This reader thinks that the writer's purpose is clear. The document has a clear focus.	This reader thinks the writer's purpose is clear for the most part.	The writer often loses focus on the main point of the document.	This reader has a difficult time determining why the writer has created this document.
Audience	The writer has written for a clearly defined audience and, in this reader's opinion, has addressed that audience expertly.	The audience for the document is clear. This reader thinks that the writer has done a good job addressing that audience.	The document's treatment of the audience is somewhat confusing.	This reader thinks that the writer's treatment of the audience appears unprofessional and/or it is not clear who is being addressed.
Organization	This reader thinks the report has a clear organizational logic. Transitions between ideas are handled well.	The report is organized effectively. This reader thinks the document's organization could be refined/tightened (headings, better transitions, etc.).	This reader thinks the document must be organized more effectively, as readers will be confused or misled.	This reader finds little coherent structure in this document. No clear rationale is apparent for why the document is set up the way it is. The document is confusing.
Evidence	This reader thinks the writer has made excellent use of research and sources, helping strengthen/build the argument with this material.	This reader thinks the writer made good use of research and sources, citing well. In a few places the document's main point could have been strengthened with additional evidence.	This reader thinks the document would be substantially strengthened with more/better evidence and/or the evidence presented is formatted in a sloppy, distracting manner.	The document is weak because of a lack of evidence and support, and/or the evidence used is formatted so poorly that it's difficult to tell what is cited.

	Excellent	Good	Fair	Poor
Sentence Style: Flow of Writing	This reader thinks the clear, concise writing in this document made it enjoyable to read. The writer uses a lot of sentence variety and strong word choices.	This reader thinks the writing in this document is good, but perhaps the writer could have introduced a little more variety and/or written in a more concise fashion.	This reader thinks some of the writing is awkward and/or the writer relies too heavily on the same kind of sentence structure.	This reader thinks much of the writing in this document is awkward, repetitive, and/or wordy. The writing was not engaging.
Correctness: Grammar and Writing Mechanics	This reader noticed few errors, if any. The document is clear, and the writer shows considerable mastery of the language.	This reader noticed some grammatical/ mechanical errors, but those errors did not interfere with the reader's understanding of the document's purpose.	This reader noticed numerous grammatical/mechanical errors, and those errors interfered at times with the reader's understanding of the document's purpose and/or caused the reader to question the writer's skill and expertise.	This reader noticed many grammatical/mechanical errors. The reader felt the number of errors made the document difficult to understand, and the reader questioned the writer's professionalism because of these recurrent mistakes.
Document Design/ Appearance	This reader thinks the document uses design elements (white space, titles, and subtitles, etc.) expertly to create a professional-looking document.	This reader thinks the document is clean, but the appearance could be improved to aid in the document's clarity and/or organization.	This reader thinks the document has an amateurish look to it and/or is in need of a more professional appearance.	This reader thinks the document appears sloppy and unprofessional, and that sloppiness may cause confusion.
Visuals	This reader thinks the document uses visuals in an expert way.	This reader thinks the writer makes good use of visuals. Perhaps there are additional opportunities for the use of such material.	The writer has missed opportunities to use visuals and/or has used visuals in a sloppy, ineffective way.	The writer needs visuals to help clarify the document's purpose, and/or the visuals are sloppy, inaccurate, or presented in an unethical manner.

Appendix B: Portfolio Contents

Business Portfolio	Career Portfolio	Quantitative Reasoning Portfolio	Writing Portfolio
Correct template Address/phone/e-mail Portfolio description	Correct template Address/phone/e-mail Portfolio description	Correct template Address/phone/e-mail Portfolio description	Correct template Address/phone/e-mail Portfolio description
BUSN 101 Case analysis summary	UNIV 101 Assessment 1— Personality	MATH 101 Final project— Questions	ENG 101 Essay 1 Essay 2
BUSN 102 Business plan Business plan reflection Financial case study	Assessment 2—Career Civic engagement Civic engagement reflection	Final project—My solutions Final project—Answers	Essay 3
Concentration courses Text contents Instructor notes Resources	CO-OP 101 or BUSN 498 Résumé Career plan Career plan reflection Article summary	MATH 102 Project 1 Reflection on the use of math in business	ENG 102 Assignment 1 ENG 103 Assignment 1
Recommended: *Assignments, research* *papers, presentations,* *group work*	CO-OP (For each co-op cycle) Co-op reflection Co-op performance appraisals Update portfolio description Update résumé	BUSN 102 Financial case study ACCT 115 Assignment 1 ECON 201 Assignment 1	UNIV 101 Book report BUSN 101 Case analysis summary COM 270 Business communication assignment
	UNIV 101 B Final career plan Final career plan reflection	Core business courses Assignments Reflections	UNIV 101 B Final career plan Final career plan reflection
	Recommended: *Interactive résumé and* *cover letter, resources,* *recommendation letters,* *work samples*	*Recommended: Math* *tutorials, models,* *assignments, work* *examples*	*Recommended: Research* *papers, business samples,* *case analyses, business* *plans, essays, marketing* *plans*

Chapter 13

Learning Portfolios in a Sophomore-Level Composition and Literature Course

Leslie Ortquist-Ahrens
Otterbein College

EIGHT FACULTY MEMBERS at Otterbein College from the departments of art, music, English, nursing, and business came together over the course of a month in 2004 to read and discuss John Zubizarreta's (2004) book *The Learning Portfolio: Reflective Practice for Improving Student Learning.* The group had set out to explore this approach out of interest, but not with the intention of implementing a collegewide program. All were enthusiastic, but only two (in English) integrated a learning portfolio component into a subsequent course.

Because I teach each year in addition to directing Otterbein's Center for Teaching and Learning, I decided to pilot learning portfolios in a required sophomore-level literature and composition course that is part of the college's four-year integrative studies core curriculum. Doing so would give me firsthand experience for future reference, if I were to recommend that others consider using learning portfolios and if the institution were to move toward e-portfolios for all students for assessment purposes. For two years, I incorporated learning portfolios into the course. Students completed all the usual required work for the quarter. They read, discussed, and wrote about love relationships as expressed in works from early Egyptian love poems to excerpts from the Song of Solomon, Plato's *Symposium* to Marie de France's medieval tales of courtly love, Shakespeare's *Twelfth Night* to Alice Munro's 1977 novella *The Beggar Maid,* stories from Chitra Banerjee Divakaruni's 1995 anthology of love stories *Arranged Marriage* to Cédric Klapisch's 2002 French film *L'Auberge Espagnole* (*The Spanish Apartment*).

In addition, they read many poems and several essays about love from sociological, psychological, and biological perspectives. Because composition is a major component of the course, students were required to write and revise several formal essays based on peer-editing feedback and my comments on early drafts; they also submitted homework assignments on readings and completed in-class writing exercises.

From the beginning of the course, students were aware (and reminded regularly) that the culminating project for the course would be a learning portfolio. To this end, they were asked to save all work—notes, drafts, homework, revisions—and to reflect on their learning throughout the course. The portfolio was designed to represent examples of students' best work, of their greatest improvements as well as their greatest challenges, and of evidence that they achieved a shared set of curriculum-wide objectives for the course. The assignment asked students to focus on three major questions: What were their greatest strengths or improvements in the course? What remained significant challenges for them as readers, writers, or thinkers (and what strategies might they use to address these challenges in the future)? And what might they identify in their own work as areas of personal, intellectual, or emotional growth in relation to the course content (love, cultural norms, human nature)—specifically, what had most challenged their own deeply held beliefs about human nature and love, and what had most affirmed their already held beliefs? Each of the three essays was to be at least one to two good paragraphs in length, and students were required to cite specifically from their own work and to submit it, carefully and clearly labeled, along with the reflection pieces in the final portfolio.

What follows are observations that have emerged from that experience. The examples are reproduced verbatim from portfolio work submitted in 2006 and 2007 and have been included with permission from the students.

Observations on Assigning Learning Portfolios

Easing discomfort Reflection does not come naturally or easily to many students. In fact, it can feel deeply uncomfortable. I have found that students must have opportunities to practice reflection in class and must receive feedback and generous encouragement on their work in progress. I also provide them with examples of strong and weak self-analysis that I do not label in advance, but rather ask them to discuss and critique with me.

Prompts No surprise: the better my prompts, the better the students' work is. Asking for analysis of work done for the course has proved to be better than asking for reflection on process (which can become a drawn-out narrative with little analysis). Requiring students to quote from their own work and clearly link appendix items to their analyses has been crucial to ground the writing and prevent vague generalizations. Prompting students to consider how they can continue to develop after the course and what resources and strategies they might call on has also been important. (See "Learning Portfolio Assignment" in Part 4.)

Some Benefits from Using Learning Portfolios

Metacognition and self-recognition Students can often (but not always) do a pretty good job of identifying areas of strength, challenge, and growth, as well as strategies to continue developing. Some students begin to move beyond identification to insightful analysis. The learning portfolio provides them with a structured opportunity to practice thoughtful, evidence-based self-reflection and thus to work on developing metacognitive skills:

> *Even though I said it was something I improved most on, summarizing is still something that is challenging for me and needs some serious work. I never know what is enough information or too much information.*

· · ·

> *This class has really opened my eyes to a new kind of writing, a style of writing in which I really push myself to think and ask questions about what I'm writing.*

· · ·

> *My biggest challenge is to "write to communicate." I tend to write to think, which makes my writing unorganized and confusing. In my second paper, "Not Necessarily a Fairytale Ending," the reader can see from my introductory and concluding paragraphs that my argument fully blossomed as I was writing, and I made marginal efforts to transition my ideas.*

Surprises Students, themselves, are sometimes surprised at what they learn (or at the patterns they identify) when they review the work from the quarter:

> *I counted the number of times the word "is" (or any of its forms) appeared in my analysis essay, and it was astonishing. I counted fifteen different places [where] I used "is" in a very short paper.*

· · ·

Well, I actually couldn't find any of my writing where I connected something to my own life—which surprised me. I guess I never flat out wrote down the connections.

Student sense of growth and values clarification   Purposeful, structured reflection gives students an opportunity to develop a sense of their own growth and to begin to clarify their values in a more explicit and conscious way:

One essay that helped me as a writer would be the Analysis Essay we did about Skolnick's "Grounds for Marriage: Reflections on an Institution in Transition." This article allowed me to critically think as a reader and interpret her work as a writer. . . . I was persuaded to believe that the institution of marriage is not disappearing. That paper was a transition point for me. It helped me to start critically thinking about everything I read.

• • •

My first attempt at writing about what I thought love was on our first day of class was not very in depth at all and dealt mainly with my unconditional love [for my brothers]: "whenever I think of [my brothers] in danger or pain, a strong feeling of fear wells up inside me." Since that initial writing, and after all that we've read throughout this course, my opinion of love has changed dramatically. First of all, reading these articles challenged me to decide where I stood on these issues. . . . One thing I realized about myself is that I'm not opposed to divorce.

Learning-focused feedback on the course   What we read in students' self-analysis is often intriguing and surprising. In any case, it is of a different nature than most of what we can learn in student course evaluations because it explicitly focuses on the students' *learning*. It can help us as teachers identify the practices that students find most transformative, and it can help us determine whether we are achieving the range of goals for their learning that we hope to achieve:

I have improved greatly in [reading] comprehension. I usually read books for school just to read them and get it over with. I never read deeper than the words on the page. Writing double column notes really helped me read into the material and its meaning. I pulled out things that caught my eye in the readings and then expanded my thoughts on it. This really helped me improve my reading skills and helped me to recognize my own thoughts about a particular topic.

• • •

One of my improvements and strengths this quarter has been my ability to take notes from readings in class and make notes of important and key events, people, and so forth. The double column notes have been a great way for me to get in the habit of highlighting important information for reading so that in class I am better prepared for discussion. I can easily read the comments I made about my reading and share in class how I felt about a certain passage, character, or comment.

Guilt reduction What we read in students' self-reflection sometimes reveals that intransigent errors and frequent problems are often the result of haste, sloppiness, or poor habits (not one's failure to cover some content or skill):

My greatest challenge as a writer is that I put all my effort into writing a paper so when I finally finish I neglect to revise the paper, especially the grammar. . . . This challenge for me can be fixed by taking a little extra time once I'm finished with my paper to reread and revise to find errors [that] spell check doesn't pick up. Another remedy could possibly be to have a peer read the paper strictly for grammar errors. Until I learn to give myself extra time to proofread my papers, I will continue to lose points and interfere with the understanding of my papers by making unnecessary mistakes.

Misconception identification Students' deeply held beliefs about learning and about their own capacities are at times revealed, and misconceptions may surface that we can address with the student (or with future students):

I think spelling is something either you have or you don't.

Some Challenges in Using Learning Portfolios

Assessment challenges It can be challenging to decide how to assess students' self-assessment to encourage reflection and honesty yet hold students to high standards in this assignment as in others. Developing careful criteria and explicit instructions can go a long way toward easing this challenge.

BS factor? If assignments aren't carefully constructed (for example, if not enough attention is given to requiring that students draw on their own work for evidence and comment specifically on it), students may be inclined to work to please the teacher and guess what the teacher wants to hear.

Discouraging evidence Sometimes it is discouraging to see how little self-awareness a student has or to hear a student say that he or she has not changed or developed through the experience in the course. This, however, is important information for us to know as teachers. If significant numbers of students in our classes were to exhibit such lack of self-awareness and growth, we would have some valuable evidence to consider as we worked to redesign the course for the future.

Time and work Incorporating learning portfolios takes time and can add a layer of work for the instructor. Streamlining the process with clear, explicit instructions and a grading rubric can help make evaluation more efficient.

Chapter 14

A Journal of Citizenship

Orienting First-Year Students to Liberal Education

Elizabeth Regosin and Ronald J. O. Flores
St. Lawrence University

IN 2003, THE ASSOCIATION OF AMERICAN COLLEGES AND UNIVERSITIES (AACU), in collaboration with the Charles Engelhard Foundation, launched the Bring Theory to Practice (BTP) initiative, which seeks to understand the relationships between pedagogies of engagement and student outcomes, such as mental well-being and civic development. The project is a "response to concerns about the increase of debilitating behaviors, such as alcohol abuse and the prevalence of chronic expressions of depression, among college students" (AACU, 2007). Harward (2007) describes the impetus for the initiative by detailing the growing disengagement of university students with their academic careers, which has led to higher levels of stress, depression, suicidal tendencies, and indifference to social concerns. St. Lawrence University (SLU) joined the BTP initiative in 2005 by introducing the Center for Civic Engagement and Leadership (CCEL), which combines academic and cocurricular activities within a living-learning community where students work together with community partners to develop and direct community projects that address locally identified needs.

We have chosen to foreground citizenship and leadership skills in our programming because the most powerful engaged learning experiences among our students center on community service and social activism. Further, the practice of citizenship and the emergence of leadership skills have strong positive effects on personal development, including improved self-confidence, self-esteem, personal agency, and accomplishment (Eyler & Giles, 1999, pp. 151–165), all of which positively affect student outcomes and behavior. Our BTP project aims at isolating and assessing the effects of pedagogies of engagement on student outcomes among two successive cohorts of first-year students who live in the CCEL and together participate in a community-based learning course that critically examines citizenship through active learning. While the course incorporates a variety of engaged learning opportunities, we focus on the role that learning journals (a close relative of learning portfolios) play as a foundational tool for engaged learning and the effects of such journals on promoting both the critical assessment of citizenship and the development of citizenship skills.

Pedagogies of Engagement, Learning Journals, and Civic Development

Although there is no consensus on what is engaged learning (Flores, 2007; Swaner, 2007), we find that Jones, Valdez, Nowakowski, and Rasmussen (1994) offer a useful and comprehensive definition that emphasizes both student responsibility for learning and creating opportunities for the application of what is learned in the classroom to real-world situations. Students set their own learning and discovery agendas, identifying problems and applying learned skills to seek solutions and advance knowledge. Since learning typically involves working with others, pedagogies of engagement stress the collaborative process, where students learn to respect and incorporate others' views in authentic situations of discovery, problem solving, and decision making. Palmer (1998) stresses this point by declaring that pedagogies of engagement are all supported by the assumption that knowledge is coconstructed by communities of teachers and learners.

In her exhaustive review of the literature on engaged pedagogies, Swaner (2007) identifies problem-based learning, service-/community-based learning, collaborative learning, and community-based research as the primary strands of engaged learning, and while she does not acknowledge learning journals/portfolios on her list, their basic features as outlined by Zubizarreta (2004) indicate that they are critical tools in engaging students with learning and, thus, in increasing the probability of successful student outcomes derived from these pedagogies. For example, Eyler, Giles, and Gray (2003) argue that while community-based learning has been associated with positive student civic development outcomes such as improved interpersonal skills, greater sense of social responsibility, increased commitment to community service, reduced acceptance of stereotypes, and greater sense of personal worth and autonomy, its success depends on how well the community experience is integrated into the fabric of the course. Such integration is best accomplished through reflection assignments, such as learning journals or portfolios that ask students to consider in writing how their experiences speak to course materials and how such materials have informed their work in the community (Bringle & Hatcher, 1999; Cooper, 1998; Kottkamp, 1990).

Aside from acknowledging that journals and portfolios have been shown to successfully bring together classroom and community experiences for students in community-based learning courses (Bringle & Hatcher, 1999), as well as evidence that such courses and assignments enhance citizenship skills, we chose a learning journal as the primary course writing assignment because it asks students to be both intentional in and responsible for their learning. Further, since the learning journal, like democratic action, is a collaborative and dynamic endeavor, its exercises dovetail nicely with the students' maturation as active citizens. The journal, then, becomes a powerful space where students are free to explore their own learning agendas as they dialogue with themselves, their instructors, and their readings. To highlight best how our efforts all come together to foster engaged learning and civic development, we briefly outline the aims and objectives of the course within the context of the larger BTP initiative.

Brown College

Since the SLU participation in the BTP initiative emphasizes community service and civic engagement, our project focuses on first-year students because they tend to be committed to personal involvement as a way of improving conditions, especially on the local level (Levine & Cureton, 2002), and they have already been involved in a variety of community activities (Duckenfield & Swick, 2002) and expect to continue such service during college. Thus, as we designed the second iteration of the first-year program course, known as Brown College, we wanted to take advantage of the typical incoming student's community service background and challenge the traditional assumption that responsible citizenship is a *byproduct* of liberal learning, that students who become lifelong learners would inevitably understand and practice active citizenship. We wanted to ask students to consider Dewey's (1916) vision of higher learning, which sees citizenship as a fundamental part of the college experience.

Following Dewey (1916), the work of the course demands that students critically engage ideas about and actually assume the responsibilities of citizenship in a diverse democracy as a fundamental part of their liberal arts education. The main "text" of the course is the students' experience in the local community. Inside the classroom, we use readings, class discussions, and group activities to examine historical and contemporary theories and examples of citizenship in American society. Issues of race, class, inequality, power, and political institutions infuse intentional teaching and learning about social responsibility and active citizenship in a democracy.

To accomplish our aims and maximize the power of engaged pedagogies, we construct a *democratic* classroom that maximizes the community experience as text and where student engagement is given primacy (Zlotkowski, 1999). Our classroom activities and discussions emphasize active learning while rejecting the assumption that learning is an individual or private endeavor. (On this last note, Howard [1998] argues that when the students' focus is on their own learning and grades, they do not see themselves as responsible for the learning of anyone else. For this reason, for example, students will look only to the professor when they speak in class, since their motive for speaking in class is to maximize their grade.) Throughout the course, we foster the philosophy that students are responsible not only for their own learning but for others' learning. Our classroom is decentered—that is, power and control are shared with our students. Class is not always predictable, but we find that our students embrace the opportunities to share in dictating the direction of the class.

Our democratic classroom and the collaborative learning that is a staple of our weekly plenaries and seminars are intimately tied to the course learning journal. The learning journal enables students to integrate the various components of the course and to make meaning of them in some holistic manner. In their journals, our students reflect on the variety of texts and experiences of the course: community service, course readings, class discussions, and activities. However, we make sure that such reflection is furthered by the guiding hand of their mentors. This point is fleshed out by Zubizarreta (2004), who recognizes the central role of collaboration and mentoring in making the learning that occurs in a journal "community property" (p. 11). Following Zubizarreta, the format of our journal assignment recognizes that while student reflection is a "private affair," it is "sharpened by the positive influence of collaboration with a mentor" (p. 12).

Prompting Learning

As part of that guiding-hand role, we open the journal assignment (actually, we open the course) with a series of advising prompts designed to get students thinking more intentionally about their learning within the contexts of a liberal arts education and our course. During the summer, we ask our students to write us an introductory letter in which they tell us something about who they are and some of the goals they hope to accomplish while at SLU. To facilitate their thinking, we offer a few questions for them to think about. For example:

- What would compel you to sign up for a course about making a difference?

- What do you hope to accomplish while you're here beyond the immediate goal of earning a diploma?

- Which among the many courses of study available at SLU interest you at the moment?

- Which among the many cocurricular opportunities at SLU might you be interested in pursuing?

- What have you done in the past that makes these particular things interesting to you?

We also ask them to review the "Aims and Objectives" statements of the university, the first-year program, and our course, and to share what they hope to accomplish during the upcoming semester, both in this course specifically and as a student overall.

Unbeknownst to these students, the introductory letter is their first journal entry and sets the tone of intentional learning within the context of honest self-reflection. Throughout the semester, we periodically pose questions designed to help them organize their thoughts in ways that promote a more conscious understanding of the nature of their learning. For example, since much of the course critically assesses the concept and practice of leadership, we ask students to define leadership and leaders. In developing their definitions, we encourage them to reflect on issues raised in class and apply their definitions to their work in the community. For example, we ask the following questions:

- Is there a crisis of leadership in society today?

- What makes an effective leader? What do you need to lead?

  - What are the characteristics of an effective leader?

  - Are leaders born, not made, or made, not born?

  - What is the difference between leadership and tyranny?

- Where are leaders most likely to be found and why?

- What is the role of the follower? What is the relationship between the leader and the follower?

- How does the evolving definition of leadership speak to your experiences in the community? Who are the leaders that you have encountered in your work in the community? Are you a leader? Are you becoming a leader? What will it take for you to be a leader? Do you want to be a leader?

What makes such journal entries a true community learning experience is that we group the students by their community placements and ask them to work together, exchange their ideas regarding leadership, and share their group's observations with the rest of the class. What we try to do is frame the learning experience within multiple learning communities: the local community placement, the classroom, and the students' small groups. The more voices we can encourage them to consider, the more likely they are going to be able to move out of the confines of their own personal life experiences.

Radical Reflections

Both of us have had the pleasure of teaching with creative writers. And one lesson that they have shared with us in the writing process is that productive, rich revision must involve what our colleague Bob Cowser calls "radical reseeing." This reseeing is a reconsideration of the basic premise of what was originally written while bringing in new ideas and perspectives in a messy and yet invigorating way. The concept of radical reseeing is exactly what the learning process is all about. Hence, we tell our students not only to reflect in their journals but to reflect radically. We want them to move away from the more conventional understanding of reflection as an act of thinking after an event, quietly and calmly reconsidering an experience or a set of ideas to come to some better or new understanding of what happened. At its root, the word *reflect* means "to bend, turn," and it has definitions such as "to throw, to bend off backward at an angle, to cause to rebound or reverberate." This sense of reflection is one that is incredibly active, where ideas are bouncing around every which way. It is precisely this definition of reflection that we employ when we ask our students to undertake our learning journal project. Rather than being a space of passive recollection, the learning journal is a chaotic, vibrant site of learning in process.

But to succeed in such radical reflection, intense collaboration with us, their mentors, is essential. Consequently, we ask our students to create double-sided journal entries where a description of their placement experiences is located on the left and their initial (or first-draft) reflections are sketched on the right. We stress that they should be sure to consider as part of their reflections how the course readings inform what they chronicle in the left-hand column. Typically, their initial passes at reflection are rather superficial, failing to consider course readings. Time for radical reflection!

Students submit the first drafts of their journals to us periodically throughout the semester. In addition to sharing our views on their observations, we also pose questions, raise hypothetical situations for them to consider, and challenge their logic—all of which is designed either to initiate or to continue a dialogue with us. With each submission, their reflections literally become works of art as each question, student response, mentor reply, and so on is written in a different color and (sometimes) font (when we run out of colors). By the end of the semester, reading through a journal is like seeing a constantly changing rainbow of learning. With each submission, every new color represents another sample, another product, another artifact of their learning experience. Thus, the visual representation of the entries emphasizes the *process* of learning, which is at the core of learning journals and portfolios. Our emphasis is on continuous reflection on the student's part and interactive dialogue between student and instructor. At the end of the course, we are interested in paying attention to the progression of learning that we can trace—can actually see—throughout the journal.

One recent example of this kind of progression of learning is in the journal of Kristen (fictional name), a student who volunteered at the local Methodist church's Free-Will Dinner program. St. Lawrence University is located in the North Country, a heavily rural area plagued by persistent poverty and economic distress. Many of the guests at the Free-Will Dinners reflect the economic profile of the county. Kristen comes from a middle-class family and has little, if any, exposure to families living below the poverty level. Although she is not from the area, Kristen has a close relative who lives and works in the local community. Initially, Kristen was somewhat disdainful of the people she encountered because of the anecdotes she had heard from her aunt. Kristen explained in her journal that she felt depressed by the prospect of her work in the community:

> *My aunt works for a pre-school in [a nearby city]. Hearing her talk about the kids that enter her classroom every day makes me feel depressed. . . . She says she has kids who come into her class with dirty clothes, which they have worn on their backs for the past week. Many times she will wash the . . . clothes because she knows that at home, these kids are not getting the attention and care they need because the . . . parents can barely care for themselves. She told me of one instance where a baby was dropped off with a bottle full of soda to drink. Why are the less fortunate having kids if they cannot even care for themselves?*

We took this opportunity to compel Kristen to reconsider her conclusions, responding in her journal: "How can you rephrase that question so that it's not a judgment but a real question about people's circumstances?" In that same entry, Kristen noted that she believed these children were not being nurtured. We responded:

How do you define "nurtured?" Are you confusing the circumstances of poverty with outright neglect? Might there be some blending of circumstances here? (I'm not saying that there aren't some really crappy parents out there. I'm just asking if people [who] don't necessarily have the means to give their families everything should be considered negligent or not nurturing).

When we received Kristen's journal the next time around, she had responded to these questions by drawing on her experiences at the dinners and a conversation we had with our class about living in poverty, which most likely precludes access to financial resources to purchase clothes or the opportunity to wash them regularly. It was clear that some students in the class had not considered that poverty typically means not enjoying the ease of having amenities such as washing machines and dryers that the middle class takes for granted. Many had not realized how difficult it is to haul a load of laundry to the Laundromat without the convenience of a car or to balance the cost of washing clothing with buying food and other necessities. In our class discussions, we also tackled common misconceptions of the poor and how the ideology of meritocracy blames the poor for their plight while ignoring the structural sources of inequality.

Of particular note were the exchanges in class between students from different social classes, especially the voices of students from the North Country who were considerably vocal about the everyday struggles of living in an area that had few economic opportunities. Further, students from poor economic backgrounds who felt uncomfortable sharing their experiences with poverty were able to reflect on those experiences in their journal in ways that demonstrated that they were developing a deeper understanding of their life experience while providing insights on life in poverty that were enlightening to their mentors.

To the question about nurturing and negligence, Kristen responded:

No I think I was being too general. Nurture means to take of someone and to make sure that they are always okay. . . . It is a support system. To be a nurturer, one does not have to have money and I do realize that for some families it is hard to wash clothes and to provide new outfits for their children. This was probably the case for the kids who came into my Aunt's classroom. The kids are probably loved[;] they might just not be as fortunate.

It was clear from an entry dated several days later that Kristen's thinking had changed in part because she had befriended a family with a baby boy. She was clearly taken with the baby and with his family's adoration of him. In one entry she described an encounter with the family. Rather than being depressed, Kristen was happy to be working at the dinner that evening: "I am in a great mood and the first person I spot is John [fictional name]. Going up to the baby he looks as happy as ever and his mother is so excited because his teeth are starting to poke through his baby gums." At this point, we responded to Kristen: "Just reflecting back on the questions above . . . here's a family without many resources who nurture and care for their baby, right?" Kristen explained how her thinking had changed:

> *Yes, and I think I spoke too soon and made a general statement about*
> *poor families not loving their kids because these people love their*
> *baby even though he wears hand-me-down clothes that smell of musk.*
> *Everyone at the Free-Will Dinner always walks over to him; he is the*
> *center of attention.*

When we read back over Kristen's journal at the end of the semester, we could pinpoint that moment and that relationship with John's family (of whom she wrote often in the journal) as the catalysts for change in her understanding of her work in the community and her position in relation to it. Here we see that Kristen was developing a sense of empathy for the people she was meeting and interacting with, a critical component of active citizenship. To help her make sense of her position, we asked her to consider Robert Coles (1993) and his message about seeing the world through the eyes of others. More importantly, in this moment Kristen herself recognized that she had changed her way of thinking. Her journal provided the space (both literally and figuratively) for her to have that kind of experience, and it simultaneously served as the means by which she could chronicle her learning.

To the extent that the learning journal is a more active, chaotic enterprise, we must note that the instructors' role in the journaling process is one that is rather invasive. We do not consider the journal a private document; it is not a diary, even though it is a space for personal reflection. We conceive of our job as instructors as one of pushing the bounds of our students' thinking; we want to call their ideas into question, to ask them to think about why they interpret an experience or a set of ideas in a particular way, to challenge them to support the conclusions they have drawn about an experience or a subject with some kind of meaningful evidence. The instructors' challenges of using the learning journal assignment are many, not the least of which are the amount of time that reading and responding to the journals takes and determining how to assess the journals and assign them grades.

The model of the learning journal works effectively in a course that employs more than a single pedagogical strategy as the mode of teaching and learning. The learning journal provides students with a site in which they can integrate the various elements of the course so that each speaks to and enriches the students' experience with the others. It would be hard to imagine that Kristen could have developed that same sense of empathy had she not been out in the community. But clearly, her work in the community alone was not enough to provide a meaningful learning experience in terms of better understanding what it means to be an active citizen. Kristen's engagement with class discussions and her interaction with her professors contributed to her learning. In the learning journal, Kristen was able to bring all these elements together to reconsider her original ideas and to draw new conclusions about the population of rural poor living in the community.

In another example of the integration of learning experiences, Alice (fictional name) was in the process of describing the state-funded nursing home in which she worked and comparing it to the private nursing home in which her grandmother had spent time. Alice was appalled by the conditions of the state-run nursing home: "We provide [senior citizens] with a run-down nursing home and call it 'senior care'—what a euphemism! Perhaps the politicians should be required to spend a week in this home before voting on its budget."

We responded to Alice by encouraging her thinking along these lines. Since our course is about how active citizens can make a difference in a democracy, we asked Alice, "Now the question is, what can *you* do about it? Any sense of how the single individual can make a difference in this situation?" In her next submission, Alice called on a reading about the civil rights movement that we had used in class to offer a historical example of Richard Couto's (1995) notion of a "citizen leader," an ordinary member of society who felt called to take action in response to problems he or she sees in his or her own society:

> *I think the book on the Montgomery [Bus] Boycott showed how a single individual could make a difference. Although [JoAnn Gibson] Robinson was only one woman, she came up with the idea of the boycott and convinced her friends in the WPC [Women's Political Council] that they could do it—if only for a day. But once again, with the elderly, there is a different, more difficult set of circumstances.*

Setting aside the question of whether the elderly have a more "difficult set of circumstances" than African Americans in 1950s Alabama, what is notable in Alice's response is the dialectical relationship between her experience in the community and the text she had read and talked about in class as exemplifying a kind of leadership. The text gave Alice's community experience specific meaning beyond what occurred at her placement; Alice's experience in the community made what she read for class about the civil rights movement totally relevant and accessible to her.

Conclusion

While we have already implied that the learning journal and learning portfolio share many common elements, in effect, the learning journal is quite different from an authentic portfolio because it lacks any of the polish and finality that the title *portfolio* evokes. At the end of the semester, the learning journal is often a messy document and one that has no clear beginning or end; it is often circular in its arguments, is littered with different colors and fonts, and offers no single or multiple formal assignments as evidence of learning. Yet the learning journal possesses all the key elements of the learning portfolio: flexibility, reflection, collaboration, evidence of the learning that has occurred, and intentional examination of the learning process. Perhaps its most important message to our students is that learning is a chaotic, messy experience that itself has no clear beginning and no end. In our effort to orient first-year students to liberal education, to the concepts of responsible citizenship and lifelong learning, the learning journal has proved to be an invaluable pedagogy.

References

Association of American Colleges and Universities. (2007). *Bringing theory to practice*. Retrieved October 2, 2008, from www.aacu.org/bringing_theory

Bringle, R., & Hatcher, J. (1999). Reflection in service learning: Making meaning of experience. *Educational Horizons, 77*(4), 179–185.

Coles, R. (1993). *The call of service: A witness to idealism*. Boston: Houghton Mifflin.

Cooper, D. D. (1998). Reading, writing, and reflection. In R. A. Rhoades & J. P. F. Howard (Eds.), *New directions for teaching and learning: No. 73. Academic service learning: A pedagogy of action and reflection* (pp. 47–56). San Francisco: Jossey-Bass.

Couto, R. A. (1995). Defining a citizen leader. In J. T. Wren (Ed.), *The leader's companion: Insights on leadership through the ages* (pp. 11–17). New York: Free Press.

Dewey, J. (1916). *Democracy and education*. New York: Macmillan.

Duckenfield, M., & Swick, K. J. (Eds.). (2002). *A gallery of portraits in service learning: Action research in teacher education.* Clemson, SC: National Dropout Prevention Center.

Eyler, J., & Giles, D. (1999). *Where's the learning in service learning?* San Francisco: Jossey-Bass.

Eyler, J., Giles, D., & Gray, C. (2003). At a glance: What we know about the effects of service learning on students, faculty, institutions and communities, 1993–2000: Third edition. In *Introduction to service-learning toolkit: Readings and resources for faculty* (2nd ed., pp. 15–19). Providence, RI: Campus Compact.

Flores, R. J. O. (2007, January). *Engaged pedagogies, liberal learning, and sustainable civic outcomes.* Paper presented at the annual meeting of the Association of American Colleges and Universities, New Orleans, LA.

Harward, D. W. (2007). Engaged learning and the core purposes of liberal education: Bringing theory to practice. *Liberal Education, 93*(1), 6–15.

Howard, J. P. F. (1998). Academic service learning: A counternormative pedagogy. In R. A. Rhoades & J. P. F. Howard (Eds.), *New directions for teaching and learning: No. 73. Academic service learning: A pedagogy of action and reflection* (pp. 21–30). San Francisco: Jossey-Bass.

Jones, B. F., Valdez, G., Nowakowski, G., & Rasmussen, C. (1994). *Designing learning and technology for educational reform.* Oak Brook, IL: North Central Regional Educational Laboratory.

Kottkamp, R. (1990). Means for facilitating reflection. *Education and Urban Society, 22*(2), 182–203.

Levine, A., & Cureton, J. (2002). What we know about today's college students. *About Campus, 3*(1), 4–9.

Palmer, P. J. (1998). *The courage to teach: Exploring the inner landscape of a teacher's life.* San Francisco: Jossey-Bass.

Swaner, L. E. (2007). Linking engaged learning, student mental health and well-being, and civic development: A review of the literature. *Liberal Education, 93*(1), 16–25.

Zlotkowski, E. (1999). Pedagogy and engagement. In R. Bringle, R. Games, & E. Malloy (Eds.), *Colleges and universities as citizens* (pp. 96–120). Boston: Allyn & Bacon.

Zubizarreta, J. (2004). *The learning portfolio: Reflective practice for improving student learning.* Bolton, MA: Anker.

Chapter 15

Representing, Not Testing
Webfolio as Final Exam

Donna Reiss
Tidewater Community College

I GAVE MY final exam in 1996 after twenty years of teaching first-year composition and undergraduate general education courses in literature and humanities. Since that time, students in all my classes have ended the semester with an electronic portfolio to represent their reading, writing, and learning. Having already embraced the interactive communication potential of personal computers—in the mid-1980s with "sneakernet," where students moved from computer to computer to share their texts; later with an internal network where text could be transmitted from one computer to another but not yet beyond the classroom; and then to the world beyond classroom walls with e-mail—I began asking all students to publish their writing to a larger audience over the World Wide Web as soon as I discovered Web page development in the mid-1990s. I called this publication a Webfolio (http://wordsworth2.net/webfolio), and this selection of compositions students have already produced throughout the semester was introduced by a new element: an introductory reflective hypertext essay from which they link to their individual works and to any relevant external Web sites that enhance the representation of their learning.

Although the technology for producing such electronic portfolios has changed and my specific criteria have evolved, my central purpose for these general education classes has not altered much. In the 1990s, students had to learn hypertext markup language (HTML); fortunately, the software for publishing content to the Web is now much easier to use with copy-paste-submit programs similar to Webmail and MySpace, so students no longer need to learn code. Today, one can publish hypertext portfolios in a variety of ways: blogs, wikis, social-networking sites, slide shows, and even word-processed documents linked to each other.

Two examples illustrate technological advancements that allow students to represent themselves through design as well as through text and media, no longer constrained by my limited knowledge of Web development. First, Judy S., a nontraditional student at Tidewater Community College in 1998, composed her Webfolio in HTML, using a simple template I provided (see Figure 15.1).

The format and design features may be simplistic, but the text of Judy's introductory reflective hypertext essay is not. Judy points out that she doesn't expect to write much in her career as a "service technician for heating and air-conditioning systems"; nonetheless, she does find she is able to "organize [her] thoughts and ideas better both on paper and in [her] head . . . to be clearer about what it is [she is] trying to express." Her technical interests are apparent in her emphasis on improved grammar; her awareness of the importance of language is apparent in her description of what she considered her best writing in our class, a profile based on an interview with a

---

FIGURE 15.1

Judy's Introductory Reflective Hypertext Essay

Writing Web English 111-18 Spring 1998

Judy S

Tidewater Community College

Reflections on Writing

Before I came to TCC's English 111 course I thought I understood how to write fairly well. My thoughts quickly went from "I know how to write" to "Yikes, I don't know how to write." The important thing is that my writing ability has improved since taking English 111. I have learned about the mechanics of grammar too. I have always been an avid reader and I believe that because I can read and comprehend so well that surely I should be able to write fairly well. Now I find myself critiquing (with what limited knowledge I have about grammar and sentence structure) what I am reading rather than just reading it for it's content. I am fascinated by mystery writer's ability to develop and make interesting an idea. My favorite mystery writer is Patricia Cornwell. I can't fully identify why I like her writing so much except to say that she keeps interest high during the length of the book. I also like that she has a strong female lead character in her books. Although I won't be using the lessons learned from English 111 too much in my career because it doesn't demand too much writing (I am a service technician for heating, and air-conditioning systems), I will benefit from it in other ways. English 111 has helped me organize my thoughts and ideas better both on paper and in my head, and has enabled me to be clearer about what it is I am trying to express when writing. Since my grammar has improved I am better able to write a properly constructed sentence, placing commas and the like in their appropriate places. If I decide to take more academic courses I feel well prepared to meet the instructors demands and criteria regarding research and essay type papers.

My English 111 Writing Projects

Following are two annotated writings that I have chosen from all of the assignments given in English 111. The first is titled "Juxtaposed Jailings". It is a paper on a contrast of a personal experience: There is a marked difference in the jails and jailers of New York City and Ottawa, Canada. After being arrested in several cities for animal rights related actions, I was jailed in New York City in December of 1995 for an arrest during a peaceful civil disobedience action protesting animals being used for entertainment. I was later arrested in Ottawa during an anti-fur demonstration. The differences in the two jails and jailers were many. In New York the jail and jailers seemed to match each other pretty well. I found New York City jails and jailers to be: rough, unkempt, in poor shape; like slobs really, cold, rude, loud, cynical to a fault and crude. The jail and jailers in Ottawa however were very different than New York City. The jail and jailers in Ottawa were: friendly, organized, clean, polite, and nonabrasive.

The second annotated writing is entitled "A Transgendered Life". It is from an assignment in which we had to write a paper based on a conversation with someone. It is about a friend of mine who considers themselves transgendered and what transgendered means to them: What is male? What is female? Can one live somewhere in the middle? Can this middle ground, often referred to as trangendered be defined, or is it so subjective it will be impossible to assign a definition. The word hasn't landed in the dictionary yet. But from the word itself it is clear that it is about crossing the boundaries of gender. Zay a friend of mine who considers themselves trangendered, says it is hard to describe what exactly transgendered means. It has more do with what is inside one that what is reflected on the outside. Zay was born female but doesn't feel comfortable in her given body. She feels more male emotionally, physically and spiritually than she does female. She presents herself in more of a typical male fashion, both in dress and personal grooming. She may even go on to become a male through surgery and or hormones. Zay says she is not entirely sure what she will decide on. One gets the feeling that the words that Zay has used to describe herself are at best inadequate, as if using them limits her soul somehow. One thing Zay did make apparent is that living the word transgendered means transcending the boundaries that society has erected to separate the characteristics, behaviors, attitudes, dress, appearance and affectations of the male and female sexes. As Zay says, living a transgendered life widens the circle that limits our sexual and emotional selves.

Source: Webfolio by Judy S., Composition I, Tidewater Community College, 1998.

transgendered friend: "Can this middle ground, often referred to as transgendered, be defined?" A link to the essay, revised for publication online, allows her audience to read the complete paper.

In contrast to the unadorned appearance of Judy's Webfolio, the entry page of Meredith's Webfolio in December 2006 (see Figure 15.2) demonstrates that a variety of design features have become available to support students' representation of themselves and their learning. In addition to selecting which writings to discuss in her introductory reflective hypertext essay, Meredith chose a color scheme and linking system (navigation bar at top, colored links within her text) that she felt would convey her character and make her Webfolio attractive as well as interesting to read.

FIGURE 15.2

Meredith's Introductory Reflective Hypertext Essay

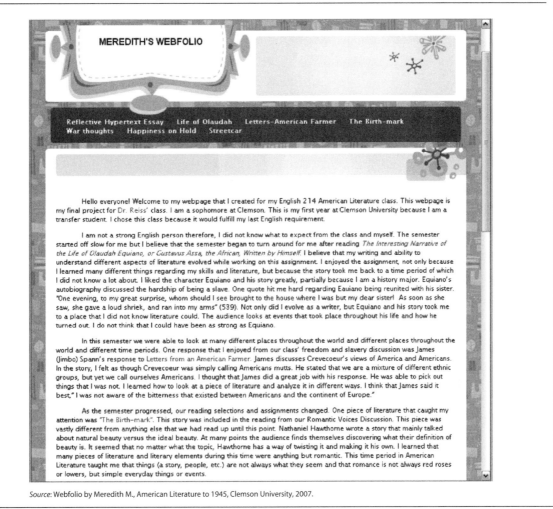

Source: Webfolio by Meredith M., American Literature to 1945, Clemson University, 2007.

Following those links takes Meredith's audience to selected compositions she has written throughout the semester as well as to classmates' writing, to our course homepage, and to relevant literary Web sites, such as audio files of poets reading their works, full texts of short stories and books such as *Walden*, and scholarly resources online.

Meredith found that neutral colors best suited her, but the snowflakes and curved frame around her name add some motion and flair. Instead of underlining, she used colored text for active hyperlinks. More importantly, Meredith explained what she learned from our readings—in particular, the strength of Olaudah Equiano, whose determination helped him overcome captivity and enslavement. From reading Nathaniel Hawthorne's "The Birthmark," she not only was engaged with the concepts of "natural beauty versus the ideal beauty" but also understood that literary romanticism is complex and does not mean "red roses or lovers."

These snapshots of their introductory reflective hypertext essays show that this final assignment led Judy and Meredith to reflect on and represent for others their own experiences during the semester: what they had read, written, and learned. This primary purpose of my class Webfolio as final exam has not changed much in more than a decade. The goal is not only to demonstrate fulfillment of course objectives but also to invite engagement with the content of the class and to encourage individual reflection on course activities and on the evolution of students' own learning and writing, using a protocol of "collection, attention, selection, composition, connection, reflection, representation, and publication" (see http://wordsworth2.net/webfolio/webfolioedu.htm). Reflection on the semester's reading and writing, including classmates' writing, preserved on our discussion boards and blogs, is the basis for students' new 750-word reflective hypertext essay to introduce their collected materials and to represent their understanding of relationships between elements of the course. Like a final exam, the project requires a thorough review of the coursework for the term as well as significant new writing. Unlike a final exam submitted only to the professor, the Webfolio is a publication to a potentially wide audience, using a contemporary medium. Each Webfolio is a work to be read, viewed, saved, shared with others beyond the class through the Web, and if students wish, revised as well as assessed. The introductory reflective hypertext essay provides coherence; active links to chosen compositions reinforce and represent the relationships between the parts. Instead of cramming for an exam where I might have asked questions about the parts of the course they knew and understood least, students strive to demonstrate to me what they have learned and understood best. Judy represented her growth as a writer by rereading and analyzing an essay she had written about a difficult topic: coping with a transgendered identity. Meredith described her journey through an American literature survey course as a series of revelations about the range and evolution of genres and styles beginning with Native American creation narratives and concluding with modernist poems. And every student illustrates the information in his or her introductory reflective hypertext essay with links to his or her own more detailed writing about each reference.

The introductory reflective hypertext essay for our Webfolios does have criteria other than the 750-word length. For instance, in American Literature to 1945, a sophomore survey at Clemson University, students were required to incorporate each literary period and genre within their introduction and among their artifacts. They were expected to include discussion of and links to their own formal and informal writing as well as examples of what they had written to classmates and what classmates had written to them or others—in other words, to represent "what [they] have taught and what [they] have learned" (see http://wordsworth2.net/webfolio/refhypertext.htm). Ashley G. explained how she selected from her own and classmates' writing: "I thought about the assignments that I liked best, both to read and to respond to, and then I thought of which of my classmates' work that I could still remember. . . . I figured that if I could still remember one of my classmates' writings as being insightful or helpful, then it must have been good."

As a bonus, I learn from reading their final introductory reflective hypertext essays, as well as from following their links and rereading their semester's work collected within the Webfolio, what changes I should make to the course in the future, both for updating portfolio criteria and for designing course activities. The context is different from reading and grading an entire set of papers on the same general topic, such as an argument for reduced tuition or a critique of Stephen Crane's "The Open Boat," as I had done during the semester. Instead, I relax and enjoy each student's oeuvre in light of his or her own reminiscences, finding out what he or she liked and learned. For instance, I found students at Clemson were particularly engaged with the writings of Thoreau. Many of them came from small towns in rural South Carolina. They identified with life in the woods and with a philosophy that was inspired and educated by nature. As a result of their Webfolio essays, I revised my syllabus to emphasize attitudes toward nature as one of the major motifs of our course as revealed in the works of Native Americans, Puritans, revolutionaries, romantics, realists, and modernists. From students in composition classes at Tidewater

Community College, I learned that they felt most engaged when writing about topics in their lives, such as child care and public education for their children, tuition costs at the universities to which they wanted to transfer, and the impact of tourism on the local economy and ecology.

I also learned about the challenges students faced preparing their Webfolios, and I revised the project criteria accordingly. To help students have confidence that I would be able to access their introductory reflective hypertext essays and all their linked works, I added a review and revision process for two outside readers to provide them with feedback on Webfolio drafts and check that all their links worked. Students chose their own reviewers, typically classmates, roommates, or relatives who were willing to read and respond to the introductory essay and to follow the links. In addition, I added a separate composition, which I called a "submission letter," to be turned in at the same time or within a few days after the Webfolio was due. This short, informal note to me is separate from the Webfolio itself, a place for students to reflect on and describe their own Webfolio development process. In his submission letter" in spring 2007, Dan L. described how he attempted to represent what he had learned:

> *I tried to show my work that best displays my ability to comprehend and analyze American literature, and that best shows the characteristics of writing style during each of the selected time periods that we studied. I tried to choose reflections that speak both about the work and about the time period. Therefore, I was limited on my choices; however, I feel confident that my selected pieces help to enhance my reflective essay.*

Dan made significant rhetorical choices as he reviewed his own and classmates' writing as well as literary works we had read, and in the process of writing this brief submission letter, he articulated his selection of his compositions during the course that "speak both about the work and about the time period."

How did my own ideas about a course-based reflective hypertext portfolio fit with the possibility that a university-wide system would be mandated for students at some point in the near future? When I left Tidewater at the end of December 2004, no institutional portfolio initiative was in development, so I did not need to consider the relationship between my class-based Webfolio and a broader program. However, when I began teaching at Clemson in January 2005, several models of university-wide digital portfolios were under consideration, and faculty from a wide range of disciplines were exploring class-based individual and collaborative electronic portfolios. I proceeded on the assumption that any electronic portfolio system worth considering would allow students to incorporate a range of media, including audio and video files. Surely, the several pages of their Webfolios from our class could be included; after all, students have practiced reflecting and linking, so they would be able to consider how their processes and products from our class connected with their other classes and, as they graduated, with their overall programs. Having saved their work on their computers and published some on the Web, they would be able to copy and paste examples of their compositions from our class to the university portfolio template. The e-portfolio at Clemson University is currently accessed within a password-protected Blackboard course management system; however, students "can select to share the ePortfolio with individuals in Clemson community (faculty, staff and students) or with external users (family or prospective employers)" (see www.clemson.edu/ ugs/eportfolio/process.html). In addition, they have some flexibility to include examples of their work in a variety of modes and media to "give [their] ePortfolio a bit more Pizzaz!" (www.clemson.edu/ugs/eportfolio/ process.html). These features of the university portfolio initiative, along with a system of tagging that allows students to connect their work from our class to general education competencies, reinforces my conviction that their Webfolio for our class is both an independent publication representing their progress and products and a valuable contribution to their university e-portfolio.

Instead of ending every semester with a self-contained and possibly stressful final exam, students have the pleasure of composing, and many readers have the opportunity of engaging with, a publication unique to each individual. I conclude with the words of Michael P., a Clemson student in what I anticipate will be the last university class of my teaching career, American Literature to 1945:

> *I first reviewed and revised the files thoroughly myself. I went back into the files that were included as artifacts and added dates in order to show my development as the class progressed. Selfishly, I took a break for a round of golf before I made my final revisions to the Webfolio. Next, I had my girlfriend look over and provide comments as to any improvements that I could make before final submission. She complemented [sic] the Webfolio and said that I definitely had a unique style of writing. She said that there were some sentences she would have worded differently, but their uniqueness accented my flow and style of writing. I also had my roommate look over my Webfolio before final submission. Like me, he is also an engineer so his literary abilities may not be as proficient [as]*

other members of society. I reasoned that if he could read and understand my Webfolio and grasp my attempt to prove my growth in critical reading skills, then anyone could. He enjoyed viewing my Webfolio. I would like to thank everyone for all their wonderful discussion posts throughout the semester; it was very enlightening and fun!

Posted online for all the class to see, Michael's submission letter was an informal, even chatty, way to reflect further on his Webfolio with its more formal introductory reflective hypertext essay as its starting point. Because Michael's class was totally online and asynchronous, I never met him; he probably never met his classmates. Nonetheless, he wrote an unsolicited thank-you note to classmates with whom he had discussed literature through discussion boards and blogs. He felt comfortable writing about his friends and his hobbies, incorporating self-deprecating humor and an admission that our required course, not part of his engineering major, was still enjoyable. Like Michael, students who finish the semester with a course-based electronic portfolio as their final exam demonstrate engagement with the class content and resources, they continue the class's ongoing conversation, and they represent their learning to themselves, to me, to classmates, and to anybody in the world with whom they share the Web address for their Webfolios.

Chapter 16

Challenging Tertiary Teachers' Beliefs and Practices

Facilitating Change and Development Through Portfolios

Rachel Spronken-Smith and Sarah Stein
University of Otago, New Zealand

TWO COURSES MAKE UP our Postgraduate Certificate in Tertiary Teaching, and each is taught part-time over a semester. The broad aim of the certificate is for graduates to be able to accomplish the following:

- Apply knowledge of research on teaching and learning to their own teaching

- Develop and justify a repertoire of teaching approaches and assessment practices

- Evaluate and consider changing their teaching practices

The first course in our certificate is entitled Critical Reflections on Tertiary Teaching and aims to enable participants to develop a critical rationale for understanding teaching and learning in tertiary education settings. The learning outcomes for the course are that graduates will have:

- Developed a critical rationale for their teaching that shows connections between student learning and teaching beliefs, practices, and values

- Acquired an understanding of key teaching and learning literature in tertiary education in general and within their specific discipline area

- Reflected on and critiqued evidence gathered about their own teaching and their own students' learning in the light of key teaching and learning theories, practices, and perspectives

- Articulated a philosophy of teaching and learning that demonstrates their capacity to reflect on their practice and to make plans for their ongoing professional development

To assess whether participants have met the outcomes, they must complete what we term a "teaching portfolio," which is really a learning portfolio, but in this instance the topic of the students' work is teaching, hence the title. Our intention is for the assessment to be a genuine reflection of the goals of the course and to be a learning task that represents an authentic teacher activity.

This chapter initially describes the certificate, the first course, and the type of participants and then discusses why we chose to use a portfolio as the summative assessment item. We provide details on the components of the portfolio, illustrated with examples of participants' work. The chapter continues by sharing insights gained from teacher and participant feedback.

The Postgraduate Certificate in Tertiary Teaching: Teaching Practice and Participants

The certificate is taught collaboratively with another institution, the University of Canterbury, within the same country. While each institution offers its own certificate, we combine the teaching so that our semester structure, content, and processes are similar. In Critical Reflections on Tertiary Teaching, we cover six broad content areas: reflective practice, the current context for higher education, the teacher's beliefs about teaching, student learning, disciplinary differences in teaching and learning, and developing a critical rationale or teaching philosophy. These topics are taught through a core set of readings, face-to-face workshops for our on-campus participants (sometimes linked with Canterbury, using a Web-based video conference), and use of a learning management system Web site (Blackboard), particularly the discussion board. Thus, our learning community is broadened, and we provide opportunities for our participants to engage in firsthand use of communication technologies to support learning. Another bonus is that we benefit from having a small group of distance participants who add another dimension to our interactions. Consequently, all participants have plenty of chances to experience and reflect on the variety of teaching and learning environments and student needs that exist in tertiary settings today.

The certificate at each university typically attracts twelve to twenty-five participants who are tertiary teachers from a variety of institutions. They include university and polytechnic academics as well as teachers from public and private training institutions and those, such as librarians, who may have teaching as one part of their role. In New Zealand, all tertiary institutions are considered to be part of the same sector, a detail that explains why our program is about "tertiary teaching" rather than "higher education," a term that is used, predominantly, to refer to university teaching and learning only. Our participants represent a wide range of teaching and academic experiences and disciplinary areas. For example, in recent years we have had a professor of marketing with many years of teaching experience and lecturers who have just taken up their first teaching positions. Other participants have had long professional lives but have changed their careers to involve teaching and academic research. Some attend because they feel that a formal qualification would be advantageous for their future career progression, while others from the polytechnic sector are compelled to attain a formal teaching qualification by their institutions. Thus, as with most courses, we have a wide variety of people in our groups with varying motivations, interests, and experiences.

For some, the process of thinking and writing like a professional teacher about teaching and learning is a huge challenge. For others, it seems to be a natural flow from their previous way of working. Often such variation is linked to the disciplinary areas from which our participants come.

Why Use a Portfolio for Assessment?

First, in our context, for our purposes, the portfolio is an authentic activity for our learners (Stein, Isaacs, & Andrews, 2004). It aligns directly with our goals for facilitating their deep and higher-level thinking about their practice and their beliefs and for setting the scene for them to question those beliefs and practices. Our structuring of the various elements within the portfolio task itself focuses their attention on documented research and others' lived experience, across contexts and disciplines. The portfolio prompts students to engage in continual scrutiny of their own lived experience and observations, in the spirit of inquiry, thereby making the ordinary and implicit extraordinary and explicit. Also, the portfolio raises to a level of consciousness that which may not have been evident previously and causes students to problematize received knowledge that they have taken for granted.

Second, the portfolio task provides participants with a practical way of demonstrating their scholarship of teaching. According to Shulman (1998), a scholarship of teaching "will entail a public account of some or all of the full act of teaching—vision, design, enactment, outcomes and analysis—in a manner susceptible to critical review by the teacher's professional peers, and amenable to productive employment in future work by members of that same community" (p. 6). In our institution, as in many other tertiary situations, we are fortunate to have formal performance review and promotion processes in which academics are expected to articulate their teaching philosophy and to demonstrate how they are continually pursuing their goals for teaching and learning through the collection and evaluation of evidence. Shulman's ideas of a scholarship of teaching are thus given credence in the environment in which we operate, and our teaching portfolio task becomes something that can be used for more utilitarian purposes while still retaining its integrity as a genuine teacher (learning) activity.

Furthermore, the third reason for using portfolios in our course consists of the considerations of what constitutes worthwhile professional development for teachers. The ideal professional development described by Cochran-Smith and Lytle (1999) should emulate a "knowledge-of-practice conception" of teacher professional development. This conception is where "teacher learning begins necessarily with identifying and critiquing one's own experiences, assumptions and beliefs" (p. 279) and where the goal of any professional development experience is "understanding, articulating and ultimately altering practice and social relationships in order to bring about fundamental change" (p. 290). Our intentions for this course include, in line with Cochran-Smith and Lytle's arguments, that teachers are led to see their classrooms as formal sites for intentional, planned research, the outcomes of which are reportable or publishable. Taking a broad view of what constitutes "reportable or publishable"—from simply talking about classroom inquiry at a departmental meeting with close colleagues, to presenting a report on the inquiry at in-house/university seminars on teaching, to developing a peer-reviewed article published in an international journal—means that all participants can engage in scholarly activity at their own level and within their own capability and capacity.

Thus, for us, the teaching portfolio task facilitates thinking and reflection. It is a statement of where the participants are now in their thinking and understanding, yet it is also forward looking and questioning, promoting an inquiry approach toward teaching. It provides an opportunity for teachers to articulate a well-founded rationale for why they do what they do and demonstrates the process of reflection as a built-in "mentoring and systematic self-analysis" activity (Zubizarreta, 2004, p. 24). Our aim is to help tertiary teachers "unearth new discoveries about themselves as teachers" (Seldin, 1997, p. 8). It provides a practical way of acknowledging and making real for the participants the central and catalytic role reflection plays in the development of personal professional knowledge (Butler, 1996). Through the process of reflection, teachers can critique the worth of public knowledge about teaching (that is, documented research about the theories and practices of teaching) in light of their worldview and then translate, integrate, and embed that knowledge into their own professional practice.

Key Elements of the Teaching Portfolio

The guidelines for our portfolio have evolved over several years in response to participant and staff feedback. The current format is fairly prescriptive— at least, for the core elements—to maintain some coherence in terms of work presented, to enable some of it to feed directly into confirmation and/or promotion applications, and to keep the portfolio manageable.

The following excerpt is part of the guidelines given to the class about the assessment task:

> *The teaching portfolio will demonstrate and document your learning achieved through participation in this [course] and indicate your ongoing intentions for further development. Essentially, the portfolio will be a critical rationale for your tertiary teaching beliefs and practices. It will be a statement of your philosophy of teaching and learning in your context, with discussion and supporting evidence drawn from the formative assessment tasks.*

Three formative tasks are set to help participants shape their ideas about teaching and learning. These tasks are well aligned with topics that are explored throughout the readings and class sessions—both face-to-face and online. Furthermore, the tasks are similar to the types of activities reflective teachers would engage in as a matter of course. Each formative task is posted online to a peer group whose members act as critical friends and provide constructive feedback on the work.

The first formative task is a report on teachers' beliefs to focus the participants' attention on their own and other tertiary teachers' beliefs about teaching and learning and how those beliefs are expressed through everyday teaching practices. In this task participants observe a colleague teaching and then have a conversation with the colleague to find out what he or she was trying to achieve, what teaching is for him or her, and how he or she goes about teaching and why. The participants are then asked to write a brief report (less than five hundred words) to outline the responses they received, relate the feedback to the literature, and include their reflections on the exercise and any implications for themselves as teachers.

The second formative task focuses attention on the approaches students take to learning. Participants are asked to have a conversation (face-to-face or via e-mail) with some of their students to find out how the students approach learning tasks and why. Again, the participants must analyze the responses, making references to the literature on learning, and then post another short report online to their peer learning group.

The third formative task has two main aims: (1) to raise awareness of the breadth of higher education literature in students' disciplinary area and its value in informing and enriching participants' teaching and learning beliefs and practices, and (2) to further develop participants' critical-thinking skills. In this task participants must prepare a critical review of two self-selected articles concerned with learning related to their teaching context and their developing area of inquiry. This task, of about a thousand words, is also posted online for feedback.

The teaching portfolio is the only summative task for this course and is designed to synthesize participants' thoughts about teaching and learning. Three key elements are prescribed for the portfolio: (1) a teaching profile, (2) a description of the student's journey through the course, and (3) supporting evidence that should include at least the formative assessment tasks. Each of these elements is briefly described next with examples of a participant's work. The criteria for assessing the teaching portfolio are given in Appendix A.

A Teaching Profile

The teaching profile is a relatively succinct summary of the learner's teaching context and teaching philosophy or critical rationale. It should draw on key theoretical concepts and insights gained through the student's experience and learning in the course. Participants are expected to make reference to relevant tertiary education literature (both mainstream and in their disciplinary area) and to draw on material from the formative assessment tasks. One of our key motivations for using a portfolio was to facilitate thinking and reflection (Butler, 1996), and the comments that follow, from participants' teaching profiles, confirm that our aims were met (pseudonyms are used):

> As with many journeys, I thought I knew where I was going as a teacher
> and how to tell that I had arrived. . . . [I]n an effort to find my way
> forward I enrolled in Critical Reflections on Tertiary Teaching, hoping
> to find, as Ramsden (2003) said other new teachers sought, a neat bag of
> tricks that would guarantee learning. What I have actually found (so far)
> are two important facts: (1) my recognition that lectures have weaknesses
> and that students . . . as has been well documented . . . are the ones who
> do the learning and (2) the mystical bag of guaranteed teaching tricks
> does not exist. (John)

• • •

My belief, before I started this course, was that there were only two capabilities that a good teacher had to have. One was to have enough [content] knowledge of the subject and the other was to deliver it well. I am now hoping to build my teaching philosophy around the following ideas: shifting my focus from what I am teaching to what students are learning[,] . . . motivating the students not only to learn but also to teach them how to learn, to see the class through the students' eyes[,] . . . using teaching methods and academic tasks that require students to learn actively, responsively and cooperatively. (Zac)

• • •

[M]y thinking took a right turn. I had a heightened awareness of my actions and beliefs which were quite different to what I'd thought they would be and what I wanted them to be. So with open eyes I began to look at how students learn. (Rose)

The excerpts provide an illustration of how participants articulated a changing view of teaching and learning, revealing a capacity to see beyond the immediate to the many complexities that make up the teaching-learning process. What the excerpts also show is that teaching and knowing about teaching are a personal endeavor, a process involving individual teachers making new discoveries about themselves (Seldin, 1997) as they integrate their experiences, observations, and understandings from the literature into their own personal professional knowledge and practice (Butler, 1996).

A Description of the Student's Journey Through the Course

The next piece—a description of students' journey through the course—is a reflexive one that should include a mind map illustrating the participant's journey and the key concepts or insights gained along the way and a discussion of this mind map that elaborates on key messages the participant wishes the reader to understand. This task provides an opportunity for participants to articulate their growing and changing perspectives and understandings (or, indeed, to reaffirm and rearticulate already held perspectives and understandings). It results in individuals exploring their beliefs and providing a rationale for how, where, and why they are changing (Zubizarreta, 2004). Participants' discussion of their mind maps thus highlights their key formative learning experiences in the course.

The journey through the course has been described as "tumultuous" by Zac, and his mind map consisted of a meat grinder (rather appropriate for a teacher of catering management), which was used as a metaphor for his journey. With particular reference to his changing perspectives of teacher and student roles, he made the following comment:

My understanding of what teaching is has been turned upside down. I grew up studying in a time where the teacher lectured, sometimes reading straight from notes and then reproducing them in exams. . . . [A]ll my previous notions on teaching as imparting knowledge that were based on my days as a student were pulverized and a new and different understanding of the subject arose [through formative task 1, on teachers' beliefs].

Similarly, Sally comments on how task 2 (an exploration of how students learn) challenged her thinking about why students either struggled or found learning easy:

As I completed task 2, I became more focused on my topics of inquiry, having sought feedback from past and current dissertation students. . . . [T]heir responses pleasantly challenged my thinking, as I realized that they all indicated a deep learning preference. I knew that some of the group had struggled through their dissertation for various reasons that were overt to me but perhaps there were some other factors that I hadn't considered?

Regarding task 3 (the comparative critique), Hannah's notions about the nature and role of teacher reflection were becoming evident:

Through my reflections and readings for assessment 3 I realized that reflection is a skill that needs support and time to develop. . . . I wanted to find out how I could change my assessment to match the development of my students.

Rebecca's mind map (see Figure 16.1) was described by her as

. . . showing a cyclic framework of interconnections that links teaching, learning, students and critical reflection. . . . [A] teacher's beliefs about teaching and learning shape how they approach teaching in a particular context. Teaching practice impacts on the learning approaches a student will use and this can bring about a change in understanding. Critical reflection about students' learning and understanding is used to reinforce or modify the teacher's beliefs to improve teaching.

Rebecca's mind map illustrates how she engaged in uncovering the many complexities inherent in teaching and exploring the intricate

FIGURE 16.1

Rebecca's Mind Map

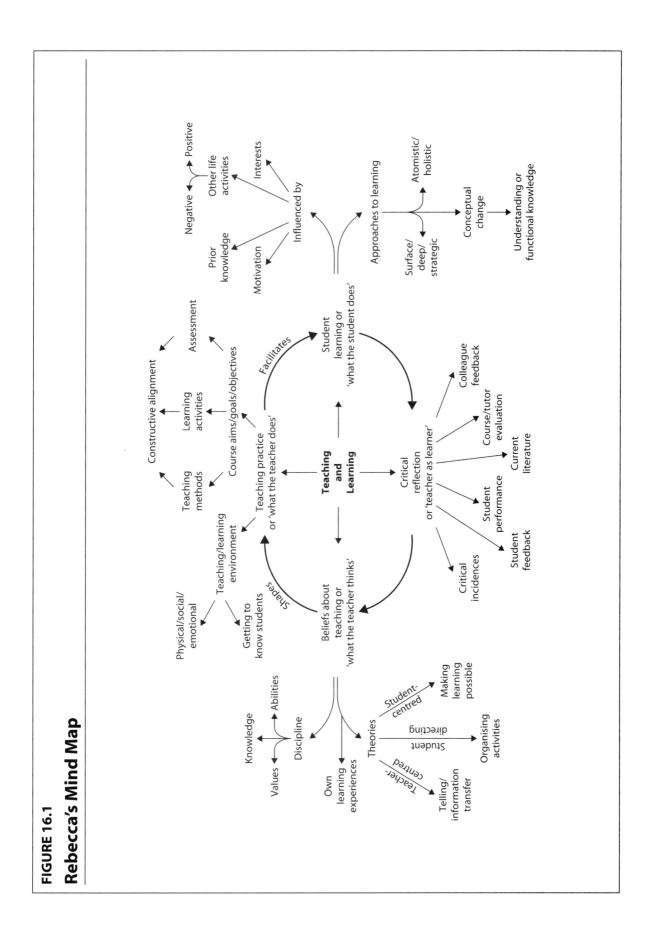

relationships that exist among teachers, students, learning, reflection, and contexts.

Emma's summary of her journey (which was represented in a mind map by a spiral path, rather like a drawing of a brain—again appropriate, given Emma is a psychology teacher) provided insight into how the portfolio elements had affected her learning. She was discovering more about herself as teacher and as learner:

> *I ended the course by starting it again. As I came to the conclusion of the course, developing a mind map of my journey, and verbalizing my teaching philosophy, I went back to the beginning of the course and reviewed the very first readings on developing a teaching philosophy and rationale. Not surprisingly, I saw these concepts again with new eyes, colored by my experiences and learnings throughout the course. I am very clear that although the course has ended, my learning and reflection in this area have only just begun. My path into the second level of the spiral staircase starts today.*

Supporting Evidence

Supporting evidence consists of appendixes that should definitely include the formative assessment tasks but could also include any written reflections from the formative assessment activities and any other evidence, such as online discussions and reflections on class discussions. Together with the mind map and the teaching philosophy, the supporting evidence provides a convincing rationale for any expressed belief. Scholarly teachers are able to articulate beliefs and provide well-founded, reasoned, evidence-based rationales for why they do what they do (Shulman, 1998).

Student and Teacher Experiences of Assessment by Portfolio

As teachers, we thoroughly enjoy reading the portfolios. Because the portfolios are so grounded in the participant's own context, we can gain wonderful insights into teaching and learning in different disciplines and settings and see the development of teachers' understandings about teaching and learning. The portfolios also provide useful and continual guidance on aspects of the course that the participants value and those that are less formative.

To gauge participants' views, we administered a survey that explored how the portfolios influenced the students' learning and whether they had used their portfolios after completing the course. The participants generally found the portfolios valuable as the process of reflecting, collating evidence, and writing became an integral part of their learning in the course:

> *For me the portfolio was the most influential part of my learning in 501. I found the process of compiling the portfolio hugely beneficial. . . . [It] was the key to my learning—it gave me my own learning space and the freedom to explore the areas that were appropriate to my context. As a new teacher, this formed my platform. (Sue)*

• • •

> *It was like writing the portfolio (and the component exercises) gave me permission to think around the subject as a whole, and relate it back to myself and my life, rather than having to learn particular facts for regurgitation in a particular assessment. It really encouraged me to use a deep approach to learning, which I think had a highly positive impact on how much I learned, and also made the whole experience interesting and enjoyable. (Emma)*

Kath, another student, found that "the formative tasks were effective at focusing on learning and driving individual research into areas of interest." Jane "particularly enjoyed the mind map." She had used this tool before and found it very helpful to focus her thinking.

The utility of the portfolio also extends beyond the course, and as we hoped, participants often use parts of the portfolio for performance appraisal, in their curriculum vitae, in job applications, and in their teaching practice. For example, Sue commented:

> *I have used parts of my portfolio in performance appraisal this year and will be doing so again at the end of this year. I have referred back to it on numerous occasions during my ongoing studies and in my everyday practice in the School of Nursing. It has been useful in my ability to contribute to discussions around teaching and learning issues. My portfolio remains an active part of my teaching practice.*

Summary

The teaching portfolio activity that we use as an assessment task for one course in our program, the Postgraduate Certificate in Tertiary Teaching, helps each participant translate and integrate research-based ideas and personal views and perspectives into personally meaningful and cohesive conceptual frameworks for tertiary teaching and learning. The activity is an authentic teacher activity. It stimulates reflection and analysis of documented research, individual perspectives, and disciplinary and institutional contexts. It provides an opportunity for participants to come to know more about themselves as teachers, to seek to understand more about their students and about learning, and to experience what it means to engage in the scholarship of teaching. The evidence we have indicates that the portfolio activity is a worthwhile learning (and assessment) tool. It provides a dramatic and influential experience for the tertiary teachers who enroll in our program.

Appendix A: Assessment Criteria for the Teaching Portfolio

The teaching portfolio should demonstrate that participants have met the learning objectives of the course. The document will need to demonstrate that you have, by active participation in the course:

- Developed a critical rationale for your teaching practice that highlights the relationships among what tertiary teachers and students do and think, their backgrounds, their characteristics and beliefs, and the quality of student learning outcomes

- Gained an appreciation of the place and value of higher education literature to inform and enrich your understandings about tertiary teaching and learning

- An understanding of key theories and approaches to understanding learning and teaching in tertiary settings, the variety of contexts in which they can be applied, and their relevance for your own context

- Recognized and documented your own progress and achievements in teaching and learning and have developed critical and reflective strategies for your ongoing professional development

To fulfill these criteria, your teaching portfolio should be grounded in your own context and in your developing area of inquiry. It will be reflective in nature. It will draw on and make explicit reference to evidence gathered through the formative assessment tasks and to literature in higher education as it relates to your own discipline and to tertiary education in general. The physical presentation of the document will be of a high standard, and writing will be appropriately structured. The text should be readable and correctly referenced.

Special thanks to Jenny Conder, Jenny Conroy, Cherie Johnson, Rachel Johnston, Dave Jull, Belinda Lawrence, Sarah Mager, Veronique Olin, Anupam Shailaj, and Maree Steel for allowing us to use parts of their portfolios. And thanks to these and other participants of Critical Reflections on Tertiary Teaching in 2006 and 2007 for providing feedback on how portfolios facilitated their learning.

References

Butler, J. (1996). Professional development: Practice as text, reflection as process, and self as locus. *Australian Journal of Education, 40*(3), 265–283.

Cochran-Smith, M., & Lytle, S. L. (1999). Relationships of knowledge and practice: Teacher learning in communities. *Review of Research in Education, 24,* 249–305.

Ramsden, P. (2003). *Learning to teach in higher education* (2nd ed.). London: Routledge Falmer.

Seldin, P. (1997). *The teaching portfolio: A practical guide to improved performance and promotion/tenure decisions* (2nd ed.). Bolton, MA: Anker.

Shulman, L. (1998). *Course anatomy:* The dissection and analysis of knowledge through teaching. In P. Hutchings (Ed.), *The course portfolio: How faculty can examine their teaching to advance practice and improve student learning* (pp. 5–12). Washington, DC: American Association for Higher Education.

Stein, S. J., Isaacs, G., & Andrews, T. (2004). Incorporating authentic learning experiences within a university course. *Studies in Higher Education, 29*(2), 239–258.

Zubizarreta, J. (2004). *The learning portfolio: Reflective practice for improving student learning.* Bolton, MA: Anker.

Chapter 17

The English Language E-portfolio

Fiona Williams, Vicki Chan, and Hokling Cheung
City University of Hong Kong

THE ENGLISH LANGUAGE CENTRE (ELC), working in collaboration with the Education Development Office at City University of Hong Kong, is a year into a project experimenting with the integration of e-portfolios with the courses run in the ELC for undergraduates to enhance their English language skills. The courses are taken by about 25 percent of the students in the university, and the students have to pass them to graduate. Each student takes between five and six of the courses (approximately two hundred classroom hours) over a period of two to three years.

Pedagogical Aims

It was important for us from the outset that the English language e-portfolio (ELP) be both a product and a learning tool. At the start of this project, we believed the ELP could do all the following:

- Be a place for students to collect work produced over their years at the university, including items such as videos of presentations and written reports

- Be a marketing tool, providing evidence of the students' English language competency and their approach to learning for future employers or graduate school

- Be a motivating tool, getting students to produce their best work by thinking of their intended audience

- Encourage reflection by getting students to assess their work and to think about how they could improve their English skills

- Encourage independent learning by getting students to improve certain skills and subskills in order to have a compelling showcase of their competencies

- Help achieve the aims of our courses, which include developing students' language skills

- Provide evidence of learning so that those viewing the portfolios would be able to see the students' effort and progress

Designing the English Language E-portfolio

We initially modeled the structure of our e-portfolio on the Council of Europe's language portfolio, but as the year progressed, other important elements started to emerge and a more individualized departmental portfolio began to take shape.

We also felt it was necessary to dictate that certain essential elements were present so the portfolios would fulfill our original aims. However, we still wanted the students to feel they had ownership of the portfolios and could personalize them, so although we created templates for the students with specific sections to which they could upload artifacts, the process was sufficiently flexible to allow for additions, alterations, and personal style.

We ended the year with five sections to the English language e-portfolio:

1. *An introduction:* an introduction by the student. We empowered students to make their own decisions about how they introduced the portfolio and themselves. The main purpose was to create some kind of digital story or presentation that would give future employers an immediate impression of their English-speaking abilities and a glimpse into their personality. This section was also the place for students to assess their own English language competency in their own words.

2. *Academic record:* an area for students to list their academic qualifications. This section could be removed if the ELP was to be part of a larger institutional portfolio. If, however, the students were giving only the hyperlink of their e-portfolios to employers to demonstrate their English language skills, then it could be left intact in the portfolio (for example, see Figure 17.1, shown later).

3. *Coursework:* five or six course portfolios (for example, see Figure 17.1, shown later). Each course portfolio contains the following: artifacts from the coursework, comments made on the work by peers, comments made on the work by instructors, self-reflections on the individual pieces of work, and self-reflections on the student's achievement in the course.

4. *Independent learning:* a section for students to assess their own strengths and weaknesses; to write plans detailing the subskills requiring improvement, how they intend to improve them, and what resources they will use; to post examples of work done at various stages; to post self-reflections of their progress; and to post recordings of consultations with their language adviser (for example, see Figure 17.4, shown later).

5. *Gallery:* an area where students showcase their best work, demonstrating their English language competency.

The ELP as Part of a University E-portfolio

Although we wanted the ELP to be a stand-alone portfolio, we also wanted students to have the option to create a university portfolio to document and reflect on their entire learning experience, from their major studies to cocurricular activities and part-time work, and then be able to have the ELP as a part of their overall achievement. The plan we envisioned is illustrated in Figure 17.1.

In the illustration, we show how a student's university portfolio consists of various other portfolios to be selected for presentation, depending on the intended audience.

The Process of Integration

The process of integrating the e-portfolio into the ELC's courses is illustrated in the implementation schedule we drew up at the beginning of the project (see Figure 17.2).

The experimental portfolio project team consisted of nine teachers working with twelve courses. The team met to discuss the uses of the e-portfolio, to confirm the additional intended learning outcomes for the courses with the added e-portfolio element (see Figure 17.3), to ponder the overall structure of the e-portfolio, and to discuss the effect of the additional requirement on students and teachers.

Project leaders also met with each teacher individually to discuss the essential elements instructors wanted in their templates in addition to those we believed should be included, such as space for uploading feedback on work received from teachers and peers and a space for reflection on the work done and students' competency at that point in time. We talked through the specific artifacts the students would be expected to produce in their courses and upload into their e-portfolios. For a course such

FIGURE 17.1

E-portfolio Structure and Linkages

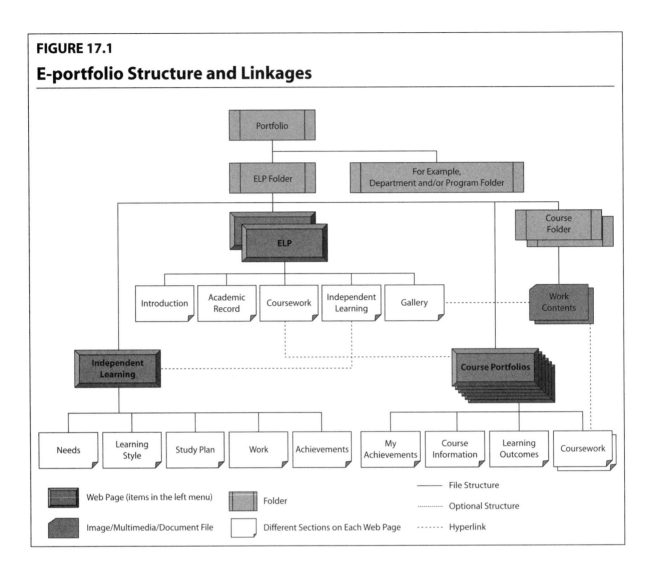

as Presentation Skills, for example, products may have included videos of individual presentations, copies of PowerPoint slides produced, and reflective digital stories.

We also discussed the technical requirements—where and how the students would be doing recordings and how the recorded material would be digitalized, made accessible to the relevant students, and stored. We communicated to teachers the need for them to have teacher and peer commentary mechanisms in place so that the students could record these comments easily and reflect on them.

In addition, we trained the teachers as students, enabling them to set up their own e-portfolios, and we briefed them on how we envisioned their role with regard to the portfolio integration in their classes. We believed their job was to brief the students on the value of the e-portfolio and the reasons behind our introduction of it; to give the students clear instructions

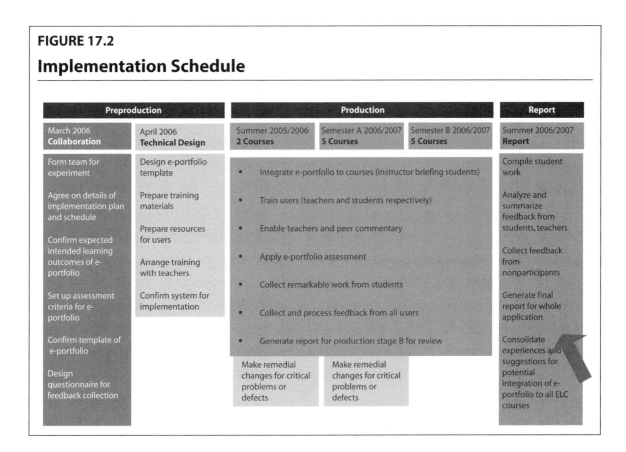

FIGURE 17.2

Implementation Schedule

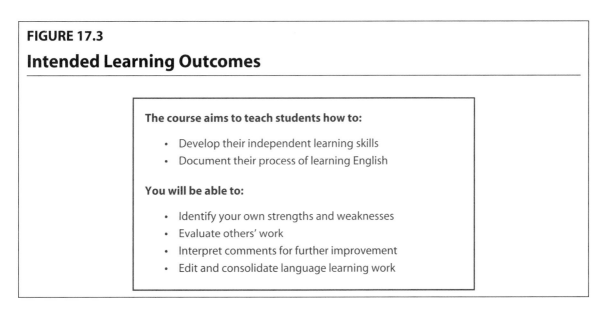

FIGURE 17.3

Intended Learning Outcomes

The course aims to teach students how to:

- Develop their independent learning skills
- Document their process of learning English

You will be able to:

- Identify your own strengths and weaknesses
- Evaluate others' work
- Interpret comments for further improvement
- Edit and consolidate language learning work

on the requirements for their courses; to guide, encourage, and help the students through the stages of posting their work and reflecting on it; to assess the students' needs; and to plan for future improvement with technical support on hand.

The project involved over 250 students. At the start of each course, the students were given initial training in constructing their e-portfolios, and we offered a series of workshops where they could learn more skills involving multimedia and advanced technology. Each class was also assigned a team of student helpers or mentors who were paid to be available to answer questions and deal with any problems that arose. We created a Web site with FAQs and sample e-portfolios produced by the student helpers. In addition, the Web site featured animated guides for all the steps required in the portfolio development, from the essential to the advanced.

Student Feedback

From our research, we discovered that nearly 40 percent of the students who participated agreed that the e-portfolio motivated them to produce quality coursework, and almost the same percentage said that the portfolios had helped them better reflect on their teachers' comments. Also, 35 percent of them believed that the e-portfolio was a better way to evidence learning than producing an exam and assessing the results. However, most of the students were focused on the product rather than the process of learning; consequently, they worked on presentations or role plays or pieces of writing based on their teachers' comments but only posted the final versions, not including the teachers' comments or their own reflections on their initial work and how they went about improving their skills. Also, because the course length was too short, there was no time for us to see them work on the independent learning parts of their portfolios; hence, it wasn't until we started to work more with individuals through one-to-one consultations that the benefits of the portfolio as a learning tool could be seen. The following is a transcript of one student's reflections concerning the e-portfolio experience:

> *I think it is good for me to develop an e-portfolio. Firstly it can be seen as a summary of my learning and I can do revision once and for all. Secondly it also drops me hints and* identifies my weaknesses and subsequently more efforts can be made to get somewhere with my shortcomings. *Making the e-portfolio is a chance for me to review all the materials and skills learned. . . .*

> *I believe it is very helpful and useful for me to find a good job. For the reflection part digital story is a good choice because I can review what I have done in a video. I think that making a portfolio helped me a lot by knowing myself more deeply in planning, collecting, and reviewing what I have learned.*

Challenges

We had two main challenges with integrating the portfolios into existing courses. The first was motivating the students and getting them to be as enthusiastic as we were, to see what we could see with regard to using e-portfolios, and to complete the set tasks. The second challenge concerned the level of technical competence required.

Motivation

For the project, we asked students to attend training on how to create the e-portfolio and how to spend time uploading the materials. The students in the courses at the ELC are already given a certain amount of learner training, and all of them attend the core courses that help them develop their independent learning skills. The only additional work, other than acquiring the technical knowledge and skills, was getting them to document their learning and demonstrate a substantive level of reflection on their work. However, for each class that was asked to complete the portfolio, at least another ten classes for the same course were not required to assemble the portfolio. Thus, the majority of the students said in their feedback that they would have been more motivated if the portfolio had been a set course requirement or if they had received some kind of reward for developing the portfolio, since they were not happy that they had to do more work than others taking the same course.

Throughout the year, we could see that motivation was an issue. We noticed that some teachers were getting better results than others, so we asked those teachers to share how they were motivating students. Some of their simple but effective techniques included getting the good students to demonstrate what they had done, praising the good students, demonstrating their own teacher portfolios and showing their own enthusiasm for the uses of the portfolio, giving guidance and deadlines at various stages, and demonstrating one small, new strategy that could be employed to make one portfolio stand out from another. We also introduced a competition, with jobs as student helpers for the summer as prizes.

Technical Difficulties

We had anticipated that some of our teachers might find the required technological expertise a little challenging, but we were surprised by the number of twenty-year-olds, in a university that has computers everywhere, who were technically challenged by the e-portfolio software. When we asked the students to outline any problems they encountered when working on their portfolios, about 80 percent of their responses referred to technical difficulties.

Since we were experimenting with different platforms and authoring tools for creating the portfolios and since we, as teachers without the appropriate technical knowledge, were relying on technicians, we did not realize until it was too late at times that we were requiring too much technically from the students. Our technical experts now better understand what our English language teachers feel comfortable with, and they are more aware that the average student's technical competency is a long way from their own professional expertise.

Lessons Learned

To achieve our initial aims—to have portfolios that are both useful products for the students' future careers and learning tools for the three years of university study—we believe the following considerations are crucial:

- The portfolios should count toward final grades in the courses and should be assessed or be part of a cocurricular achievement award scheme.

- The portfolios need to be easy to create.

- The students need to see the value of the portfolio as both a product and a learning tool.

- The teachers must put forth the time required to train the students to reflect meaningfully and to take pride in their portfolios.

We have much more to learn about the role of the e-portfolio in helping promote and document English language learning among our unique students in the ELC at City University of Hong Kong. But one outcome already is very clear: students benefit from the reflection, organization, documentation, and mentoring that go into the development of e-portfolios. We conclude by letting one of our students have the last word through a shared portion of his ELC e-portfolio (see Figure 17.4). His learning in the e-portfolio speaks for itself, in his own unedited voice.

FIGURE 17.4

Darry's Independent Learning

| Needs | Learning Style | Study Plan | Work | Achievements |

My Needs

My reasons for learning English—I believe the skills I have learned from the course will be significant in my future career and social interaction with others!

My weaknesses—I was not confident to express my ideas and to participate in discussion with others. It is because my weakest areas is the pronunciation.

My Learning Style

From the Brain Works test, my learning style tends toward the auditory. I really like to listen to something but not seeing them. I also like to know all the detail and process inputs sequentially and classify each before moving on to the next.

My Study Plan

I plan to spend three hours in note taking and listening skills. For the speaking and discussion skills, I plan to practice them for another three hours. I also plan to join the PLA for three hours in order to improve my confidence in speaking English. Lastly, I will practice my speaking and listening skills from watching a two hours movie.

Skill to work on	Specific area of focus	Resources I will use	Amount of time I will spend	When I will do this
Listening and note taking	Take note on key issue and ability to summarize the news	BBC news Web site	3 hours	October
Speaking	Practice the pronunciation of specific words from the songs	English songs	1 hour	October

(Continued)

FIGURE 17.4 (*Continued*)

Speaking and discussion skills	The opening of discussion; the conclusion and the skills during the discussion	Practice discussion skills with some friend (exchange student for first priority)	2 hours	October
Conversational skills and improve confidence in speaking English	Try to practice my pronunciation and vocabulary (special terms) that I have learned	Join the conversation club Join the traveling and dining club	3 hours 1 hour	November
Speaking and listening	New vocabulary and pronunciation	Watch a movie I like with no Chinese subtitle and write down new vocabulary; practice pronouncing words	2 hours	November

Resources recommended by my language learning advisor (LLA)

Reading: BBC Web site
Listening: BBC Web site
Speaking: Discussion worksheet and practical language activities (PLAs)
Pronunciation: English songs and movies
Vocabulary: PLAs, movies, BBC Web site

My Work

Task 1: BBC news

Firstly I choose for the news part of BBC news and select some hot topic in order to improve my listening and note taking skills.

Download: Scanned documents in a zipped file

What I have learned

I have learned some new words and how they are pronounced, but I am still weak at listen different countries' English tone.

What I will do next

As I think there should be many speaking style in English. To go on with this, listen more others' English will improve my listening skill.

Task 2: Practice discussion skills with some friend

FIGURE 17.4 (*Continued*)

First to select a worksheet to discuss with my classmates. In part 1, I have draft some notes for the presentation of the topic. To give a summary of what I read to my partners. In part 2, to hold a discussion with three other classmates.

Download: Scanned documents

What I have learned

I knew which part of the discussion is my weakest point—the counter challenge—and I will put more effort on it.

What I will do next

Try to practice English speaking and build up confidence in speaking or pronunciation.

Task 3: Listen to songs

First to listen to the songs two times and read the lyrics, then find the word I don't know how to pronounce or the meaning.

Download: Scanned documents

What I have learned

During I practice the word; it is much easier to sing it instead of read it. It should be a benefit of listen songs. I think this can improve my pronunciation.

What I will do next

I will try to do more speaking activities with others in order to build up confidence in speaking.

Task 4: Join the PLA

Join the PLA activities that I like. I have joined the conversation club and traveling and dining club so as to practice a real discussion with others.

What I have learned

For the traveling and dining club, I have practiced how to conclude my feeling about a topic. I can also gain some ideas about how to express and summarize feeling via the activity. For conversation club, I have learned how to counter and express the ideas during the discussions. Also, try my best to give a social conversation with others can gain some confident. At last, summarize the points from the notes also gain much confident as usual.

What I will do next

After the PLA, I find that I am still weak at pronunciation of some special terms. I will try to read more newspapers like SCMP to know more wordings.

Task 5: Watch movie

I have watched the *Edward Scissorhands* and use the guideline from the worksheet. To making notes about the film, especially the new wordings. After that, practice those words.

Download: Scanned documents

What I have learned

(Continued)

FIGURE 17.4 (*Continued*)

The activity can improve my listening and note taking skills. For speaking, I practiced to follow the pronunciation of the character said. I have also knew some new words from the film.

What I will do next

Like the task 4, I will try to read more new words via watching the film.

My Achievements So Far

As a whole, the most important issue I got from the independent learning is really build up my confidence in speaking English. As from the activities, I have learned the counter/express ideas skills. And I found that another weak point is the pronunciation/meaning of the new words. I still need to read more newspapers or watch movie so as to reach more new wordings.

Chapter 18

Upon Further Review

A Second Look at the Student Learning Portfolio

Alan Wright and M. Heather Hartley
University of Windsor, Canada

IN THE EARLY 1990s, the teaching portfolio gained prominence and relatively widespread use in higher education institutions in Canada and the United States (Anderson, 1993; Edgerton, Hutchings, & Quinlan, 1991; O'Neil & Wright, 1991; Seldin, 1991; Seldin, Annis, & Zubizarreta, 1995a, 1995b; Zubizarreta, 1994). A sharp increase in the use of student learning portfolios in colleges and universities has followed over the past ten to fifteen years (Waterson, 2001; Wright, 2001; Wright & Barton, 2001; Wright, Knight, & Pomerleau, 1999; Zubizarreta, 2004). Empirical and action research in the use and benefits of the student portfolio have led to growing and increasingly credible literature on the subject and have inspired guidelines for implementation of innovative student portfolio policies and programs. The first edition of this volume brought together many of the lessons learned concerning the learning portfolio in a consolidated collection, underlining effective practices and outlining future possibilities. Many of our institutions now use the student learning portfolio as a matter of course, as it were, in a variety of ways and in a variety of academic departments as well as in student services. Given that there is often little communication from one institutional department to the next regarding the outcomes of specific portfolio programs, policies, and practices, and given that there is a tendency to become complacent with regard to innovations that have been in place for a number of years, it is time to review the design and usage of first-generation learning portfolio initiatives against the findings published over the past decade and the lessons drawn from experience in the higher education environment.

The potential strengths as well as the potential problems and pitfalls in the use of the student learning portfolio have been well documented. An article that appeared in 1999 provided a list of potential strengths based on a review of the work of some thirty authors (Wright et al., 1999). Portfolios have the potential to document student growth and achievement, to encourage student reflection and self-evaluation, to empower students to set learning goals, to encourage students to integrate understanding and evidence from many sources, to provide evidence of learning processes as well as the products of learning, to help align instructional goals and assessment practices, to provide evidence of learning outcomes, to provide for nonwritten components, to encourage career preparation, to stimulate improved faculty-student rapport, to provide a suitable alternative to examinations, and to improve academic and career guidance (Adamchik, 1996; Ashforth, 1990; Assister & Shaw, 1993; Bimes-Michalak, 1995; Birenbaum, 1996; Collinson, 1995; Elbow & Belanoff, 1986; Fenwick, Assister, & Nixon, 1992; Fontana, 1995; Gordon, 1994; Hannam, 1995; Jasper, 1995; Knight, 1995; Mills, 1990; Moersch & Fisher, 1995; Newman & Smolen, 1993; Nieto & Henderson, 1994; Slater & Astwood, 1995; Stephenson & Laycock, 1993; Trowler & Hinett, 1994; Wolfe, 1996). Since our specific contribution to this volume involves a portfolio in the area of communication studies, it is useful to recall that many authors see the potential to accommodate a wide variety of media as one of the portfolio's potential strengths. In particular, Angelo and Cross (1993) see the annotated portfolio as inviting "the assessment of visual, musical, and other expressions of creativity and synthesis, since the portfolios can include photographs, drawings, slides, sound recordings, videotapes, or software" (p. 182).

The potential of the student learning portfolio as a favored pedagogical approach in the context of institutional efforts to engage the undergraduate and to provide a learning-centered environment is clearly indicated in the strengths just listed. By the same token, the literature of the past decade highlights problems and potential pitfalls in portfolio practice. These include possible faculty and student confusion over the ultimate purpose of the portfolio in a given context, uncertainty regarding portfolio review procedures and effective portfolio assessment, insufficient faculty preparation and planning for effective use, unreliable or poorly articulated standards for summative portfolio evaluation, high student resistance toward and lack of readiness for the demands of portfolio projects, lack of institutional support and resources for portfolio initiatives, and lack of acceptance of portfolio-based evidence by employers and graduate admission committees (Adamchik, 1996; Ashforth, 1990; Assister & Shaw, 1993; Bimes-Michalak, 1995; Birenbaum, 1996; Collinson, 1995; Elbow & Belanoff, 1986; Fenwick, Assister, & Nixon, 1992; Fontana, 1995; Gordon, 1994; Hannam, 1995; Jasper, 1995; Knight, 1995; Mills, 1990; Moersch & Fisher, 1995; Newman & Smolen, 1993; Nieto & Henderson, 1994; Slater & Astwood,

1995; Stephenson & Laycock, 1993; Trowler & Hinett, 1994; Wolfe, 1996). (Elements of these potential pitfalls are reviewed using the communication studies student portfolio, described later in this chapter.)

Institutional Portfolio Scan

How do the various student portfolio programs in use in a given institutional setting measure up when they are reviewed in the light of the list of potential strengths and possible pitfalls as outlined previously? How might we reexamine our practices in established student portfolio programs, perhaps comparing notes from one model to the next? How can we, in short, review our current practices to ensure that the second generation of student portfolio programs incorporates lessons from the literature and from practice?

A scan of programs at a midsize comprehensive university indicates widespread use of student portfolios across the curriculum and at every level from first year to doctoral studies. An overview of initiatives provides insight into the scope of current portfolio use and provides the starting point for review, cross-fertilization, and interdisciplinary dialogue regarding strengths, problems, and renewal in portfolio policies, programs, and practices. Portfolio usage ranges from evaluating performance in a given course to showing readiness for a program or level of study through demonstrating career preparation and leadership. In the following review of campus uses of the portfolio, we limit our study to portfolio use beyond the confines of a specific course.

Department of English

At the University of Windsor, the Department of English requires a creative writing portfolio for admission to each of its five creative writing courses from the first to the fourth years of studies. The student candidate must complete an application form and submit a ten- to twenty-five-page portfolio (depending on the level of the course) containing writing samples that represent the student's best work. A team of professors then reviews the portfolio for quality and potential. Students majoring in fields other than English are invited to apply, and applicants are informed that an impressive portfolio may gain entry to a class but does not predetermine a stellar course result.

Centre of Co-op Education Program

The Centre for Co-op Education Program in the Centre for Career Education also provides a portfolio assessment for students. The center offers guidance regarding some thirteen components to the portfolio, ranging from a statement of career objectives and learning objectives for work terms through a profile of skills and work term reports (Centre for Co-op Education Program, n.d.).

Education Studies

The joint PhD in educational studies requires a comprehensive portfolio that students develop collaboratively with a dissertation committee. The portfolios typically include items such as literature reviews, publications, conference presentations, and other evidence of scholarly activities. Furthermore, students must reflect on how information in the portfolio substantiates achievement of stated criteria and then prepare for an oral examination that certifies them as doctoral candidates (Faculty of Education, n.d.).

Educational Development Centre

The student development center invites up to thirty students involved in extracurricular activities and students who hold formal leadership positions to apply to the WindsorLEADS professional portfolio development program. The program is designed to help students showcase their skills and abilities, and it includes learning goals, plans, and reflections to document progress and an emphasis on extracurricular and curricular university experiences. The promise of the program is that it is unto itself a "valuable learning experience," an aid to "set [students'] goals and evaluate how [they] are doing" as well as a great tool for "future use." The program stresses the dynamic, evolving nature of the portfolio (Educational Development Centre, n.d.).

Fine Arts

The bachelor of fine arts program does not require a portfolio for admission into visual arts. But it does require a successful portfolio evaluation for admission to year three of the program. An unsuccessful portfolio evaluation may result in entry into year three on a conditional basis (subject to reevaluation) or transfer to the general bachelor of arts–visual arts program. A similar portfolio practice has been adopted by communication studies. (The evolution of practices with regards to the communication portfolio will be the subject of a closer look next in this chapter.)

The overview of portfolio use on one campus indicates widespread use of the student learning portfolio concept beyond the context of a given course. In some cases, students must demonstrate a very high degree of learner autonomy, independence, and self-reliance to assemble a credible and successful portfolio. The annotated portfolio is an example of an approach designed to "stimulate students to create, and allow faculty to assess, original intellectual products that result from the synthesis of the course (or program) content and the student's intelligence, judgment, knowledge, and skills" (Angelo & Cross, 1993, p. 181). The portfolio requires creative thinking as the student develops his or her capacity for synthesis. This suggests that faculty responsible for the framework, criteria, and assessment of student portfolios developed in this context must be especially careful to review portfolio policies and procedures to ensure that the design provides students with sufficient guidance to allow them to meet the objectives of the exercise.

The Portfolio in Communication Studies

The Department of Communication Studies of the University of Windsor requires a successful portfolio review for student admission to advanced production courses. Students submit the application form and creative work samples at the end of their second year of university studies. A faculty committee reviews the portfolios in May, and the results are released to the students in time for them to register for the fall semester of their third year.

The first version of the portfolio framework document consisted of a cover page, a two-page application form, and a three-page attachment on creating a portfolio. The cover page explained the eligibility requirements, the selection criteria, and the process of the portfolio review. The application form asked students for essential contact information, academic status, and production coursework completed. It also contained three short-answer questions. An attachment listed required components of the portfolio (including an artist/personal statement), objectives of portfolios in general, and information concerning the gathering and presentation of work samples. Students were allowed to submit a maximum of eight samples of work.

Faculty Reflections About the Communication Portfolio

In the 2006–2007 academic year, the portfolio process was reviewed and revised to move from a primarily product-driven approach to a method that asks students to reflect on and think critically about their studies and creative work. As a new faculty member in communication studies, one of us authoring this chapter, Heather, had not worked with learning portfolios before but had created a teaching portfolio and participated in workshops on reflective practices. She implemented reflective exercises in several undergraduate courses she taught at the Pennsylvania State University and the University of Windsor. She had seen students solidify and comprehend at a deeper level their learning and growth when asked to think about, articulate, and assess their studies, assignments, and creative work. These reflections demonstrated critical-thinking skills, mastery of content, and the development of self-understanding and self-awareness.

The first step in the review and revision of the learning portfolio practices in communication studies entailed an examination and assessment of the original portfolio document and process. Was the purpose of the portfolio writing and submission process clear to all parties concerned? Was information clearly conveyed to students? What impact did the process have on faculty workloads? The review identified several problems to address in revising the department's portfolio policies and practices.

Connecting Evidence to Purpose

While the purpose of the portfolio process had been clearly stated in the portfolio framework and application document—a successful portfolio was a prerequisite for admission to advanced filmmaking and video production courses—the directions to students were not sufficiently clear, and no solid connection was established between the purpose and the materials and evidence students were asked to submit.

The portfolio was intended to enable faculty to assess each student's learning to date and his or her potential and readiness to engage with theories, critical thinking, creative activities, and technology at the advanced undergraduate level. But the process seemed primarily to be asking for a collection of information and work. This could easily lead to a portfolio in its most rudimentary state—a shapeless catchall of products and experiences without form, perspective, reflection, or commentary. Students listed production courses completed; enumerated volunteer, employment, or extracurricular activities; and submitted up to eight samples of work. But there was little in the process that asked students to reflect on their learning, assess their creative work, or articulate their growth and goals as scholars and artists. In such a framework, students were not prompted to make their own case for moving on to advanced production courses. They collected and compiled information and work samples, and the faculty members on the committee went about ranking the student applicants. But given the lack of student reflection and analysis, the faculty adjudicators often found themselves inferring potential and conjecturing about readiness.

We should note that the required artist/personal statement and one of the questions on the original application form might have resulted in students' critical reflections on their learning, creative processes, and work. However, the guidelines in the attachment about what could be included in that statement were too broad and did not ask students to consider and articulate carefully their thoughts on creativity and artistic direction. The application form asked students to comment on their portfolios, but the general nature of the question did not provide students with enough direction to assess and reflect on their work in a meaningful way. What's more, we know from a review of portfolios at other institutions that the results produced by the students sometimes fall short of our expectations. An academic from a major university in Indiana reports that "even excellent student writers wrote mediocre reflections on the significance of their work." She concludes that students clearly "need more guidance on how to do this kind of critical thinking" (Banta & Hamilton, 2002, p. 80). We found, then, that applying such caution to the specific context of the University of Windsor was a wise strategy.

Articulating the Information

Particularly problematic in the original portfolio framework and application document was the confusing attachment meant to assist students in developing their portfolio packages. The attachment was general in nature and presented an unclear and, at times, inaccurate description of what a student should include in his or her portfolio. While the attachment specified components each student was to submit, the bulk of the information was entitled "Portfolio Preparation Tips" and applied more to employment and teaching portfolios than to learning portfolios intended to present readiness for advanced coursework.

In the section "Potential Portfolio Items," the attachment correctly listed standard examples of creative work, including scripts, photographs, and Web pages designed by the student. The piece went on to explain how to submit film and video work on a tape. But the attachment also specified that the portfolio could include a variety of items such as recommendations, evidence of service activities, and records of conference presentations or workshop attendance. Certainly, conferences and workshops are included in teaching portfolios, and commendations may be included in employment applications, but these do not constitute creative work samples in the context of our student clientele.

Quantity Versus Quality

Student portfolios, according to Angelo and Cross (1993), normally "contain a very limited amount of creative work supplemented by the student's own commentary on the significance of these examples" (p. 208). Another source provides the following advice: "Limit the number of products required in a portfolio" (Fenwick & Parsons, 2000, p. 151).

Permitting eight samples of creative work from each student seemed to emphasize quantity over quality and did not take into account that most students submitting portfolios had one year or less of hands-on, creative-production coursework. While students were not *required* to present eight work samples, some candidates felt compelled to pad their portfolio with work to meet that magic number. In fact, the document attachment encouraged that tendency with broad invitations to add any number of potential items to the portfolio.

Accepting eight samples per student also produced a heavy workload for faculty members who were asked to review the work. With the submission of between forty and sixty portfolios each year, faculty members on the review committee could be required to review and evaluate up to 480 creative samples.

A Second Look at the Communication Portfolio Framework

The revisions in the portfolio document and process adopted for the 2007 review were designed to address the identified problems and afford students the opportunity to demonstrate the critical-thinking and analytical skills needed in advanced coursework. The creative work sample submitted demonstrates certain technical and creative skills. The reflective components of the new portfolio process allow students to document their growth, encouraging them to reflect on, analyze, and articulate how their learning has had an impact on their lives, their motivation for pursuing advanced production, and their creative goals.

The attachment document was eliminated, and the necessary information and instructions were consolidated and included on the cover page of the revised portfolio framework and application document. The new process no longer requires students to list courses taken: a degree audit supplies that information and allows the faculty to view each student's academic standing.

The requirement to write a personal/artist statement has been maintained. The directions ask each student to discuss his or her creative process and artistic goals. These traditional elements of a personal/artist statement focus on concepts students should appreciate if they have engaged meaningfully with their early production coursework.

The revised process allows a student to submit creative work in only one form: a film or a video project, a script, a series of photographs, a short story, or a series of poems. The student must also assess, in a 250- to 300-word essay, this work, including its strong points and potential weaknesses. The new approach to the creative work sample limits faculty adjudicators' workloads and, more importantly, requires students to engage more deeply in the self-presentation process of the portfolio and to demonstrate ability in critique and project analysis. Such skills are increasingly necessary in advanced production courses.

Tangentially, the requirement to assess the weaknesses of the creative sample lets students know that the focus of the portfolio review is not strictly on the technical quality of the work. In revising the portfolio requirements, faculty acknowledged that the students applying for upper-level courses were still learning technical skills, the creative process, and project development. This notion relates to the benefit of portfolio use as a means to "show learner growth over time" (Fenwick & Parsons, 2000, p. 152). The portfolio submitted by Windsor communication studies students at the end of their second year is intended, then, to provide a snapshot of a "work in progress" and to offer an insight into "the process of learning" for students and faculty alike (Fenwick & Parsons, 2000, p. 152).

Critical Analysis and Reflection

Two essay-style questions on the new application form are designed to compel students to think critically and broadly as they contemplate continuing into advanced production. The first asks student to reflect on their learning and its impact on their worldview. Many proponents of the portfolio approach put a premium on the assessment of "reflective practice," reserving their highest ratings "for those portfolios where reflection was common and typical, not sporadic" (Walvoord & Anderson, 1998, p. 87). The new question involving critical reflection makes this aspect a specific requirement for portfolio writers.

A good example of the benefits of such critical reflection is found in one student's portfolio. In 2007, Fran (not his real name) in part analyzed the weaknesses of the film he submitted as his creative work sample by writing:

> *I found that one of the flaws of this piece came from the music. The music to me was overly dramatic and I felt it was telling the story instead of our characters. . . . [W]hen I first showed my work to family members,*

*they did not get the ending or were confused about how our main char-
acter ends up at a cemetery. I thought I should have made the transition
from his living form to death smoother, instead of just telling the audience that he was dead with his voice-over.*

Fran's analysis displays his understanding of important elements of
visual storytelling and his awareness of areas where his film fell short
of achieving excellence. Rather than focusing strictly on technical problems,
such as bad exposure or poor focus, Fran recognized and articulated that
the "overly dramatic" music was substituted for authentic character and
plot development. He also correctly pointed out that it is better to show
the audience important moments in a film than to tell them facts. Fran also
learned the importance of communicating effectively to an audience.

While Fran's film had many strengths, it was his insight into the weaknesses and how the film missed the mark of strong visual storytelling that
demonstrated his ability to critique his work and the work of his colleagues
thoughtfully. He also displayed learning and retention of key concepts
from his early theory and production courses.

Many of the courses in communication studies also aim to teach students how to analyze media—its construction, its modes of representation,
and the political and economic agenda often contained in its messages. We
want students to understand that film, television, radio, newspapers, and
the Internet are constructed forms of communication that shape our view
of life, transform our perceptions, and affect the ways we participate in the
world around us.

Ideally, students integrate into their portfolio the knowledge and perspective gained in all their communication studies courses, not strictly their
production courses. In addition, successful applicants relate their early
coursework to their own lives and worldview, offering them the opportunity to grasp and to articulate the growth and change that their early university work has created in their lives. Such reflection allows them to show
the faculty evidence of their learning processes.

In reflecting on his learning in communication studies courses and
what a difference they made in his view of the world, Fran wrote:

*The one important thing that Communication Studies has taught me is
how advertisements manipulate our . . . minds into consuming useless
products. This has made my outlook in the real world vastly different.
When I see an ad related to a product, I often question the motives behind
that ad. . . . What purpose does this have? Will this ad have an effect on
my life?*

Fran's response shows that he is not narrowly focused on the technical aspects of media making. He has grasped a crucial lesson about media and the influence that it can have. Fran has become a more critical media consumer, and the faculty believe that such a revelation will have a positive impact on his creative process and the media projects he undertakes in advanced production courses.

Student Motivation

The second new question on our application form asks students to present an effectively organized analysis of their inspiration, drive, and commitment to advanced creative work.

Ali (not his real name) answered this way:

I would . . . like to learn the art of documentary filmmaking because I feel it is the most direct and effective way of informing the audience about certain issues. My goal is to search, explore and tell untold stories from around the world and promote unity among humans. Having learned the importance of the media to our society I wish to become a successful media practitioner and pursuing advanced production will help me gain the skills that I need to do so.

Again, we see a student make a case for learning and practicing more than the technical aspects of filmmaking. Ali conveys his awareness that studying documentary filmmaking will enable him to communicate effectively to audiences and ultimately reach his goals of bringing complex issues to audiences and advancing global harmony. Ali's motivation is not focused on fame or financial gain; rather, he emphasizes his dream of having a positive impact on the world.

Conclusion

The University of Windsor provides one institutional example of the widespread use of the student learning portfolio beyond the confines of a single academic course. University faculty responsible for the implementation of program-based portfolios must take collaborative action to monitor the outcomes of the programs, policies, and practices in force. The review of the portfolio process in communication studies at the University of Windsor provides one example of the kind of second look at the student portfolio we advocate in the title of our contribution to this volume. The "further review" undertaken by faculty has moved the portfolio process toward increasing student self-assessment, valuing student reflection and evidence of learning, and encouraging the integration of knowledge and experience from many sources. Ideally, such change in emphasis will affect the learning outcomes adopted in first- and second-year production courses. The introduction of the new process means that faculty must stimulate reflective practices in early creative and production coursework as they encourage students to develop the analytic, critical-thinking, and writing skills that will eventually help students create a successful learning portfolio. As we refer to the listing of the potential strengths and weaknesses of the portfolio approach as established in the literature, we conclude that we are moving in the right direction.

The communication studies portfolio process will continue to evolve. The method and materials cannot be established and then allowed to become stagnant and unresponsive to changes in student demographics, pedagogy, or faculty and student goals. Regular critical review and assessment of the purpose, methods, and outcomes will ensure that the student learning portfolio framework and process continue to prompt student reflection, the articulation of student learning, and the provision of evidence to demonstrate student readiness to pursue advanced coursework.

The authors wish to thank Jessica Raffoul of the University of Windsor's Centre for Teaching and Learning for her contribution to assembling the references and citations for this text.

References

Adamchik, C. F., Jr. (1996, June). The design and assessment of chemistry portfolios. *Journal of Chemical Education, 73*(6), 528–530.

Anderson, E. (Ed.). (1993). *Campus use of the teaching portfolio: Twenty-five profiles.* Washington, DC: American Association for Higher Education.

Angelo, T. A., & Cross, K. P. (1993). *Classroom assessment techniques: A handbook for college teachers* (2nd ed.). San Francisco: Jossey-Bass.

Ashforth, D. (1990). *Records of achievement in the marketplace.* Windsor, England: NFER/Nelson.

Assister, A., & Shaw, E. (Eds.). (1993). *Using records of achievement in higher education.* London: Kogan Page.

Banta, T., & Hamilton, S. (2002). Using portfolios to coordinate teaching and assessment of student learning. In A. Doherty, T. Riordan, & J. Roth, *Student learning: A central focus for institutions of higher education* (pp. 77–88). Milwaukee, WI: Alverno College Institute.

Bimes-Michalak, B. (1995, May). The "portfolio zone." *Education Digest, 60*(9), 53–57.

Birenbaum, M. (1996). Assessment 2000: Towards a pluralistic approach to assessment. In M. Birenbaum & F. D. P. Dochy (Eds.), *Alternatives in assessment of achievements, learning processes and prior knowledge* (pp. 3–30). Dordrecht, Netherlands: Kluwer.

Centre for Co-op Education Program, Centre for Career Education, University of Windsor. (n.d.). Retrieved October 2, 2008, from www.uwindsor.ca/cce

Collinson, V. (1995). Making the most of portfolios. *Learning, 24*(1), 43.

Edgerton, R., Hutchings, P., & Quinlan, K. (1991). *The teaching portfolio: Capturing the scholarship in teaching*. Washington, DC: American Association for Higher Education.

Educational Development Centre, University of Windsor. (n.d.). *WindsorLEADS*. Retrieved October 2, 2008, from http://uwindsor.ca/leads (see "Professional Portfolio" at Program Outline link)

Elbow, P., & Belanoff, P. (1986). Portfolios as a substitute for proficiency examinations. *College Composition and Communication, 37,* 336–339.

Faculty of Education, University of Windsor. (n.d.). *PhD handbook.* Retrieved October 2, 2008, from http://web2.uwindsor.ca/courses/edfac/morton/phd_handbook.htm

Fenwick, A., Assister, A., & Nixon, N. (1992). *Profiling in higher education*. London: Council for National Academic Awards.

Fenwick, T., & Parsons, J. (2000). *The art of evaluation: A handbook for educators and trainers*. Toronto, ON: Thompson Educational Publishing.

Fontana, J. (1995). Portfolio assessment: Its beginnings in Vermont and Kentucky. *NASSP Bulletin, 79*(573), 25.

Gordon, R. (1994, May). Keeping students at the center: Portfolio assessment at the college level. *Journal of Experiential Education, 17*(1), 23–27.

Hannam, S. E. (1995). Portfolios: An alternative method of student and program assessment. *Journal of Athletic Training, 30,* 338.

Jasper, M. (1995). The portfolio workbook as a strategy for student-centred learning. *Nurse Education Today, 15,* 446.

Knight, P. T. (1995). *Records of achievement in further and higher education*. Lancaster, England: Framework Press.

Mills, R. P. (1990). Using student portfolios to assess achievement. *Education Digest, 55,* 51–53.

Moersch, C., & Fisher, L. M. (1995). Electronic portfolios—Some pivotal questions. *Learning and Leading with Technology, 23*(2), 10.

Newman, C., & Smolen, L. (1993). Portfolio assessment in our schools: Implementation, advantages, and concerns. *Midwestern Educational Researcher, 6*(1), 28.

Nieto, R. D., & Henderson, J. L. (1994). Using portfolios to assess student performance. *The Agricultural Education Magazine, 66*(9), 22.

O'Neil, C., & Wright, W. A. (1991). *Recording teaching accomplishment: A Dalhousie guide to the teaching dossier.* Halifax, NS: Dalhousie University, Office of Instructional Development and Technology.

Seldin, P. (1991). *The teaching portfolio: A practical guide to improved performance and promotion/tenure decisions.* Bolton, MA: Anker.

Seldin, P., Annis, L., & Zubizarreta, J. (1995a). Answers to common questions about the teaching portfolio. *Journal on Excellence in College Teaching, 6*(1), 57–64.

Seldin, P., Annis, L., & Zubizarreta, J. (1995b). Using the teaching portfolio to improve instruction. In W. A. Wright & Associates, *Teaching improvement practices: Successful strategies for higher education* (pp. 237–254). Bolton, MA: Anker.

Slater, T. F., & Astwood, P. M. (1995, May). Strategies for using and grading undergraduate student assessment portfolios in an environmental geology course. *Journal of Geological Education, 43*, 216.

Stephenson, J., & Laycock, M. (Eds.). (1993). *Learning contracts in higher education.* London: Kogan Page.

Trowler, P., & Hinett, K. (1994). Implementing the recording of achievement in higher education. *Capability, 1*(1), 53–61.

Walvoord, B. E., & Anderson, V. J. (1998). *Effective grading: A tool for learning and assessment.* San Francisco: Jossey-Bass.

Waterson, K. (2001). Did Socrates have transferable skills? Or Dalhousie University's skills transcript project. In G. Tucker & D. Nevo (Eds.), *Atlantic universities' teaching showcase 2001: Vol. 6* (pp. 21–33). Halifax, NS: Mount Saint Vincent University.

Wolfe, E. W. (1996). *A report on the reliability of a large-scale portfolio assessment for language arts, mathematics, and science.* Paper presented at the annual meeting of the National Council on Measurement in Education, New York.

Wright, W. A. (2001). The Dalhousie career portfolio programme: A multi-faceted approach to transition to work. *Quality in Higher Education, 7*(2), 149–159.

Wright, W. A., & Barton, B. (2001). Students mentoring students in portfolio development. In J. E. Miller, J. E. Groccia, & M. S. Miller (Eds.), *Student-assisted teaching: A guide to faculty-student teamwork* (pp. 69–76). Bolton, MA: Anker.

Wright, W. A., Knight, P. T., & Pomerleau, N. (1999). Portfolio people: Teaching and learning dossiers and innovation in higher education. *Innovative Higher Education, 24*(2), 89–103.

Zubizarreta, J. (1994). Teaching portfolios and the beginning teacher. *Phi Delta Kappan, 76*(4), 323–326.

Zubizarreta, J. (2004). *The learning portfolio: Reflective practice for improving student learning.* Bolton, MA: Anker.

Part Three

Sample Learning Portfolio Selections

PART 3 INCLUDES representative and adaptable examples of actual selections from learning portfolios. Some of the items are reprinted from the first edition of this volume, and some are new. For a vast number of examples of actual student portfolios, remember to browse the numerous institutional portfolio programs listed in Chapter 4 of this volume and the many links to student electronic portfolios available on the Web.

Chapter 19

Education Technology Web Site

Robyn Allen
Wake Forest University

HI. MY NAME is Robyn Allen, and I would like to welcome you to this site that explores my experiences with technology in the Master Teacher Fellow Program at Wake Forest University. This year, I am preparing to become a biology teacher at the secondary level. This particular career has been a dream of mine since my junior year of high school, and it is very exciting for me to watch it come true. This Web site will contain my technology portfolio, which is not only required for licensure in North Carolina but will also teach me many areas of pedagogy and technology. People who might be interested in this site are other future teachers who want to view a technology portfolio, members of the licensure committee, and friends and family.

Components of My Technology Portfolio

Standards Newsletter

Field Trip Planning

Professional Presentation

Instructional Design Project

Technology Philosophy

Resources

North Carolina and National Educational Technology Standards

Some aspects of this portfolio will need Acrobat Reader software to view. Click here to download Acrobat Reader: www.adobe.com/products/acrobat/alternate.html#50

Personally...

I am a graduate from the "university of the people," the University of North Carolina at Chapel Hill. (GO HEELS!!!!) As a born and bred Tar Heel, I am finding life at another Atlantic Coast Conference school difficult—not academically, of course, but more along the lines of when it is appropriate to wear a Carolina Blue T-shirt without getting mobbed by a jealous crowd (just kidding, to my Wake Forest friends).

Needless to say, I love watching sports, especially my Heels, but I also enjoy reading, watching movies, and being outside and enjoying nature. My newest and favorite love, though, is my husband, Rodney. Together we are forming the other important aspect of my life—family. My parents, brothers, and now Rodney have kept me grounded (with sarcasm mostly), which will hopefully help me in the classroom.

| The interaction of animals and plants drives the cycle of nature. | The birth of new life reveals the wonder of genetics and evolution. | Habitats like this coral reef are important areas of biodiversity on our planet. | Raptors, like this bald eagle, are at the top of the food chain. | Plants are the beginning of life due to food and oxygen production. |

I hope that you enjoy your stay and will return soon! Get out there and enjoy SCIENCE!!!

Reflection on the Creation of My Standards Newsletter

In preparing the standards newsletter, I was able to see and to understand the skills necessary in publishing something for parents. Before this task, I assumed that things of this nature were relatively easy, but now I realize the time and energy that using the Microsoft Publisher software requires. Once I knew it a little better, I was able to manipulate text and picture with greater ease, but it was still time consuming. This exercise showed me that when producing an involved newsletter or other letter to go home, much thought and preparation must be put into it. For instance, I had to know the technology standards for both teachers and students as well as the biology standards so that I could express to parents the way that science teachers were going to integrate technology into the biology curriculum. To find out about each of the standards required for both students and teachers, I went to the North Carolina Department of Education Web site to find requirements for both groups and content areas. The National Education Technology Standards for students and teachers was at the Web site for the International Society for Technology in Education.

I also learned to think about who my readers were going to be. Parents need to know that teachers are going to do everything to help their students succeed, so I included information such as class technology activities, projects that are new additions to the curriculum, technology training of teachers, and students' use of computers while at school (availability times in and out of class so that no parents thought they would have to buy a computer for the home).

Another aspect of parent communication is readability and attractiveness. One would hope that all parents would automatically read any papers sent home, but sometimes this does not happen. To combat this, I included graphics in the newsletter, as well as different colored fonts, to give the reader something to look at besides words. These pictures and text boxes also sum up the given information so the parent can know immediately what he or she is about to read. I also worked on picking a font that was easy to read and tried to make my language easy to understand and as narrative-like as possible. I wanted my parents to get the needed information quickly with as little effort as possible. Any correspondence with parents should not be preachy or too erudite to avoid offending them; teachers and parents must work together to ensure a quality education. Any publication to students or parents—such as a syllabus, newsletter, conference request, discipline notice, or positive announcement—should be as professional as possible with aspects that show your creative and caring sides as well.

I believe that the Microsoft Publisher software is a useful tool for producing documents within the classroom setting. From awards to calendars, a teacher has so many wonderful options at his or her fingertips. I am lucky enough to have this on my personal computer, but if it is not included at a school site, a teacher could be missing out on one of the easiest ways to create paper products that are great supplements to any classroom environment. The communication aspect is probably where it is most important, especially for items like newsletters to parents, calendars for a class or club, and letterhead for professional communications. This program is also easily teachable to a class of students who could themselves use it for presentations on topics in biology by using brochures, newsletters, Web sites, or posters. Publisher will be an excellent way for me to communicate with parents or students and will be an important way for me to teach my own students technology skills as I try to integrate computers in my content area.

Competencies Covered by This Project

NC Competencies—Basic

3.1. Word processing

3.2. Copy and move blocks of text

3.3. Change text format and style, set margin, line spacing, tabs

3.4. Check spelling, grammar, word usage

3.5. Create a header or footer

3.6. Insert date, time, page number

3.7. Add columns to document

3.8. Insert clip art into document

8.1. Produce print-based products

8.6. Role of media in effective communication

NC Competencies—Advanced

10.1. Use computer skills curriculum

12.3. Use computers to communicate effectively

NETS

    I. Technology operations and concepts—A and B

   II. Planning and designing learning environments and experiences—A

 III. Teaching, learning, and the curriculum—A

 IV. Productivity and professional practice—B, C, and D

Technology Philosophy

Learning to use technology effectively has given me many options for teaching opportunities as well as chances to improve my personal productivity. With only training in word processing and the Internet, I knew that my skills were insufficient to not only use technology for learning but also to teach tech skills to my students. This class has provided me with the knowledge to both use and teach many programs in my classroom.

With so many things for a teacher to do, it is necessary to find ways to do large tasks easily. Communicating with parents becomes quick and easy, yet very professional, with mail merge options within software. Also, publishing software allows me to create powerful newsletters for parents. Students can use this program to make productions for projects to show what they have learned. Creating lessons, notes, and concept maps are simple with word-processing programs and other software, such as Inspiration. These can be saved and used year after year as well as have changes made easily to them upon reflection of the lesson. Programs like Inspiration also provide methods to make ideas visible; visualization is a way to reach all learners with one aspect of a lesson. Using these many programs also allows the teacher to use multiple methods of presenting content, such as pictures, written instructions, and so forth.

It is important also to remember that teaching technology must be coupled with lessons concerning Internet safety and copyright issues. Students must be taught by both example and instruction from me about how to use the Internet to gain the information they need or want without exposing themselves to the questionable people and Web sites that exist today. Though most schools will participate in filtering programs, I believe that an education program is much more important and effective to teach students the proper way to use technology. This program should also include in-depth information concerning copyright information so that students will understand its implications and repercussions. In dealing with access for all students, it is necessary to be supported by an administration that believes in spending money on technology for all classrooms and labs so students can get lots of experience both in and out of the classroom.

I look forward to using technology to help teach all students in my classroom to the best of my ability. Technology offers so many more options for teachers to try and reach all learning types than ever before. It also assists teachers in presenting many key aspects in learning science, such as problem solving and analysis. Programs and software also make most lesson plans more intricate with less work if proper training and practice are employed. I feel that my training has given me the start that I need to use technology in my classroom.

Chapter 20

Learning Portfolio

Alicia I. Gilbert
Arizona State University

Table of Contents

18. Advertisements from Graduate Student Forum of the Society for Latin American Anthropology

19. My Path to My Dream Job

Finding a Cactus Flower: My Educational Journey (BIS Autobiography)

When I began my collegiate career, I had a murky perception of what I wanted to do in my adulthood. Because I am the granddaughter of a pastor and civil rights advocate, my maturation occurred in the public eye. Although I tried constantly to resist it, people seemed fascinated with my family's life. Until this point, the careful guides of my family and church had molded all my experiences.

Before my high school years, the only career I wanted was in the arts. During my childhood, everything I did led me in this direction. I was a singer, a musician, a dancer, and an actress. I did some typical childhood activities, such as school plays, choir, and band. However, I also did some atypical activities: songwriting, playwriting, and broadcasting. Until I was about fourteen, I never imagined any other way of life.

Doubt set in when I was about fourteen because my mother discovered something: my journal. I had been writing since I was about eleven. I kept a journal that had diary entries in it, but it also included my sketches, my songs, and some of my other work. My mother had been in my room and had discovered it. It must have taken her a couple of hours to look through it and to read everything in it.

Then she did the unthinkable: she wrote a lengthy response in it. I thought I had safely concealed some of my doubts and fears in that journal—the main one being that I had no other career ideas for my life. One of the statements she wrote was, "You seem to be a good reporter, and you should try journalism."

She had a point. I had been writing for school, church, and community newspapers for a long time. It was something that I enjoyed doing. However, my mother also wrote that I was wasting my time thinking that I could have a career in the arts. I recall her stating that musicians usually end up using drugs and that she did not expect me to have such a life.

So my participation in the arts slowly decreased, and my intrigue in journalism increased. By 1989, I was graduating in the top of my class. I had many college scholarship offers, even one to West Point, but I am an Air Force brat, and I didn't want to be in the military at any level. This was completely against my family's wishes. People from the church thought I had lost my mind. A good family friend recommended that we tour Western Kentucky University. She is an alumna and she offered to go with us on the tour.

Because of the tour, I found myself on Western Kentucky University's campus in August 1989, away from all I had known for the first time in my life. The overachieving, people-pleasing little girl was terrified of failure.

For me, failure meant attending college for four years, graduating, and working a job instead of having a career. Somehow, I lost the will to be the best journalist that I could be during my junior year. I was under pressure to choose a minor. There were many subjects that I was interested in, but I still felt I had to meet my family's approval. After all, they were helping me pay some of my college expenses. Although I had taken classes in French, Portuguese, and Spanish, I felt that I could not choose any of these as a minor. I enjoyed studying these languages, but I was living in the south and had little opportunity to improve my skills. Also, I am an Arizona native who first learned to speak Spanish as a child while playing with Spanish-speaking children. When we moved to Tennessee, I lost the ability to speak Spanish. In other words, I did not have the confidence during my time at Western to choose a language as a minor.

Although I continued to take ballet classes, I felt that my dancing wasn't as good after a foot injury during my sophomore year. I had to consider the personal struggles a professional dancer experiences. I had witnessed what friends of mine were going through in that world. I decided that I would not minor in dance.

At that time I had thought about anthropology, but I was honestly worried about my family's opinion. Worse, what would the church think about this? Once again, I decided not to minor in anthropology.

My ballet professor's ex-husband was the head of the theater department, and I decided to go talk to him. I wanted to know what his thoughts were about a journalism and theater combination for my studies. He thought it was an interesting idea. Therefore, I pursued theater as my minor, without my family's knowledge until a few months before graduation. I began to study languages more, and I also began to study Latin America. In reality, my interdisciplinary studies began about ten years ago. My last two years at Western were an improvement over the first two. Although I graduated quite high in my class, I felt like a failure. I had a journalism degree, yet I was not looking forward to working in news. Before venturing off to work, I was going to attend graduate school in England. During this time, I fell in love. We were supposed to get married. When the relationship broke up, I stayed in the states. I was not able to find the kind of journalism job that I wanted. After only a few months in the field, I decided that journalism was not for me.

My undergraduate studies at Western were not entirely in vain. The university's motto is "The Spirit Makes the Master." Now that I am an alumna, I realize how true that statement is. During my time there, I had a poor spirit. I had no idea how to take risks. At the time, I was too cowardly to stand up for my convictions.

After I canceled my study-abroad plans, my parents decided to move back to Arizona. At the time, my mother had been working for Sprint for five years. Sprint's center in Nashville closed unexpectedly. She was offered the chance to transfer. She asked me whether I wanted to move to Arizona with them. One thing that I had wanted to do for a long time was to return to Arizona. I missed living in the Southwest. I felt that this was a chance for me to have a more normal life. I decided to move to Arizona.

In September 1994, I moved back to Arizona. My plan was to move to Arizona and to attend Arizona State University the following year. About three months after I moved back, my paternal grandmother died suddenly. Her death was the first event that made me think about my own life. Because of her death, I changed jobs. I worked in public relations for a brief time, but I knew it was not what I should be doing. I wanted to learn more about Latin America, and I wanted to improve my ability to speak Spanish. In November 1995, I began working at Sprint. Because I work at Sprint's international dialing center, I've known people from numerous cultures. I've learned more not only about Latin Americans but also about how well diversity can work in a company.

The second event was the theft of my identity by someone I know very well. I found out about it in December 1997. My journalism skills helped me greatly during that ordeal because I was able to find out who used my information to make purchases with it. It was a difficult time for me. However, after this happened to me, I became more focused on how I wanted my life to change. I worked diligently for two years on discovering who I really am. When someone takes your identity, the theft makes you question what makes you, you.

The third event that happened to me was early in 1999. A childhood friend was gunned down in his own home. We were a year apart in age. Because this happened to someone I had known for over twenty years, I was more determined than ever that my life would not be in vain. I specifically remember that two weeks after his death, I honored his memory by going to Arizona State University (ASU) and getting all the information

I could about communications, anthropology, and Latin American studies. I applied to ASU's undergraduate and graduate programs. I had no idea how I was going to do it, but I was determined to return to an academic life for a while because that is where I belong.

Although it would be easy just to get a master's degree and go on with my life, I found out that I could earn another bachelor's degree fairly quickly. I decided to do this because the interdisciplinary studies programs at ASU appealed to me as a path that could lead me to a combination of areas. Reading Gary Zukav's *Seat of the Soul* also made my decision easier. Once I discovered that I needed "to align all of my other ships with my Mother Ship," I knew that I must stop conforming to what others wanted me to do. I began to stand up for my own convictions. It was simply time for me to be myself. If my family and my church could not understand, then I felt the failure was their problem. At twenty-eight, I decided that I would not think of others this time. I would think of myself and do what felt right.

To study anthropology and Latin American studies is a natural part of my life. Anthropology is the one area in which I can explore *all* the things I've ever been interested in. I can do work in this field and not feel as if it's work. Confucius said that if you do what you love, you'll never work again. I've always had a love for Latin American culture. I am of Latin American descent (Haitian), so I suppose my attraction is natural. In the past couple of years, I've realized that language and culture have always captivated my attention. When I was heavily participating in the arts, I was participating in culture. Recently, a friend of mine helped me realize how interested I am in religion. I've always been interested in the role religion has in our lives. Just last year I wrote a paper about the religious restraints on our appearance. I'm interested in not just Christianity but other religions, too. By attending ASU, I've been exposed to many religions. I've learned more about Islam, Judaism, the Baha'i, voodoo, Santeria, and countless others.

I am not just an interdisciplinary studies student now. I have an interdisciplinary *life*.

Reflection on Values Checklist

A career as a cultural anthropologist matches well with my core work values. Both of my concentration areas use the values that are significantly important to me. I am able to work on long-term projects, work independently, work with ideas, work with people, and work with a flexible schedule.

Because I enjoy doing extensive research, I am able to work on long-term projects. I enjoy visiting libraries, visiting newspaper morgues, researching online, and interviewing people. All these activities are vital to doing extensive research. One of my goals is to do research during my academic career. However, I would also enjoy a research job in the field of cultural anthropology. A dream come true for me would be to do extensive research in Latino communities in the United States. One idea I have is to research the impact that the "English for the Children" propositions will have on non-English-proficient Latino public school-children in the Southwest. Another is to research organized religion's restrictions on appearance. I have researched both topics before, but the research was marginal. The kind of research I want to do will take years. Even if I do not have a career that allows me to do such research, I intend to continue it on my own.

Often one must work independently when doing a long-term project. Cultural anthropology is conducive to such work. When anthropologists write an ethnography, often they work alone to collect and organize data. I do not require constant supervision, so cultural anthropology would be a good career, allowing considerable autonomy to gather data.

Because I have a background in print journalism, creative writing, and the fine arts, I enjoy working with ideas. The ideas do not have to be my own. If I am doing teamwork and someone else on the team has an idea, then I will collaborate with that person. In the end, each person should receive credit for his or her contributions to the work. Ideas are essential to cultural anthropologists because they are a starting point for meaningful research. . . .

A cultural anthropologist must have a flexible schedule. Often the anthropologist must arrange his or her schedule according to when inform-ants are available. Also, some cultural events are unexpected, not neatly scheduled. A cultural anthropologist can study how people in a particular group respond to such events.

Such basic values complement my ambition to be a cultural anthro-pologist. The basic values may also work well in other careers, but I cannot imagine myself doing anything else at this point in my life.

Chapter 21

Learning Portfolio Reflections

Diana Lynde
Columbia College

THE FOLLOWING ARE excerpts from a comprehensive learning portfolio that included reflections on class notes, learning style, course content, online reflective writing in a threaded discussion, formal essays, drafts, research papers, oral presentations, classroom discussions, group work, and creative projects.

Class Notes

I doubt I could have contrived to fit more blank sheets of paper into my note-ready binder, stuffed in preparation for the beginning of ENG 102. I anticipated sitting quietly in class, taking endless notes on the subtleties of novels with exciting names like *The Stranger* and *Aura*. Now, at the end of the semester, however, the grand results of my note-taking endeavors are four sheets of notebook paper with scattered questions and now meaningless words:

Narrative, universal themes?

YHWH.

Padre y hijo.

Conscious heroism?

Dr. Z's tie.

Why did I abandon my usually meticulous note-taking habits? The answer to that question comes down to a matter of learning. I based my initial expectations on the assumption that my professor would supply the class with questions, insights, and answers. According to this assumption, our role as students would be passive and receptive.

My assumption proved a far cry from actuality. Our professor began the semester with a brief foray into the realm of theory and types of analysis, explaining the workings of Joseph Campbell's model of the monomyth. This initial emphasis on theory launched us on the cyclical path of the monomyth, finally releasing us into the world of literature. After this traditional presentation of Campbell's theory, our professor expected us to make our own connections in the pieces we read and studied. With the monomyth as a starting point, we delved into the various class readings. Thus, the class roles that lead to extensive notes—the roles of teacher and pupil—became obsolete. Learning happened through the exchange of ideas between students and professor. One person started class with a question, a thought from a reading; another quickly followed with an insight or additional examples.

The best word to describe the class is *community*. We became a community of active and reflective learners. Note taking in such a situation would have been a hindrance, slowing down the exchange of ideas. When I tried to take notes, I felt torn between transcribing and exchanging ideas. So I gave up on notes. I often found myself sitting quietly as others talked, just absorbing ideas, savoring them like a good cup of coffee, comparing them to other ideas, adding my own comments back into the mix. Notes, for me, are the product of simply observing; we, on the other hand, participated. My physical evidence may be limited to four sheets of lined paper, but I know I learned far more from my participation than I would ever have learned through simple transcription.

Online Discussion Forum

Interestingly, this English class alerted me to the fact that I prefer not to communicate through writing, enjoying verbal communication far more. With this newly discovered preference in communication styles, I found it difficult to sustain a steady output of thought. However, I did notice that when I succeeded in writing a thoughtful, somewhat insightful post, not only did I learn far more than reading about the topic, but I *enjoyed* the result.

Summary

The overarching theme of this class, with respect to my own personal experiences, is the idea of growing away from passive living, waking from the realm of shadows into an active existence. Through our readings, I began to develop opinions on subjects that previously did not interest me, areas I initially passed over because I did not take time to see their impact on the world. I naturally follow those who have strong opinions, allowing them to make decisions. If anything, this class taught me to balance this reserve with action. Certain parts of life require involvement and risk—learning is a prime example. As this class draws to a close, I know that the lesson of action—from avoiding passive verbs to seeking out opportunities to get involved—will last beyond this semester and carry on through my entire life.

Chapter 22

PowerPoint Portfolio

Lindsay Perani
University of North Florida

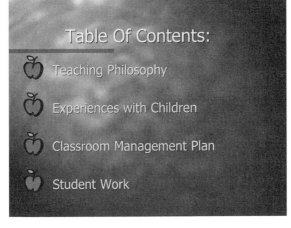

Teaching Philosophy

My classroom is an environment which fosters critical thinking, a positive self-image, responsibility, and an understanding that effort and cooperation will lead to success in preparing for tomorrow's world.

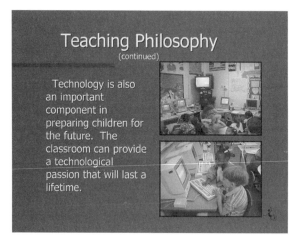

Teaching Philosophy
(continued)

Technology is also an important component in preparing children for the future. The classroom can provide a technological passion that will last a lifetime.

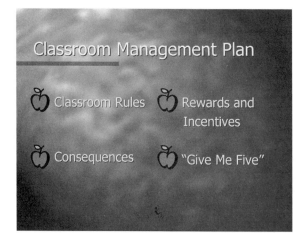

Classroom Management Plan

🍎 Classroom Rules   🍎 Rewards and Incentives

🍎 Consequences   🍎 "Give Me Five"

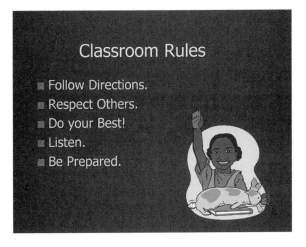

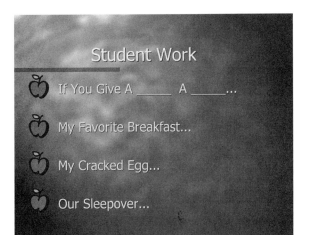

If You Give A _____ A _____...

The idea for this writing lesson was inspired by author Laura Joffe Numeroff and her zany stories. During the week of March 8-12, we read her three books, "If You Give a Mouse a Cookie", "If You Give A Moose A Muffin", and "If You Give A Pig A Pancake". After that, we wrote a class story, individual stories, made mouse cookies, pancakes, and blueberry muffins.

"If You Give A Toucan A Taco..."
By: Our Class

If you give a toucan a taco, he will want some hot taco sauce to go with it. So, you will bring him some of your grandmother's homemade sauce. When he is finished eating the taco, he will want another, and another. When they are gone, you will have to go to Taco Bell to get some more...

"If You Give An Intern A Skillet..."
By: Miss Perani

If you give an intern a skillet, she will want some pancake batter to go with it. Once she gets the batter, she will want a spatula. After she makes the pancakes, she will want a hungry class to eat them.

My Favorite Breakfast...

George Shrinks, by William Joyce, was one of our favorite stories this year. In the story, George gets to eat whatever he wants for breakfast. We decided to write about our favorite breakfasts and illustrate them.

"Eggs, Grits, and Toast"
By: Hosea Cason

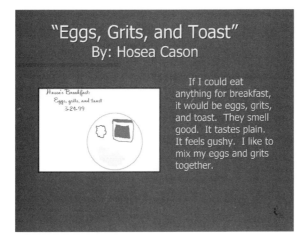

If I could eat anything for breakfast, it would be eggs, grits, and toast. They smell good. It tastes plain. It feels gushy. I like to mix my eggs and grits together.

Our Sleepover...

On February 26, six first grade classes at Lone Star had a sleepover from 11 - noon. Two stories, "A Great Place for Llama" and "Never Wake a Sleeping Snake" inspired us to have our sleepover. We also read to the Duval County School Board employees in our pajamas. This showed everyone that to reach our goal of reading 25 books, we read each night before going to bed.

Chapter 23

Honors Portfolio

Connie Thackaberry
Kent State University

Reflection Paper: Becoming an Actor

Expression. Art. Drama. Theater. Acting. The scope of expression and the form vary for each individual. Actors from ancient Greeks to current Hollywood favorites have struggled with the process of becoming an actor. For me, much of the struggle down the path toward life as a professional actor has taken place in the past three years of my life. Reflecting on where I was and how far my journey has taken me has allowed me to recognize some of the forces and ideas that have shaped this time of growth for me. The legendary actor Uta Hagen writes about modern-day applications of method acting in her now famous book *Respect for Acting*. She discusses the characteristics a young actor should possess:

> *Talent alone is not enough. Character and ethics, a point of view about the world in which you live and an education can and must be acquired and developed. Ideally, the young actor should possess or seek a thorough education in history, literature, English linguistics, as well as the other art forms—music, painting and dance—plus theatre history and orientation. (p. 21)*

Hagen's statement was so true to me, so real, that without realizing it I took it as my guide. This portfolio has given me the chance once again to reflect on Hagen's words. Both Hagen and my father constantly quote Stanislavsky's favorite line: "Love the art in yourself, not yourself in the art." To me, this means that you should not pursue acting because you have a large ego and want attention but because it is your vocation. As many actors become distracted by thoughts of fame, they must know what they are searching for at all times. As my mother reminds me, "You just need to keep your eyes on the prize." I guess I have been fortunate to be able to do so.

To me, the "prize" or the goal is to become a professional actor. For this portfolio, I have chosen works that reflect my interests, my knowledge, and my soul. I want to reflect further on how Hagen's words have shaped my university life. Reflecting on the last three years, I find that my classroom education, my travel in and experience of the world, and my dedication to my art have helped me in becoming an actor. . . .

I first read Hagen's book while in an acting class my freshman year. I took the course mainly because of Dr. Frese, who had been my professor for an honors course the prior semester. I think that she realized I had a great deal of energy and interest in what we were doing in class. Consequently, she always pushed me to give all that I had. I felt that I must have landed in this class for a reason. I knew that I chose it to give my acting some focus and to determine what I needed more work on at that point. But the opportunity to work with Dr. Frese and to learn new acting techniques and theories was invaluable. Hagen's words reassured me that first year that I was doing the right thing in pursuing an English major. Before this time, I had realized that I wanted to act but did not want to be stuck in the confines of a university theater program, acting only in campus productions. For me, English was the most logical choice.

I have always been awed by literature; the texts themselves, especially plays, contain abundant meaning even without the performance. I remember reading *Romeo and Juliet* in my high school freshman English class. I was puzzled when other students had trouble understanding it, even when it was read aloud in class. I was forgetting that I was practically raised on Shakespeare's works. I was taken to my father's acting company rehearsals, and with actors for parents, Shakespeare became material for bedtime stories. I realized that I could not get away from the desire to understand more of the text, more of the language, and to have a chance to examine drama from a literary perspective.

The education part of the past three years has been tied directly to my acting. I think this is the most important aspect of the Hagen quotation, for to be an actor, you must be educated. Acting, like every art form, is based only partly on talent. If you have a natural affinity for doing something, it will perhaps be a bit easier for you. But talent alone will not take anyone anywhere. Choosing an English major was not the simplest choice. I was also fascinated by journalism and photography, and I still am. I also liked the idea of becoming a lawyer. I have recently realized that while I adore the idea of playing a lawyer or a journalist, I am not as interested in having those careers as I am in the characters themselves. I often wondered, during my first year, if a more traditional undergraduate theater major would not be more beneficial. I quickly realized that I had the time and freedom to do theater wherever I wanted. I began acting professionally, working toward my equity card, the summer before I started at Kent State. I have acted in four other professional productions since then. It was not until last fall that I acted in a show at Kent State.

Choosing the English major was also difficult because compared to the more focused BFA in acting, the English BA required more language, more math, and more science. All these areas involved studying topics that did not seem so crucial to my acting. Still, I tried to remain focused. When I have to study science notes every night to grasp a concept or endlessly practice calculus problems, I imagine that I will someday play an astronaut or a calculus professor and that these skills and knowledge will become character resources. I find that I often become interested in ideas and concepts that I never thought I would care about. . . .

In January of my freshman year, I was cast as Cecily Cardew in Oscar Wilde's *The Importance of Being Earnest.* I first read this play when I was ten or twelve and remember adoring Cecily. I thought her so humorous; she pretended things just as I did, only she was practically grown up. The play turned out as fairy-tale-ish as anyone could imagine. Rehearsals were a bit of another story. For the first two weeks, I struggled desperately with the lines, trying to be funny and adorable and sweet all at once and attempting to master an authentic British accent. It was the first run-through of the play when things finally started clicking. I finally was applying some of the knowledge of both the philosophy material I had read and the textual analysis. I used Zen, method-acting techniques I had learned in Dr. Frese's class, and Buber's advice about having an I-Thou relationship. I focused. I studied. And then I let all this go. By forgetting, by allowing myself just to *do,* something could begin to happen. And it did. My struggle was rewarded because I had chosen to free myself of pressure and to rely on the knowledge that I had within me. . . .

The journey of a thousand miles begins with a single step. (Lao-Tze)

There have been many beginning steps on the journey toward becoming an actor. I am sure that steps I took in childhood, steps such as studying Suzuki violin and classical ballet, were activities that drew me closer to my art. My college education was also a beginning step.

The first step that I took by myself in my life journey was the decision to spend last year studying abroad. More recently, I have taken another step, perhaps the first major one on the road to becoming an actor. Almost a month ago, I went to Chicago for graduate school auditions. I wish to pursue a master's of fine arts in acting next fall. I was in Chicago to audition for ten professional actor-training programs. Ms. Albers, my acting mentor, told me that this trip was a real beginning for me. She encouraged me to find all the joy I could in it because I had chosen this path for my life. Ms. Albers said that Chicago was the first step in my journey toward life as a professional actor. Then she said that the trip to Chicago was also an extension of my life journey. She pointed out that I'd started it last year when I went to the University of Leicester as an exchange student and traveled in Europe. I was confused at first. I had acted professionally before. I had already begun earning equity points toward my actor's union card. I had just appeared in a professional production at the Cleveland Playhouse. So what could Ms. Albers have meant when she said this?

After Chicago, after all the auditions, I began to realize what she meant. In stepping out of my comfort zone last year, I was able to begin to delve deeper into my own psyche and my own future. Chicago then became a continuation of my journey. My own hopes for the future are clear to me. I, like any other graduate, have many dreams. I have been fortunate enough, as a Kent State student, to have had opportunities to learn in the classroom, to experience life in the vast world around me, and to dedicate a great deal of time to my art form. The combination of all the artistic, theatrical, literary, and travel experiences has led me to where I am today.

But I also need the chance to continue to grow, to learn, to experience and to follow those brilliant words of Ms. Hagen. I know that talent is not enough. I feel that my education, my travels, and my dedication to my art have prepared me for my career. I am certain that in the future all the knowledge, insight, and moments of enlightenment I gained here at Kent State will help me become the actor and person I want to be.

Chapter 24

Career Portfolio

Josee Vaillant
Dalhousie University

Table of Contents

Purpose

Experience is the finest teacher in one's journey through life. I believe everything happens for a reason and each one of us is put on this earth to fulfill a purpose. My portfolio is a reflection of my experiences and how they have contributed to my strengths and weaknesses along my journey thus far.

My ultimate goal is to become a teacher, and this portfolio is a preliminary step toward achieving that goal. It shows how all my encounters have helped me acquire a clearer picture of what opportunities will most benefit me and shape the course of my future to help me eventually become a successful teacher. . . .

Portfolio Process: A Retrospective

What?

When I first heard about creating a portfolio, I was anxious to get started. The concept of having my own portfolio got me excited to get my stuff organized. I say "stuff" because that is all I had before I created the portfolio—simply different materials scattered and disorganized. The process of creating my portfolio was an interesting journey that led me in to personal reflection about my past, present, and planned future. It also gave me a chance to reexamine the theorists we have studied throughout the course.

So What?

When the process first began, I was unsure of being able to create a concrete and complete portfolio, yet I soon discovered differently as I revisited my experiences and how they were of value to me. I was also unsure about the purpose my portfolio was to convey, but this is where my mentors were of help to me: they helped me get focused. After gathering the relevant materials and organizing my sections for them, it was time to evaluate, assess, and analyze what the materials represented to me and how they accurately reflected the purpose of my portfolio. This is what really got me thinking about my future plans. My challenge was no longer about the *what* and the *so what*, but the *now what!* Now that I had realized what my experiences meant to me, it was time to decide how I could apply my new knowledge to my future endeavors.

Now What?

I look back at when I first started creating my portfolio and realize how far I have come. When I first began, the finished product seemed far beyond my reach, and now here it is and I cannot wait to continue building it into a great tool that will be of great benefit to me in the future. I am excited about setting goals and adding to my achievements.

I now possess a tool that is essentially a self-portrayal. The purpose of my portfolio will eventually change and help me get into a bachelor of education program. One of the greatest features of a portfolio is that even if it is a finished product, there is no limit to what an individual can continue to bring to it.

Part Four
Practical Materials

PART 4 CONSISTS of a wide collection of practical materials—assignments, guidelines, criteria, evaluation rubrics—that various individuals and institutions have used as part of developing print and electronic learning portfolios from across disciplines, programs, and types of higher education institutions.

Chapter 25

Self-Assessment

Albion College

Exercises

Self-assessment exercises help you examine who you are and where you are headed. Start with one in the following list, or come up with your own. After completing an exercise, reflect on what you have learned about yourself and how you might apply what you have learned to your goals and plans. You may want to place the exercise and your responses, or maybe just your reflection, in your portfolio. Since you and your portfolio are ever changing, you are encouraged to revisit the self-assessment stage periodically.

- Discover your interests, abilities, and values

- Ask yourself why

- What have you done, what did you learn, and how will you grow?

Discover Your Interests, Abilities, and Values

With the help of DISCOVER, an interactive computer-based self-assessment program available in the student computer labs on campus, you will be able to assess your interests, abilities, and values and to learn how these relate to the world of work. After completing the Interests, Abilities, and Values Assessment, reflect on how you responded to the questions and how you can use the outcomes of this assessment as you plan for your future.

Ask Yourself Why

Why? Getting to where you are right now was based on a series of choices. What was your rationale for making one decision or choice over another? What were the consequences of those decisions?

1. Why did you decide to go to college?

2. Why did you decide to come to Albion College?

3. Why did you decide (or have you not yet decided) to pursue a particular major, concentration, or discipline?

4. Why did you select the courses in which you are currently enrolled?

5. Why did you join the organizations, clubs, and groups that you did?

6. Why do you spend your leisure time the way you do?

Whether this is the first or fourth time completing the Ask Yourself Why Assessment, reflect on your responses. What have been the consequences of your decisions? What have been the positive and negative outcomes? How have these decisions impacted other decisions you have made, and how will they impact future decisions? How can you use what you have learned about yourself through this assessment as you plan for your future?

What Have You Done, What Did You Learn, and How Will You Grow?

List five experiences you have had and at least one thing you learned from each experience. Identify whether what you learned is a new skill or moment of self-awareness. Write a reflection paragraph on each of these experiences, including what led you to the experience, how you can use what you learned now and in the future, and what future experiences you may want to explore or avoid as a result of this experience.

Making a Plan

Where are you, and where are you going? The purpose of your portfolio is to help you bring together your personal, academic, and professional experiences. Self-assessment exercises will help you reflect on how you got to where you are now and where you are going. Goal setting will help you be intentional about how you get to where you are going.

During the first year in college, it is very common for personal, academic, and professional experiences to be separate or loosely connected. Eventually, there should be natural links that demonstrate how the three come together. For example, a student who has always been very interested in animals may volunteer at the local humane society, work for a veterinarian, and declare a major in biology.

The best way to get where you are going is to make a plan. Your academic, personal, and professional plans will serve as the tool or location for sharing the public side of your portfolio. Start out by making a paper plan with the headings *Academic, Personal,* and *Professional.* Next, jot down topics or concepts that come to mind when you see each heading listed on the page. Finally, decide the topics and concepts that are most important to you, and expand on those or highlight why they are important.

Goal Setting

What do you want to do with your life? This is a question high school and college graduates are constantly asked. This question is much easier to answer if it's broken down into smaller parts. That is what goals are.

How Do I Begin?

1. Start with a long-term or short-term desired outcome. This becomes your *goal statement.*

2. Now break your goal statement into smaller parts or steps that describe an action that will contribute to achieving a goal. These are *objectives.* It is important that your objectives are specific and measurable.

3. Then, to fulfill an objective, you need to have an *action plan.* The action plan is made up of the steps that lead to completing an objective. It is helpful to include target completion dates in your action plan.

4. Finally, make sure you complete the steps listed on your action plan.

Once you begin to take the steps to achieve your goals, you may find out that you need to revise and add to your original objectives and action plan. Set a minimum of three goals, followed by a minimum of two objectives, and then the action plan, or the actions that will actually get the objectives accomplished. You might think of your goals in terms of one academic, one personal, and one professional goal:

Example

Academic Goal

Go to graduate school to get a PhD in clinical psychology.

Objective

To get an undergraduate major in psychology.

To graduate with at least a 3.5 GPA in order to be selective regarding graduate schools.

Action Plan

Speak with the chair of the psychology department to get advice regarding course selection (October).

Speak with my academic adviser about my plan (September).

Set aside time to study, and stick to a study plan (August).

Join Psi Chi, the psychology club (August).

Get help from the writing center whenever I have a paper to write because that is my weakest area academically (as needed).

How to Set SMART Goals

Specific: Does your goal provide a direction as well as a means?

Measurable: How will you measure the progress of your goal?

Attainable*/active: Is your goal within reasonable reach? Do you provide a means to achieve your goal?

Realistic*/relevant*: Can your goal be achieved? Does your goal keep you on task?

Timetable: What is the time frame in which you will achieve your goal?

*Not necessarily stated in goal—it is something you keep in mind while creating the goal.

Example

Fall semester 2000 (time table), I will obtain a GPA above 3.8 by increasing study time through dedication and time management (specific and active). My progress will be measured through set evaluations (measurable).

Chapter 26

Four-Year Portfolio Development Plan

Albion College

First-Year Portfolio

During your first year, you will be learning the basics of portfolio development. Incorporate what you learn from self-assessment exercises and goal setting to develop academic, personal, and professional plans.

- Self-assessment exercises
- Self-assessment reflection statements
- Academic, personal, and professional goals, objectives, and action plans
- Course schedule
- Student organization membership
- Hobbies
- Interests, abilities, values
- Athletics
- Extracurricular activities
- Volunteer activities
- On- and off-campus jobs
- Portfolio development timeline

- Home or index: Introduce yourself and welcome viewers by telling them a bit about what they can view in your portfolio.
- Academic: Share what you have done and what you plan to do with your coursework, highlighting what you learned from your favorite course or project.
- Personal: Share what you are involved in outside the classroom, highlighting an interesting experience.
- Professional: Share some of your professional skills and traits, how you obtained them, and how you use them, highlighting one of which you are especially proud.

Sophomore Portfolio

During your sophomore year, you will be building on the basics. You are at a new stage of development, so reassess who you are with self-assessment exercises. Check up on the goals you set, and set new ones. Continue to develop your academic, personal, and professional plans.

- Self-assessment exercises
- Self-assessment reflection statements
- Academic, personal, and professional goals, objectives, and action plans
- Course schedule
- Progress on core coursework
- Student organization membership
- Hobbies
- Interests, abilities, values
- Athletics
- Extracurricular activities
- Volunteer activities
- On- and off-campus jobs
- Leadership opportunities
- Progress toward declared major
- Externships/internships
- Portfolio development timeline

- Home or index: Modify your introduction and welcome, if needed.
- Academic: Expand on what you have done and what you plan to do with your coursework. Without removing your course or project highlight, share what your major is and how you came to that decision.
- Personal: Expand on what you are involved in outside the classroom. Without removing your highlight of an interesting experience, share how an out-of-class experience has helped you with your academic or professional development.
- Professional: Expand on some of your professional skills and traits, how you obtained them, and how you use them. Without removing the highlight of a skill or trait that you are especially proud of, share how your choice of a major will impact your professional future.

Junior Portfolio

During your junior year, you can begin to think more about audiences off campus than those on campus. Content is still important, but how you present your information becomes equally important. Since you will most likely not be present when someone views your portfolio, you want to be sure your information flows and is easily found and understood. While you want to make a visual impact, you want to be sure that impact is a positive one.

- Self-assessment exercises
- Self-assessment reflection statements
- Academic, personal, and professional goals, objectives, and action plans
- Course schedule
- Progress on core coursework
- Student organization membership
- Hobbies
- Interests, abilities, values

- Home or index: Modify your introduction and welcome, if needed.
- Academic: Expand on what you have done and what you plan to do with your coursework. You may want to expand on your course or project highlight and what your major is and how you came to that decision. Add a philosophy or mission statement. Highlight involvement in centers for interdisciplinary study and/or institutes. Offer samples of your academic work.

- Athletics
- Extracurricular activities
- Volunteer activities
- On- and off-campus jobs
- Leadership opportunities
- Progress toward declared major
- Center for Interdisciplinary Studies involvement
- Institute involvement
- Writing and research samples
- Portfolio development timeline
- Externships/internships
- Previous briefcase documents

- Personal: After looking at all the out-of-class experiences you have had, highlight the ones that have had the greatest impact on you. You may want to expand on your highlight of an interesting experience and how an out-of-class experience has helped with your academic or professional development. Add a philosophy or mission statement.

- Professional: After looking at all your professional skills and traits, highlight a few that are especially important to your chosen profession. Expand on your reflections regarding your major and the skill or trait of which you are especially proud. Add a philosophy or mission statement and a copy of your résumé.

Senior Portfolio

During your senior year, your portfolio is primarily for an off-campus audience. Content is based on who is viewing your portfolio. Since you will most likely not be present when someone views your portfolio, you want to be sure your information flows and is easily found and understood. While you want to make a visual impact, you want to be sure that impact is a positive one.

- Self-assessment exercises
- Self-assessment reflection statements
- Academic, personal, and professional goals, objectives, and action plans
- Course schedule
- Progress on core coursework
- Student organization membership
- Hobbies
- Interests, abilities, values
- Athletics
- Extracurricular activities

- Home or index: Modify your introduction and welcome, if needed.

- Academic: Expand on what you have done and what you plan to do with your coursework. You may want to expand on your course or project highlight and what your major is and how you came to that decision. Add a philosophy or mission statement. Highlight involvement in centers for interdisciplinary study and/or institutes. Offer samples of your academic work. Highlight involvement in an off-campus program or internship, if you participated in one.

- Volunteer activities
- On- and off-campus jobs
- Leadership opportunities
- Progress toward declared major
- Center for Interdisciplinary Studies involvement
- Institute involvement
- Writing and research samples
- Externships/internships
- Portfolio development timeline
- Previous briefcase documents

- Personal: After looking at all the out-of-class experiences you have had, highlight the ones that have had the greatest impact on you. You may want to expand on your highlight of an interesting experience and how an out-of-class experience has helped with your academic or professional development. Develop a philosophy or mission statement.

- Professional: After looking at all your professional skills and traits, highlight a few that are especially important to your chosen profession. Expand on your reflections regarding your major and the skill/trait of which you are especially proud. Include a philosophy or mission statement and your résumé. Highlight involvement in an off-campus program or internship, if you participated in one. Reflect on what you are planning for your next step, whether that means graduate school, a job, volunteer work, and so forth.

Chapter 27

Portfolio Evaluation Form Contents Checklist

Arizona State University

Required (45 points)

- Title page
- Table of contents
- Mission statement
- Autobiography/BIS 301 plan of study and concentration reports
- Skills evaluations lists (three lists):
    - Career Center Values Checklist
    - Skills Checklist I
    - Skills Checklist II
- Skills learned/developed from courses in emphasis areas
- Skills developed from life/job/internship experiences
    - Indication of where and how you learned each skill
- Personal strengths/weaknesses inventory list

Three of the Following Plus One-Page Narrative (10 points)

- Strong Interests Inventory Test/one-page narrative
- Myers-Briggs/Voices of Discovery/one-page narrative
- System of Interactive Guidance and Information/one-page narrative
- Investigating Academic Professional Literature I or II
- Search for integration/interdisciplinary concepts/buzzwords
- BIS 301 résumé/path to dream job

Extra (5 points)

- Résumé
- Writing sample (with favorable evaluations, if possible)

- Academic accomplishments within areas of emphasis
- Letters of recommendation
- Academic transcript
- Awards or certificate of merit or accomplishment
- Samples of artwork/design/project
- Write-up/evidence of volunteer activity
- Other

Appearance (40 points)

Materials

- Attractive, appropriate binder
- Plastic sheets/page covers
- Dividers

_____ Excellent _____ Very Good _____ Fair _____ Needs Improvement _____ No Effort Made

Neatness

_____ Excellent _____ Very Good _____ Fair _____ Needs Improvement _____ No Effort Made

Organization

_____ Excellent _____ Very Good _____ Fair _____ Needs Improvement _____ No Effort Made

Creativity

_____ Excellent _____ Very Good _____ Fair _____ Needs Improvement _____ No Effort Made

Overall Effort

_____ Excellent _____ Very Good _____ Fair _____ Needs Improvement _____ No Effort Made

Chapter 28

Showcase/Electronic Portfolio Evaluation Form

Arizona State University

Content

- Title Page
- Table of Contents
- Mission Statement
- BIS Web Page
- Sample Work
- Internship Experience
- Work Experience
- Résumé
- Skills
- Reference Letters
- Sample Work

1. Portfolio statement clearly answers the question, "How do I want prospective employers to think of me and my work?"

    YES!   Yes   Average   No   NO!

2. Selection: Do the artifacts in your showcase portfolio represent your qualifications for the position?

    YES!   Yes   Average   No   NO!

3. Interdisciplinarity/synthesis/integration: Did you represent your interdisciplinary education adequately? Did you include evidence of interdisciplinary work? Did you indicate that you have done interdisciplinary work/research/projects?

    YES!   Yes   Average   No   NO!

4. Language mechanics: Is your portfolio free of spelling, punctuation, and grammatical errors?

YES! Yes Average No NO!

5. Organization: Is your showcase portfolio appropriately organized?

YES! Yes Average No NO!

Design

Typography: Treatment of font size and style support your design

Balance of design: White space, centered, graphic/picture placement

Consistency of   Reader can access work easily; consistent page
design: layout

Conciseness: No extra artifacts that don't support your message

_____ Excellent _____ Very Good _____ Fair _____ Needs Improvement
_____ No Effort Made

Appearance

Professional quality: Easily accessible, attractive, and appropriate

Materials: Binder, dividers/plastic sheets

_____ Excellent _____ Very Good _____ Fair _____ Needs Improvement
_____ No Effort Made

Creativity:

_____ Excellent _____ Very Good _____ Fair _____ Needs Improvement
_____ No Effort Made

Self-representation:

_____ Excellent _____ Very Good _____ Fair _____ Needs Improvement
_____ No Effort Made

Overall effort:

_____ Excellent _____ Very Good _____ Fair _____ Needs Improvement
_____ No Effort Made

Chapter 29

Webfolio Assignment

Clemson University

Introductory Reflective Hypertext Essay

The opening or entry page for your English 214 Webfolio is an introductory reflective hypertext essay of at least 750 words to introduce your Webfolio and to demonstrate your learning and progress.

- Present your essay as a contribution to our shared learning this semester. Keep the audience of your professor and classmates in mind as you revise your drafts and prepare your final essay. Aim for an engaging style that encourages people to read your essay: friendly, conversational, neither too formal nor too colloquial.

- Include a little information about yourself—such as college, curriculum, and career information—either incorporated into your essay or linked to a separate Web page.

- If you publish your digital portfolio on the Web, your online audience expands to include additional readers whom you invite or who come across your Webfolio.

To plan your introductory reflective hypertext essay, reread your own writing and that of your classmates to reflect on what both you and they wrote.

- Consider what you learned about American literature and the evolution of American literary theory.

- Consider ways that your reading of and writing about American literature might affect your future reading and writing.

- If you so desire, identify and explain the literature and activities you liked most and least as well as that which you learned from so long as you emphasize what you learned from reading and discussing the works.

This introductory reflective hypertext essay should be persuasive, demonstrating that you have understood the works for this course and fulfilled the course objectives listed on the course overview Web site, supported by your explanations and evidence and by your effective writing. (The essay is not an evaluation of the class or your classmates or the teacher.)

Be clear and be specific: explain what and how and why, give examples, and incorporate short quotations from the literary works, from your own writing during the semester, and from classmates' writing.

Give complete and accurate credit to all work that is not your original composition, including images and media. You can do so informally or formally.

The final essay should be carefully revised, edited, and proofread for accuracy to show you took the project and the composition seriously.

Your introductory reflective hypertext essay must demonstrate clearly your understanding of the literature of the United States as well as individual works that contributed to that understanding. Within this essay, include at least one work from each of these literary periods:

1. Early American voices (Native American, colonial)

2. Romanticism, transcendentalism, realism (nineteenth-century prose and poetry)

3. Early twentieth-century literature (modernism)

Also include at least one work from each literary genre:

1. Fiction

2. Poetry

3. Drama

You can overlap periods and genres as appropriate. Be sure to refer by author and title to at least five works from our reading list, using accurate names and punctuation.

Incorporate into your discussion at least six of the following required exhibits in a meaningful way that makes clear what and how each artifact contributed to your learning of the literary works:

- Four or more of your own substantial compositions, which must include at least two written works but also may include drawings or media, selected to illustrate your contribution to the class community of learners (what might classmates have learned from you?).

- Two or more class discussion board or blog entries by two or more other students, selected because they were helpful to you during our class, explaining how and why they were helpful.

- Use classmates' first names rather than full names.

- Quote briefly within your essay, and link to longer passages.

- You are welcome to include optional additional artifacts that support your argument—for example, other compositions for our class, compositions for other classes or situations that relate to your essay, and any external Web sites that relate to your essay (integrated within the essay, not presented as a list of links).

You can present and discuss these exhibits in any order so long as your presentation is complete and well organized. You should quote briefly from each one within your essay and establish links to the complete artifacts on separate pages.

Chapter 30
Learning Portfolio Project

Columbia College

ONE OF THE MOST VALUABLE projects in our class is the opportunity to pull together your writing in a coherent learning portfolio that will demonstrate the content, scope, and quality of your work along with your substantive reflections on what you've learned, how you've learned, why you've learned, and what value your learning has added to your intellectual and personal growth. Remember that the portfolio, a major grade in the course, will consist of evidence of your writing accomplishments and the important reflective component that is where deep and lasting learning will really occur. When you simply acquire information or knowledge, you have activated only a part of your learning potential. Going beyond knowledge to comprehension, application, analysis, synthesis, and evaluation engages you in a richer, fuller, deeper, more lasting learning experience, and that is what you have done in your essays and online writing. When you reflect on your learning, you enhance the meaning of what you've learned and its relevance to your intellectual, social, personal, and ethical development. Your learning becomes authentic. Please take a look at my thoughts on the value of learning portfolios at www.columbiacollegesc.edu/faculty/dev/learningportfolio.asp.

In reflecting on your learning throughout the class and in your various writings, ask yourselves questions such as these in composing your reflective narrative:

1. *What* have I learned or not learned from my work in the class, from my formal and online writing?

2. *How* have I learned or not learned best in the class?

3. *Why* did I learn or not learn from the kind of work we did in the class and in the online discussion forum?

4. What have I learned about *myself as a learner* from our written work in this class?

5. How has my writing in this class *connected* to my learning in other classes? To my personal life?

6. In what ways has my writing and learning in this class contributed to my *practical* learning and career goals?

7. Did I have *fun* writing and learning in this class? What do I mean by "fun"?

8. What about the content of the course and my engagement in the course *surprised* me?

9. If I were to do the class all over again, what would I do differently to *enhance* my learning and *improve* my writing?

You do not have to answer all the questions, but they are guides to help you reflect on your learning experience in the course.

The sections that follow discuss some of the nuts and bolts of the learning portfolio.

How Long Should I Make My Reflective Narrative(s)?

Some students may wish to write a few pages as a single reflection, while others may wish to write shorter reflective statements scattered throughout their compilation of written work, addressing a particular piece or group of pieces and the meaning and value of their work. Either way, the thoughtful, analytical, metacognitive writing in your reflections will be a useful, coherent way of organizing, understanding, and evaluating your own learning. You should end up with at least five hundred words of reflective narrative, either as a single piece or as interspersed pieces.

What Should I Include in My Portfolio?

1. A written, reflective analysis of your learning. Again, your reflections can be a single narrative or various pieces interspersed throughout your portfolio. The reflective component is the heart of your portfolio, the most valuable and challenging core of the portfolio in which you tap the power of reflection in deepening and extending your learning.

2. Print-outs of your pieces from the online threaded discussion pages. You can either expand your own entries within the full list of postings and print, or you can copy and save your entries to Word and print. If you think adding others' responses or questions in a threaded series of entries enriches a particular post or helps clarify or enhance your reflection about an individual entry, then feel free to include it. As you revisit your online writing, look for patterns of learning and growth as a writer and student. Focus not only on what you've learned about the course content (for example, a short story) but also on what you've discovered about yourself as a learner.

3. Copies of your essay drafts—especially with evidence of feedback from your instructor or peers and how your writing improved—and final versions of formal papers.

4. Evidence of research for formal papers, especially the longer research paper: written notes, copies of articles with your marginal notations, and e-mail exchanges on your topics.

5. Copies of your class notes, revealing your thoughts, insights, and questions throughout the course. If you have any work you've achieved toward completion of your final creative group project, also include it.

How Should I Organize My Portfolio?

I suggest that you design sections of the portfolio that will collect the different types of writing and other learning activities of the course. For instance, you may have a section on online threaded discussion writing, a section on formal essays, a section on research, a section on notes, and such. If you choose to write a single reflective narrative piece, you could have a section for it. If you choose to write several shorter reflective pieces about your growth as a learner, commenting on your growth at various selected moments throughout the portfolio, you can add the pieces at intervals throughout the portfolio, identifying them in some notable way.

What is more important than which particular way you want to organize the portfolio is that you collect, select, reflect, and connect in a way that is meaningful and coherent for you! I will read your portfolio carefully, but ultimately, the portfolio is your record of learning in the course, and you should organize it to help you understand your learning best.

When Is My Portfolio Due?

Submit your portfolio on Monday, December 3, the final week of class.

A mindful, honest, thorough portfolio demonstrates learning at its best. I'm confident that your learning portfolios will be delightful, instructive histories of your intellectual growth. Thanks for your hard work.

Chapter 31

Online Reflective Writing
Instructions for Threaded Discussion

Columbia College

REMEMBER THAT THE threaded discussion will be a powerful, important component of our collective learning in this course; it will also figure prominently in your evaluation and final grade (22 percent of your course grade!). Please pay attention to the following guidelines. I look forward to your engagement.

Ground Rules

1. Each student should contribute a minimum of fifteen entries spread consistently and evenly throughout the semester. The online reflective writing assignment receives two grades. One is the average of three or four unannounced, periodic assessments throughout the semester, suggesting the importance of being consistent in your writing (don't wait to the last minute to write a bunch of entries all at once!). The other is an overall assessment of the extent and quality of your online reflective writing.

2. Each entry should be at least a hefty paragraph's length or two, twenty to twenty-five lines on your screen. My interest is not in counting words or lines, really, but in encouraging some development of your ideas. My experience has been that students usually far exceed the requirements of number and length of entries because they instantly and enthusiastically recognize the extraordinary learning that occurs on their threaded discussions.

3. Try to make most entries critical pieces in which you reflect carefully about an idea, issue, topic, text, class discussion, outside reading, related learning in another class—something connected to our class's work. Some entries grounded in personal experience or opinions are OK, but the premium is on critically thoughtful, challenging pieces that focus on the intellectual content of the course. I encourage you also to reflect regularly on the process of learning—that is, what you are learning about learning itself through the medium of online reflections.

4. Use specific examples and quotations to support and enhance your discussions. When quoting texts, practice MLA style of citations to continue developing good habits of sound, accurate documentation. Personal topics can be useful and helpful, but try to tip the balance toward critical thinking and writing.

5. As much as possible or appropriate, demonstrate your motivation and independent learning by bringing into your discussions references to helpful outside sources. Collaborate with others in finding, analyzing, and evaluating secondary sources that add valuable dimensions to our discussions. Remember that in addition to a wealth of library print and online resources, we have a substantial reserve reading collection at the library circulation desk. If you discover a cogent journal article, book chapter, or Web site, share it with the group.

6. Your entries will be appreciated and evaluated mostly for content, for creativity, for depth of thought, for substance of reflection, for critical engagement. Grammar, spelling, punctuation, and mechanics are not evaluated, though you should strive to communicate in clear, clean prose of which you can be proud. "Why level downward to our dullest perception?" asks Thoreau. Not a bad philosophy.

7. The online threaded discussion is a medium for challenging, creative, thoughtful reflection and engagement in intellectual growth and genuine learning. Let's respect each other as scholars and encourage risk, critical inquiry, diversity of perspectives, tolerance, and acceptance.

8. Finally, be sure to save your entries to a disk or make print copies as insurance against lost or damaged communications. Let me know if you need help in learning how to copy to disk from Internet applications. I openly reveal that I am *not* sympathetic to today's students' all-too-common my-computer-crashed or the-Internet-was-down explanations. Completing your assignment for engaged, consistent, excellent reflective or formal writing in this or any other class does not depend entirely on computers or networks. I appreciate your work in pencil and paper as much as in digital form, and I look forward to your bright ideas, shared resources, critical questions, analytical observations, and creative writing.

9. All your hard work in developing your reflective learning skills in our threaded discussion tool will compose a significant portion of your learning portfolio at the end of the term. The online reflective writing in our course Web site will help you document, assess, and evaluate

your progress as a learner. And the best news is that your learning portfolio will be almost complete by the time you assemble it at the end of the course if you are serious and regularly engaged in our threaded discussions. The learning portfolio, an alternative to a final exam in the course, is built largely around your faithful online reflective writing. A strong effort on the threaded discussion means a strong learning portfolio. Go for it!

Sample Online Reflective Entries: Handouts in Class

As a useful guide to writing meaningful reflective entries that enrich your learning, I include here some further comments on reflective online writing and references to a few selected models I will share in handouts.

The Student's Voice

Remember that writing in the asynchronous environment of a Listserv/ threaded discussion will be a powerful, important component of our collective learning in this course; it will also figure prominently in your evaluation and grade. As I have stated earlier in the syllabus, online reflective writing is a medium for challenging, creative, thoughtful reflection and engagement in intellectual growth and genuine learning.

Take a look at the sample postings I will share in handouts that illustrate compelling, thoughtful student entries. Your entries do not necessarily have to be as long or the same in content or style, but the models offer high standards for creative, collaborative, and critically engaging writing. They are excellent examples.

The Teacher's Voice

The last few entries in the samples included in your handout are examples of the kind of feedback you can expect from me. I try hard to respond to every posting, though at times I will combine several student entries and reply collectively to them. Still, I want you to know that I read and value every entry written by each of you. Hopefully, my feedback will encourage you to read, think, and write critically and enthusiastically, to contribute often and meaningfully to our community of learners. Learning at its best!

Chapter 32

Portfolio Reflections

Dalhousie University

Each of the required five sections of your portfolio must contain some introductory statements explaining why you have chosen to include these artifacts or documents, how they relate to the purpose of your portfolio, and how they relate to the career development theory we have studied.

Your portfolio will be assessed at three levels of critical reflection. As MacIsaac and Jackson (1994) explain, the most elementary reflections include simple labels, descriptions, and so forth. As they describe in their article (in your reading package), at this level you are simply remembering the what, when, and how.

The next level demands that you move beyond the remembering stage and demonstrate how you analyze, interrelate, and synthesize your materials. At this level you are reflecting on the meaning your section has for you.

At the highest level of reflection, you are not only remembering and reflecting on the meaning of your materials and experiences but also discussing your future—the next steps in your learning. At each level of reflection, it is important for you to think about and discuss your gap analysis. A gap analysis is simply a reflection on what you have yet to learn as it relates to your section and your purpose statement. It could be that you've identified weak areas that you plan to improve or knowledge gaps that you plan to overcome. *When these reflective comments also reference and integrate personally relevant career development theories, you are demonstrating mastery of the material.*

When introducing your sections for the purposes of this course, or to any audience interested in your learning and personal reflection, you may find it helpful to frame your commentary as "This is what I've learned from . . . *and* this is what I'll do with what I've learned." Your reflective commentaries are best when they answer each of these three questions:

1. What?

2. So what?

3. Now what?

The answers to these questions reflect the experiential learning model of your classes and labs.

See me for consultation about the depth of your reflections, privacy issues, the use of your reflections as they relate to interview preparation, and editing your portfolio to use in your job search. Remember the marking matrix is available for your review before your submission.

References

MacIsaac, D., & Jackson, L. (1994). Assessment processes and outcomes: Portfolio construction. In L. Jackson & R. S. Caffarella (Eds.), *New directions for adult and continuing education: No. 62. Experiential learning: A new approach* (pp. 63–72). San Francisco: Jossey-Bass.

Chapter 33

Honors Senior Portfolio Option
Contract and Guidelines

Kent State University

PROFESSOR AND STUDENT: Please read the guidelines accompanying this contract. This completed form must be returned to the honors office for approval as indicated. The student will then be registered for one credit hour (HONR 40085).

Contract

This completed contract must be submitted to the Honors College by the end of the first week of classes during the semester in which the portfolio project is to be completed.

_____ Semester 20 _____

_____   _____

Student's Name   ID Number

_____   _____

Address   Phone Number

As described in the guidelines, this project involves the selection, editing, and preparation in final form of a collection (approximately eight to ten artifacts) of work from the past four years; a fifteen- to twenty-five-page reflective paper that explains how each artifact contributed to the student's intellectual and/or personal growth; and an exit interview.

_____	_____
Signature of Student	Signature of Professor
_____	_____
Signature of Honors Adviser	Professor (please print)
_____	_____
Department	Date
_____	_____
Dean, Honors College	Date

During the first two weeks of the semester, the student, the professor, and the Senior Portfolio Review Committee should meet to discuss the details and expectations for the portfolio project. The student should contact the portfolio program coordinator in the Honors College at x2312 to arrange this meeting.

For Honors College use only:

Initial Meeting Date _____   Exit Interview Date _____

Guidelines for the Honors Senior Portfolio

Introduction

The senior portfolio provides an opportunity for students to review their work from the past four years and to select from that work eight to ten artifacts that provide the best evidence of meeting the following Honors College goals: academic excellence, campus and community service, global awareness, appreciation of cultural events and institutions, and personal growth.

The portfolio will consist of two parts: (1) documentation of these carefully selected milestones over the past four years in the context of Honors College goals, and (2) a reflective paper that integrates this collection with current personal observations of educational growth and development. The documentation may take many forms (e.g., outstanding papers, supervisor's letters, taped work, journal entries, brief response papers to cultural events attended). The reflective paper should be fifteen to twenty-five pages long and should interpret the college experience as represented by the documents. The portfolio will conclude with an exit interview.

The student must receive written permission (see accompanying form) from the instructor under whose guidance the portfolio collection and paper will be completed and who will chair the exit interview. The instructor will be responsible for grading this one-credit-hour project.

Student's Responsibilities

The portfolio collection should include examples of work drawn from across the four years that represent meaningful experiences as they relate to the Honors College values. The eight to ten artifacts in the collection may include written, visual, and taped entries. Specific suggestions for possible portfolio collection pieces include the following: an outstanding colloquium paper, a brief reaction paper to a cultural event, and samples of work that are sources of particular pride or that represent significant growth. Summary narratives describing special learning experiences and evaluations from supervisors of relevant volunteer or learning activities are also appropriate. An annotated listing of extracurricular activities that describes campus and community service and any awards received is also acceptable.

The fifteen- to twenty-five-page reflective paper by its very title suggests that this essay will contain highly subjective and personal material. In this overview and critical analysis of your years of individual experiences as an honors student at Kent State University, the challenge is to integrate a collection of outstanding work with a carefully considered evaluation of academic and personal growth. The portfolio is a retrospective effort to *make meaning* of the student's college career.

The student will provide three draft copies of the portfolio to the Honors College one week before the exit interview. The student may choose to submit a final copy to the Honors College. Upon completion of the portfolio, the student will be asked to submit a short (one-paragraph) summary of the experience for the *On Our Own* publication.

The completed contract must be submitted to the Honors College by the end of the first week of classes during the semester in which the portfolio project is to be completed.

Faculty Adviser's Role

The faculty portfolio adviser will be selected by the student and typically will be someone familiar with the student's best academic work. Ideally, the adviser will also know and be interested in the student's more general educational goals and activities. The portfolio adviser will help the student determine the specific goals of the project, review the items for the final collection, discuss the physical layout of the portfolio, help identify themes and directions of the work, discuss how to integrate the reflective paper with the collected documentary work, and review drafts of the reflective paper.

The faculty adviser will be responsible for grading the one-credit-hour portfolio and should plan regular meetings with the student to assess progress, ask probing questions, and offer guidance. The faculty adviser should also plan to attend the initial meeting as well as chair the exit interview. At any point during the process, the faculty adviser should feel free to contact the portfolio coordinator in the Honors College with any questions or concerns. The adviser should also keep a copy of these guidelines for reference.

Honors College's Role

Upon receipt of the completed form (by the end of the first week of the semester), the Honors College will register the student for HONR 40085. An initial meeting will be scheduled with the student, the faculty adviser, and the Senior Portfolio Review Committee during the first two weeks of the semester to answer any questions and provide any details about the project that are not apparent in these guidelines. Sample portfolios will be available at this meeting. The Senior Portfolio Review Committee consists of the student's honors adviser and the honors portfolio coordinator, with an invitation to the honors dean. The portfolio coordinator will be available during the semester to answer any questions the student and/or faculty adviser may have about the portfolio guidelines.

The exit interview will be scheduled for sometime before the twelfth week of the semester. The exit interview will also include the student and the Senior Portfolio Review Committee. The Honors College will reimburse the student for the three copies required at this interview. The Senior Portfolio Review Committee may make suggestions regarding the compiling, editing, and presentation of the final portfolio.

Chapter 34

Criteria for Evaluating Learning Portfolios

Otterbein College

Total points = 100

Quality of reflection (70)

	Thoughtfulness, insightfulness, honesty, accuracy of self-assessment
	Writing quality

Nature and use of evidence (20)

	Comprehensiveness of evidence (contains all required parts)
	Aptness of evidence
	Connection of evidence to reflection
	Labeling and highlighting
	Evidence of improvement (before-and-after/development examples)

Table of contents and neatness (10)

	Contains a comprehensive table of contents
	Neat and careful

As with all rubrics for the class, I provide students with a copy of this one, along with the instructions, before they complete the work.

Since the portfolio is the final work submitted for the term, since it comprises work that has been previously submitted, commented on, reviewed by peers as well as by me—and, above all, since most students don't choose to come and collect their work after the beginning of the next quarter—I only assign point values and make no comments. This is a pragmatic, time-saving choice. The learning, I believe, has gone into the process. The occasional student will, however, want to collect the work, and I am always happy to sit down and discuss the portfolio at that time.

Chapter 35

Double-Column Notes for Reflection

Otterbein College

DOUBLE-COLUMN NOTES are designed to help you pay attention to readings (so that you remember important ideas and details better) but *also* to help you begin to go beyond what the reading says and to formulate your own ideas, questions, interests, and connections. Doing this second part is a key step to making meaning—which is really the point of most writing anyway. It's important that you give the original text its due and that you seek to understand it correctly and thoroughly. But it's equally important for you to go beyond what that text says and to think about where *you* want to take the ideas. Do you see connections to other things you've read in this or other classes? If so, what do you make of those connections? Is there a pattern there that you can draw a conclusion about? Or maybe what you see is something that completely contradicts what another author has said—or what you, yourself, believe. Double-column notes are an informal way to begin making records of the fleeting ideas that run through our heads when we are really thinking about what we read.

Here's an example of how they might look:

Plato's *Symposium*	
NOTES from readings	My responses, ideas, questions, connections, etc.
p. 25 three kind of human beings man/man; woman/woman; man/woman → cut in half	This is a really weird idea! Reminds me of the Rufus Wainwright song. I wonder if there are other examples in his stuff?
	I <u>love</u> the idea of two halves finding each other = love
etc.	etc.

How long should such notes be? I would shoot for an average of one typed or two written pages per reading. Length is not the most important goal, however. Rather, it's important for the notes to reflect that you are getting some of the main ideas and noting some of the important details from the reading in the left-hand column *and* that you are raising your own questions, making your own connections, and thinking about how the detail or idea hits you (for example, do you agree, disagree, object, love it—and why?).

Models of Students' Double Column Notes

Notes from Readings (quotes or keyword summaries)	Responses (responses, ideas, questions, connections)
Sternberg, "The History of Love Revealed Through Culture"	
Love is a combo of passion, intimacy, and commitment.	This is one of the best descriptions I've heard! Incomplete, but still good.
Love is a social construction, which means that people construct their perceptions of it with culture as their guide.	I think this is true in a lot of cases but that love would still exist regardless of culture—we just might not understand or experience it the same way.
"People actively construct their perception of the world and use culture as a guide" (p. 60).	It's insane to think about how many different cultures there are and how they came up with their ideas about what is right or wrong.
Ackerman, "The Middle Ages" Sex in marriage was kept quiet and was not passionate, just for reproduction (p. 59).	Besides in biblical writings, was sex always a bad thing in marriages? Don't understand why it was such a terrible thing if they were married.
Ideas of love came from Christian thinkers…view of love started to change (pp. 59–60).	What else happened in the Middle Ages that caused the views of love to change?
"God so loved the world that he gave his only son" (p. 59).	Do you always have to give something up to prove your love?
"While the men were off fighting, it often fell to the women to manage the estate—thus raising their confidence, social contacts and …"	When I think of the crusades, this never came to mind. However, this kind of relates to what happened in WWI and WWII.
"One of the great changes of the Middle Ages was a shift from unilateral love to mutual love."	A turning point for love Where would we be now if this didn't happen?
Social constructivist perspective—societies differ in understandings of love as well as time periods (p. 61).	Reminds me of the ancient Egyptian woman of Diane Ackerman's article.
Rufus Wainwright, "Origins of Love" Blood in face "The pain down in your soul was the same pain down in mine."	Blurs vision and allows us to make mistakes on who we think we should be with. Seems like the "heavenly" connection of love.

Chapter 36

Learning Portfolio Assignment

Otterbein College

> In a learning portfolio, students assume responsibility for documenting and interpreting their own learning. Through reflection, students make their thinking visible. (p. xi)
>
> [S]tudents explain what the evidence shows about what they have learned. They tell their own stories, assess their own strengths and weaknesses as learners, evaluate their products and performances, reflect on past learning, and think about future learning. (p. xii)
>
> —John Zubizarreta, *The Learning Portfolio: Reflective Practice for Improving Student Learning*

Purpose
- To give you a chance to take stock of your own learning in the course
- To ask you to reflect on and document your learning
- To invite you to set goals for future learning

Audience
In this case, I am your audience. You can assume we share a body of common knowledge (thus, you have to explain a bit less than you would for a reader with no familiarity with our class and readings).

Contents
Include the following in a folder with two pockets:

Left-hand pocket

1. Reflection essay 1: improvements/strengths

2. Reflection essay 2: challenges/future actions

3. Reflection essay 3: personal growth

Right-hand pocket

1. Table of contents (evidence)

2. Evidence to support reflection essays

3. Evidence of achievement of course goals

Reflection Essays

Write short essays in response to each of the following questions. These paragraphs should be typed. Instead of a title, put the topic header above the paragraph. In supporting your claims, provide specific evidence by quoting from the documents you include in your portfolio, from your reading experience, or from your contributions to class discussion.

1. *Improvement and strengths* (one to two good paragraphs): Where have you improved most in the course? Where do you see your greatest strengths as a reader, writer, or thinker?

2. *Challenges* (one to two good paragraphs): Where do you still see your greatest challenges as a reader, writer, or thinker? What strategies can you use to address these?

3. *Personal, intellectual, and emotional growth* (two pages):

   - What have you learned about the following things (choose at least three to discuss specifically):

     - Love

     - Cultural norms

     - Yourself (especially in relation to the course)

     - Human nature

     - Literature (and reading different kinds of texts—poems, stories, plays, essays)

   - What has challenged you most in terms of your deeply held beliefs about human nature and love?

   - What have you most affirmed in your beliefs about human nature and love?

Evidence

What Counts as Evidence?

The evidence of your learning in IS 270 can come from homework assignments, in-class writing (drafts and revisions), formal work, even notes you have made for yourself that you may not have submitted for a grade—in short, any written work you have done for the course.

What Should I Choose and Include?

1. *Essay-related evidence:* Each of the three reflection essays should incorporate evidence (you will "quote" from your own work); in addition, the source of that evidence should be included in the portfolio. That

means the pieces that provide the best support for your short essays will represent one important set of evidence for your portfolio.

2. *Course-goal evidence:* You will also include work that shows that you have achieved the following course goals. This set of evidence may be included in your essay reflections (it overlaps in some places) or may constitute a separate section all its own. In any case, please label the pieces according to which category you believe they fit:

- Critical thinking (specifically manifested in good analysis and strong arguments)
- Strong communication of your thoughts in writing, including strong revision
- A greater sense of understanding of what it means to be human (in relation to the theme of love)
- Understanding of several different and important ideas about love relationships from different times, cultures, and disciplines
- The ability to understand and tell about a story or poem in relation to its context
- Connections between your own life and texts you read (essays, stories, poems)

Other Advice

- Be very selective. Choose the best examples of whatever you are aiming to show (that may include choosing the best example of weak work). Shoot for quality and clearly representative work rather than quantity.
- Be sure to include some before-and-after examples (showing improvement)—whether that improvement is from one draft of a paragraph/essay to the next or from early work to late work in the course.
- Label your work so that I know what each piece represents. If you are pointing out just one portion of a piece of homework or a longer essay, circle that portion with a bright highlighter, and then also label it with a brief note, so that it is easy and quick to recognize. Also be sure to include a list of all these pieces in the table of contents.
- Don't hesitate to be honest in your opinions and your self-assessment (including weaker as well as stronger examples). As always in the course, you will be evaluated on the quality of your work, not on what position you take and whether it agrees with anyone else's position

(as long as you are fair and accurate). Furthermore, you will be evaluated on (1) the quality of your current reflection pieces, and (2) the degree to which you have chosen evidence that really shows the point it's intended to show. This means that sometimes a weak piece of work may provide the best evidence.

Chapter 37

Sample Student Reflections

Otterbein College

This course has taught me many things about writing a good paper that I did not know before. One thing I have learned is how to provide support for claims made in a paragraph. I have improved on structuring my paragraphs to include specific examples to support my work. In the rough draft of my first essay, I used almost no specific examples. I made broad generalizations like "the media portrays love in a romantic way." I did not give any examples of media portraying love in this way. In the revision for this essay, I went back and cited the specific TV shows and movies where I got my ideas from. For example, I used quotes from the TV show Sex and the City *and summarized the movie* Love Actually. *Also, in a paragraph we wrote about in class about interesting things we learned about love, I used very little support for my claims. When we were able to go back and revise it, I used more specific examples from readings done in class to support my opinion. I used Sternberg, Plato, and readings about courtly love to improve my paragraph. I have been able to make this improvement by not rushing through my work. I used to tend to just say what I think. Now I really think about what I am trying to say and what evidence I can use to support it. This can allow me to have stronger communication of my thoughts in writing.*

—IS 270 student, winter quarter 2006

• • •

Throughout the quarter I have developed myself greatly as a reader and a writer. I lead an extremely active life and rarely have the time or attention to sit and read. I have always been relatively proficient in writing, and I have always been able to get by with minimal effort. This quarter, I learned that developing my reading skills broadens my writing skills. Being exposed to a variety of writing styles has allowed me to sort through them and integrate them into my own style. This has allowed me to become a more effective writer, not only in my delivery, but in keeping my reader's attention. The most important skill that I have developed is the ability to develop meanings, arguments, and insights out of readings and other materials. This also greatly benefits my writing. For example, upon analyzing Sternberg's thoughts on the history of love, I found myself making arguments in my head. This may not seem like a big deal to most, but it was a turning point for me. Sternberg makes the argument that only humans have the ability to know right and wrong. In the notes I took on this reading, I pointed out that this may not be true. Nature seems to do an excellent job governing itself, so why are human beings distinguished as something above nature? Before this course, I would have never taken the time or the effort to do this. I would have read the material, took the author's word for it, and gone on with my life. Another example of this came from notes that I took while reading Ackerman's writing on love in the Middle Ages. She speaks of Plato abandoning the delights of the flesh. I found this to be a wildly misinterpreted piece of information. Plato had relationships with young boys. Therefore, he gave in to the desires of the flesh. Again, this is another issue that I would have let pass me by, but due to my newly acquired reading skills, I actually took something away from the reading.

—IS 270 student, winter quarter 2006

• • •

This may seem like a strange selection, but I have included all of my double-column notes as a demonstration of my personal growth in this course. I felt that these assignments best showed my thoughts and beliefs as they related to the topics we discussed in class. Some of the readings included concepts and beliefs that were totally foreign to me, and the double-column notes gave me the chance to express my response to these ideas the second I had them. It also helped me better collect my thoughts for the discussions in class. By making small notes about how I felt, I was better prepared to make my case in class. We covered some touchy subjects in class, and at the very least, my horizons were broadened simply by being exposed to these ideas. And there were times when I disagreed with some of the opinions shared, and sometimes people said ridiculously stupid things that made me want to explode, but this class has helped me realize that people don't always have to agree. It's a matter of respecting different opinions and not getting so upset about them, because if everyone could master that, we'd all be a lot better off. Not only have I grown intellectually, but my love life has been changed as well. I look at my relationships in an entirely different way now. All of this analysis of love has helped me to understand what it is I'm looking for in the opposite sex, which I'm sure will cut down on a lot of unnecessary, awkward, uncomfortable dating situations, and hopefully will help me avoid any sort of disastrous relationships. And I've learned all this without the nasty consequences that come along with ex-boyfriends—a definite bonus.

—IS 270 student, winter quarter 2006

• • •

When I began IS 270, I had low expectations as to what the class could do for me as a college student. I feared that I had fallen into a course that was baseless and had no benefits towards my major or towards my development as a college student. Luckily my first impressions were very inaccurate, and I found that this class improved my writing and also allowed me to form more open-minded opinions in a wide range of topics pertaining to love relationships and cultural norms all over the world.

Arranged marriage is a topic that I had seldom thought about or discussed. However, this class helped me gain information about this type of marriage, information that was essential to forming new ideas about arranged marriage. IS 270 helped me to realize that arranged marriages in current societies are often not forced, and are instead an extremely planned out process that seeks to reach the ultimate goal of combining two loving families. Overall, I decided that this was a very good idea, something that I would've never predicted at the outset of the course. After Dr. Ruparel talked to us about arranged marriage, I realized that his culture had the answer to many of the marriage woes in this country. A frequent topic of conversation for our class focused on reality television, and its inability to match partners in a meaningful relationship. We came up with several reasons why this happened; however, the most frequent focused on the fact that the taping of the show wasn't enough time to form a strong bond between two people. We also discussed how ineffective cultural norms could be when depicting love relationships, while also exploring how different types of love can be fulfilling even when they don't contain all the typical aspects of perfect relationships. Arranged marriages not only avoid the problem of uninformed matchmaking, but they also take many of the pressures off the shoulders of teenagers, which in turn allows them to focus more time on studying and the pleasures of being an adolescent.

[An example] of writing that showed my expanding ideas with the help of literature were my double-column notes for Billy Merrill's Talking in the Dark. . . . *Billy Merrill's poems provided an inside look at the trials and tribulations of a gay man struggling to form an identity throughout adolescence and into his adult life. In my double-column notes for this reading, I comment that "I have always felt that if I had a close friend who was gay, I wouldn't have ever noticed or minded (in that I wouldn't have acted different around him, etc.). However, these poems made me realize I might not have been as comfortable as I thought."*

—*IS 270 student, winter quarter 2006*

Chapter 38

Review and Revision Process and Submission Letter for Webfolios

Tidewater Community College

THESE TWO STAGES of the Webfolio project give students an audience for their work in progress. They are responsible for ensuring not only that the Webfolio represents their learning and fulfills the project criteria but also that I will be able to access the introduction and the supporting links.

Review and Revision Process

Have at least two people, either classmates or others, assist you in the review process so that you have time to make any necessary changes. It's important for you to know before you submit it to me that the Webfolio displays as you wish on a computer other than your own.

- E-mail your Web address or your compressed files to at least two people who are willing to read the Webfolio project expectations and to give feedback on the contents and design, including the introductory reflective hypertext essay and the links.

- Visit the Web site yourself from a different computer than the one you used to create it. That way, you'll have a better sense of how it looks to others as well as how the links work.

Submission Letter

When you submit your Webfolio, also submit your submission letter of two hundred or more words.

- Describe your Webfolio composing and development process, including:
  - Previous experience constructing Web pages
  - Software programs you used to develop the Webfolio

- Selection and organization process for your artifacts (how and why you made the choices)

- Design decisions and reasons

- Challenges, successes, and/or surprises

- Describe your review and revision process:

  - Identify by name and connection to you (my classmate Pat Smart) or other designation, if you prefer not to give a name (my sister in Kansas), the two or more people who reviewed your Webfolio draft for you.

  - What were their recommendations, and what changes did you make based on their comments?

  - Summarize your own review process and any changes that resulted from your own review.

- Provide access information for your audience: the complete Web address (URL) or, if you are submitting a file attachment, file details.

Chapter 39

Rubric for Evaluating Webfolios

Tidewater Community College

TO MAKE CLEAR from the beginning of the course that students' compositions, both formal and informal (and their multimodal work such as drawings, videos, audio files, photographs, and slides), will become part of their final exam, I make the primary expectations available at the beginning of the term, via an active link from their hypertext course schedule, which I publish on the World Wide Web. Having my own Web presence, not just posting the syllabus online as a document, demonstrates my own commitment to online academic publication.

Your final exam Webfolio represents 25 percent of your grade for this course:

- Twenty percent is based on the completeness, substance, and effective writing of your introductory reflective hypertext essay. Because your introductory reflective hypertext essay is the most important element in your Webfolio, devote most of your time and energy to developing and submitting the essay by the deadline.
  - Compose the essay in your word processor, and save it there.
  - Compose the essay early in the Webfolio development process so you'll have time to revise, edit, and proofread.
- Five percent is based on your portfolio's organization, navigation, and design.
- If you have last-minute problems linking to or submitting your artifacts, you should still submit your introductory reflective hypertext essay as a single document so you can receive credit for that portion of your grade.
  - Incorporate selected artifacts within the essay, and use a visual signal to identify them, perhaps indented text or colored text.
  - Don't count the words in the artifacts within your word count.

A Webfolios exceed the expectations of the assignment; have an engaging essay with a strong sense of purpose; focus on illustrating your learning about American literature, including your own thinking; emphasize interpretation rather than summary; include all the required components in the essay and all the required artifacts; are clearly and logically organized; include no major and few, if any, nonstandard usages and grammatical decisions; adhere to all review and submission process expectations; and have design and navigation features that complement the essay and artifacts.

B Webfolios meet all the expectations of the assignment; have an interesting readable essay with a clear sense of purpose; focus on illustrating your learning about American literature, including your own thinking; emphasize interpretation with little summary; include all the required components in the essay and all the required artifacts; are logically organized; include few major and minor nonstandard usages and grammatical decisions; adhere to most review and submission process expectations; and have design and navigation features that for the most part complement the essay and artifacts.

C Webfolios meet most expectations of the assignment; have a readable essay with a relatively clear sense of purpose; focus on illustrating your learning about American literature, including your own thinking; include as much summary as interpretation; include most of the required components in the essay and in the artifacts; include some nonstandard usages or grammatical decisions; adhere to most of the review and submission process expectations; and demonstrate an effort to use design and navigation features that complement the essay and artifacts.

D Webfolios meet some expectations of the assignment; have an essay with some sense of purpose; show an effort to demonstrate your learning about American literature, but not much of your own thinking; include more summary than interpretation; include most of the required components in the essay and in the artifacts; include some nonstandard usages or grammatical decisions that make reading difficult; adhere to most of the review and submission process expectations; and demonstrate effort to use design and navigation features that complement the essay and artifacts.

F Webfolios meet few or no expectations of the assignment; have an essay with little sense of purpose; illustrate little learning about American literature and not much of your own thinking; include more summary than interpretation; include some of the required components in the essay and in the artifacts; include an unacceptable number of nonstandard usages or grammatical decisions that interfere with reading; neglect some or all of the review and submission process expectations; and lack design and navigation features that complement the essay.

Chapter 40

Reflective Writing Assignment

University of Oklahoma

REFLECTIVE WRITING ACTIVITIES can range from simple one- or two-sentence thoughts taken at the end of a lecture or assignment (the "one-minute paper"), to running commentary throughout the course (the learning log or diary), to a synthesis document prepared at the end of a major topic or at the end of the semester (the learning portfolio). In this course, we will use a variation of each.

Implementation

Starting with the section of the course devoted to water distribution systems, we will begin an experiment with reflective writing. At the end of every other week, we will ask each student to visit the class Web site and write a short paragraph (one to five sentences) in which he or she reflects on the past week's activities. These will be read only by the faculty, who will provide some feedback. (This will also help us gauge the effectiveness of our classroom activities.) When writing, consider such questions as:

- What is the most important concept that you learned since the previous reflection?
- What is the relationship of this material to other topics?
- What material do you understand the least?
- What gaps do you see in the material?
- How do you feel about open-ended design problems?
- Do you understand how to use the software as an analysis and design tool, and do you recognize its limitations?
- Do you feel comfortable identifying an approach to a problem and making good engineering assumptions?

At the end of each major topical section in the course, we will ask each student to prepare a one-page essay. In preparing this essay, students will consider three aspects of learning—content, context, and process—by addressing these three questions, respectively:

- What have you learned about the topic?
- How does this learning fit into your life's goals (professional and personal)?
- What have you learned about how to learn, particularly as the process of learning relates to open-ended design questions?

For this essay, we encourage each student to look back over his or her weekly reflections and to synthesize these thoughts and any new ones into a coherent statement. Please prepare your essay with your favorite word processor and then cut and paste it into the form dialogue box on the Web. We encourage you to circulate your drafts among your peers to get feedback. In fact, you will probably be surprised that others share similar concerns and frustrations about the course or material.

Since we are starting this process a little late, we would also like you to prepare a two-part essay that looks back at the first part of the course (that is, the material that formed the basis for homework 1, 2, and 3). The first part will be reflective in nature, as described in the second paragraph of this "Implementation" section. Be sure to comment on what things you have learned well (and why) and what things you do not feel you learned well (and why). The second part should be more substantive in nature; it should comment on how the topics that formed the basis of the homework assignments are part of an integrated whole. This midterm essay should be about one to three pages in length and submitted via the Web, as previously instructed.

At the end of the semester, we would like you to pull the midterm and topical essays together into a single document that reflects on the entire course. In preparing this document (three to five pages), consider the following questions:

- What key ideas or information have you learned about water resources engineering?
- What have you learned about how to use or apply the technical content of this course?
- In what areas do you have the most and least confidence? Why do you suppose this is the case?
- What have you been able to integrate inside or outside this course?
- What have you learned about the human dimension of the subject, regarding yourself and/or your interaction with others?

- What new interests or valuing (that is, the importance of the topic relative to your past experiences) have you acquired as a result of this learning experience?
- What did you learn about yourself as a problem solver?
- What have you learned about how to learn?

This final document should be bound together with your homework assignments to form a completed learning portfolio for the course.

Grading

Only the midterm and final essays will be assigned a letter grade. The grade will be based on the depth of your reflection and not the depth of your understanding of the technical material (the latter will be covered by the homework scores and the final exam). We expect your essay to be grammatically correct and thus readable, although we will not significantly penalize you for minor grammatical mistakes.

Chapter 41

Report Guidelines
Sample Questions for Reflection
University of Saskatchewan

THE FOLLOWING QUESTIONS are meant as an outline to guide you in your reflection about the work experience and what you learned. For each, consider and describe the source of the learning—employer, colleagues, self, clients, others.

1. Give a detailed description of the significant work you did and why. Compare two days or weeks at your job—one from the beginning of your placement and one from the end:
   - How did you progress both in terms of the quality and quantity of the work you did?
   - How did your confidence grow?

2. Explain what you learned about the employer:
   - Who are its suppliers, customers, clients, competitors?
   - What is its place in the industry or larger context of agriculture in Saskatchewan, Canada, the world?
   - How did the working environment affect your learning?
   - What type of company is it—multinational, family-owned, government?
   - What is the company structure—lines of authority, hierarchy?
   - Did you experience any conflicts in the workplace, and what did you learn from the way they were handled?

3. Everyone learns from mistakes, trial and error, or practice:
   - What did you learn in this way?
   - Were your colleagues and supervisors supportive and tolerant of you as you learned?
   - How did the feedback you received assist in your professional and personal development?

4. Describe how your work experience and your classroom learning complemented one another:

- How well did your university courses prepare you for the workplace?
- How will the work experience fit into your future university learning?

5. Describe what you learned about work:

- Do you prefer to work independently or as a team member?
- How often do you like to interact with the public? Do you prefer office/lab work or meeting customers and clients regularly?
- Do you enjoy/feel confident about giving advice and suggestions to supervisors, colleagues, clients?

Chapter 42

Promoting Intentional Learning Assignment

University of Virginia

Model Portfolios Evaluation Rubric

Create a portfolio of written work to represent your evolving thinking in this course. Because the learning portfolio is intended to be consciously and carefully selective, you should choose up to five pages of passages from your writing, from the writing of your classmates, or from critics and authors you have come in contact with. In fact, you should include a few passages from others that inspired you or helped you think more deeply about an issue. Those passages should, however, not exceed 50 percent of your total selection. For all passages, be sure to identify the source (e.g., reading journal, class notes, online discussion group posting, papers, posting on child_lit Listserv, etc.).

Then write a reflective essay (five to seven double-spaced pages) explaining what this collection as a whole means to you and how this portfolio reflects changes in your thinking about children's literature, about your writing, about connections between disciplines, about your education as a whole, about you as a learner, about the way you understand yourself and others, and so on. Your learning experience is the subject of this essay. You may want to focus on two or three specific questions, such as these:

- How has your writing evolved? Which assignments were more comfortable and productive for you? Why? What have you learned from reading the writing of your peers?

- Looking back at your responses to the *Measure of Epistemological Reflection,* how did your particular ways of knowing affect you during the semester? Did you notice any changes? If so, how would you describe them? What do you make sense of your observations?

- What major ideas, themes, and threads do you find in your writing and the writing you selected from others? How have you developed these ideas over the course of this semester? What does this development mean to you?

- How do your ideas connect to those you developed in other courses? How does this course fit into your overall undergraduate education?

- How do your insights connect to your life, your personal values, and your convictions? How might these connections affect your future learning?

Use your selected works as evidence for the arguments you want to make.

In reviewing your essay, I will look for the following as they apply to the questions you choose:

- Critical analysis of how and why your writing and thinking about the subject of the course has changed (or not changed)

- Evidence of your preparedness to take an active role as a participant in the discourse of our field of study, including accuracy of discipline-specific facts and principles

- Ability to connect the course material to other fields you have studied and to your personal interests in different areas of your life

- Depth and specificity of reflection

- Persuasiveness of your evidence-based argument

- Clear organization; engaging and comprehensible style; correct grammar and vocabulary

As was the case for all previous projects, this is not the place for flattery or arguments you don't believe in. I am not interested in shallow statements about how good the course was (you can do this in your course evaluations). I am interested in deep reflection and strong arguments. Essays that compellingly and convincingly argue that this course has been a waste of time and otherwise conform to the standards of excellence described in the evaluation rubric will receive an A. You will have to seek peer feedback and turn it in together with your portfolio. This final assignment counts for 15 percent of your course grade.

References

Adapted from McGregor, J. (Ed.). (1993). *New directions for teaching and learning: No. 56. Learning self-evaluation: Fostering reflective learning (p. 102)*. San Francisco: Jossey-Bass.

Chapter 43

Evaluation Rubric for Reflective Essays

University of Virginia

	Excellent	**Good**	**Satisfactory**
Analysis/Reflection	The essay offers an in-depth analysis of and reflection on the question(s) it investigates. It wastes no time stating the obvious and is specific and personal: apt quotations are selected, appropriately introduced, and fully analyzed.	The essay offers a good analysis of and reflection on the question(s) it investigates. It offers a unique perspective: good quotations are selected, appropriately introduced, and well analyzed.	The essay offers considerable analysis and reflection. Quotes are not always fully analyzed, and the argument is often rather general.
Course Concepts	The essay consistently demonstrates an excellent understanding of the concepts and terms it discusses.	The essay demonstrates a firm grasp of the concepts and terms it discusses.	The essay demonstrates a considerable understanding of the concepts and terms it discusses.
Argument	The essay provides a surprisingly strong, coherent, and compelling argument with a clear point and sound logic, and it offers vivid detail and highly specific examples. This paper makes an insightful argument with force and clarity.	The essay presents a strong argument supported by good evidence. It offers sufficient detail and uses examples to illustrate a point.	The argument is solid but general. At times, the essay lacks specific evidence, examples, and detail.

	Excellent	**Good**	**Satisfactory**
Investment	It is obvious that the argument matters to the writer. The writer employs a highly developed personal vocabulary and clearly articulates the connection between his or her persuasions and scholarly pursuits.	The argument is convincing. The writer employs a well-developed personal vocabulary and articulates the connection between his or her persuasions and scholarly pursuits.	Overall, the argument is convincing but lacks at times a clear articulation of the connection between the writer's persuasions and scholarly pursuits. The language is at times generic.
Awareness	The essay exhibits a keen self-awareness and consistently avoids broad generalizations of individual experiences. It takes into consideration other perspectives and carefully examines their potential value.	The essay exhibits self-awareness and mostly avoids broad generalizations of individual experiences. It takes into consideration other perspectives and examines their potential value.	The essay exhibits some self-awareness and rarely generalizes. It refers to other perspectives but does not fully examine their potential value.
Organization	The essay is very well organized. The ideas flow with elegance and ease, building a coherent whole.	The essay is well organized. The ideas flow logically and with energy.	The essay is reasonably well organized. At times, the transitions are missing or unclear.
Writing	The essay possesses graceful sentence structures, creative use of language, sophisticated and precise diction, and almost flawless mechanics.	The essay is generally graceful with few mechanical errors, and the few that do appear arise from the complexity of the sentences (i.e., the errors are more sophisticated than those in a C essay).	Sentence structures are not very sophisticated (they are short and choppy, are run-ons, and/or fail to vary in form), but they are free from serious errors in grammar and punctuation.

Chapter 44

Reflections in Technology Portfolios

Wake Forest University

Reflections

Reflections are personal narratives that express critical thought about the instructional design and/or productivity skills developed while preparing technology portfolio evidence. Each reflection should communicate what you've learned about the software/hardware and demonstrate your ability to think beyond the final product and technologies you used. The key to a quality reflection is to spend some time considering the value of the technology as a tool to enhance instruction, student learning, or personal productivity through the lens of a teacher in your content area and grade level. Reflect on what you learned by completing the project and how your experience might affect your instruction or professional practice in the future. Review the National Educational Technology Standards for Teachers (NETS*T) you address in the creation of the project to help stimulate thought about the value of the technologies to teaching and learning. Organize your thoughts carefully to increase the effectiveness of your communication about the value of what you've learned.

Think about real uses of the tools to support meaningful and relevant future instructional practice, and include specific integration ideas to help illustrate the value of the technologies. Keep in mind that your future instruction must take into consideration the standard course of study curriculum and computer skills curriculum. Use the standard course of study to identify relevant content for your instructional examples. Communicate honestly and use your knowledge of best practices (methods courses) and learning theory (educational psychology) to support the relevance of your integration ideas. Avoid iterations of skills/techniques you learned. Strive for evaluation, synthesis, and creative thought.

A reflection must accompany every major project included in your technology portfolio and must include references to the NETS*T and relevant learning theories. You may use up to two double-spaced pages to communicate your thoughts.

Chapter 45

Technology in Education Web Page

Wake Forest University

THE TECHNOLOGY IN Education courses are a requirement for all students seeking initial licensure through the Department of Education at Wake Forest University. Although both courses are designed to help candidates meet state licensure requirements and the National Educational Technology Standards for Teachers, the courses taught in the fall semester place more emphasis on technology integration in secondary classrooms, while the Technology in Education courses taught during the spring semester focus on the integration of technology appropriate for elementary classrooms. Speak with your program or content area adviser for recommendations on course requirements. General course sequences are provided in tables 45.1 and 45.2.

TABLE 45.1
Course Sequences for Undergraduate Elementary Program

Sophomore (Spring) or Junior (Fall)	Junior (Spring)	Senior (Fall)	Senior (Spring)
Educational Foundations	Children's Literature	Elementary School Curriculum	Special Needs
Educational Psychology	Technology in Education	Methodology:	
Field Experience	Field Experience II	• Language Arts	
	Methodology:	• Mathematics	
	• Social Studies	• Arts and Movement	
	• Science	• Student Teaching	
	• Reading		

General Goals

Prepare candidates to:

• Use technology to improve personal productivity and communicate with the school community

TABLE 45.2
Course Sequences for Undergraduate/Graduate Secondary Program

UNDERGRADUATE			
Sophomore (Spring) or Junior (Fall)	**Junior (Spring)**	**Senior (Fall)**	**Senior (Spring)**
Educational Foundations	Educational Psychology	Methods: • English • Foreign Language • Mathematics • Science • Social Studies Technology in Education	Student Teaching Seminars: • Special Needs • Diversity • Classroom Management • Student Teaching
GRADUATE			
Summer	**Fall**	**Spring**	**Summer**
Psychology of Diverse Learners Sociology of Diverse Learners Research and Statistics	Methods Technology in Education Descriptive Research	Student Teaching Student Teaching Seminar Special Needs Seminar	Professional Development Seminar Educational Leadership

- Integrate technology appropriately into instructional design
- Design instruction that uses technology: to provide multiple representations of content
- Design instruction that uses technology to provide multiple opportunities for expression of knowledge
- Design instruction that addresses the needs of diverse learner groups
- Plan alternative assessment strategies that integrate technology appropriately
- Model ethical use and appropriate use of technology
- Meet the North Carolina technology licensure requirements
- Use their technology skills and resources to become educational leaders

Technology Portfolio

A technology portfolio is required for licensure in North Carolina, and all candidates seeking this license create the majority of the evidence for this portfolio in the Technology in Education course. Each spring, portfolios are evaluated by a team of local educators, technology specialists, and university faculty from outside the Department of Education.

For more information about the course(s) or the technology portfolio, please contact Dr. Ann Cunningham.

Our students learn to develop Web sites using Adobe Dreamweaver CS3. Beginning fall semester 2001, all teacher candidates seeking initial licensure publish their technology portfolios online. Evidence of technology proficiency can be found in student reflections and a variety of other documents, often available as PDFs.

References

AAHE launches communities of practice. (2004, January). *AAHE News.*

Adamchik, C. F., Jr. (1996, June). The design and assessment of chemistry portfolios. *Journal of Chemical Education, 73*(6), 528–530.

Allen, M. J. (2006). *Assessing general education programs.* Bolton, MA: Anker.

American Association of Colleges for Teacher Education, Technology and Innovations Committee. (2007). *The handbook of technological pedagogical content knowledge for teaching and teacher educators.* Mahwah, NJ: Lawrence Erlbaum Associates.

Anderson, E. (Ed.). (1993). *Campus use of the teaching portfolio: Twenty-five profiles.* Washington, DC: American Association for Higher Education.

Angelo, T. A., & Cross, K. P. (1993). *Classroom assessment techniques: A handbook for college teachers* (2nd ed.). San Francisco: Jossey-Bass.

Annis, L., & Jones, C. (1995). Student portfolios: Their objectives, development, and use. In P. Seldin & Associates, *Improving college teaching* (pp. 181–190). Bolton, MA: Anker.

Arter, J. A., & Spandel, V. (1992). NCME instructional module: Using portfolios of student work in instruction and assessment. *Educational Measurement: Issues and Practice, 11*(1), 36–44.

Ashforth, D. (1990). *Records of achievement in the marketplace.* Windsor, England: NFER/Nelson.

Assister, A., & Shaw, E. (Eds.). (1993). *Using records of achievement in higher education.* London: Kogan Page.

Association of American Colleges and Universities. (2007). *Bringing theory to practice.* Retrieved October 2, 2008, from www.aacu.org/bringing_theory

Banta, T., & Hamilton, S. (2002). Using portfolios to coordinate teaching and assessment of student learning. In A. Doherty, T. Riordan, & J. Roth, *Student learning: A central focus for institutions of higher education* (pp. 77–88). Milwaukee, WI: Alverno College Institute.

Barr, R. B., & Tagg, J. (1995, November/December). From teaching to learning—A new paradigm for undergraduate education. *Change, 27*(6), 12–25.

Barrett, H. (2000). Create your own electronic portfolio: Using off-the-shelf software to showcase your own or student work. *Learning and Leading with Technology.* Retrieved October 2, 2008, from www.electronicportfolios.com/portfolios/iste2k.html

Barrett, H. (2000). *Electronic portfolios = multimedia development + portfolio development.* Retrieved October 2, 2008, from www.electronicportfolios.com/portfolios/EPDevProcess.html#eval

Barrett, H. (2000). *Using Adobe Acrobat for electronic portfolio development.* Association for the Advancement of Computing in Education. Retrieved October 2, 2008, from www.electronicportfolios.com/portfolios/sitepaper2001.html

Batson, T. (2002, November 26). The electronic portfolio boom: What's it all about? *Campus Technology.* Retrieved October 2, 2008, from http://campustechnology.com/articles/39299_2

Bauer, W. I., & Dunn, R. E. (2003, Fall). Digital reflection: The electronic portfolio in music teacher education [Electronic version]. *Journal of Music Teacher Education, 13*(1), 7–20.

Baxter Magolda, M. B. (1999). *Creating context for learning and self-authorship: Constructive-developmental pedagogy.* Nashville, TN: Vanderbilt University Press.

Baxter Magolda, M. B. (2001, November/December). A constructivist revision of the measure of epistemological reflection. *Journal of College Student Development, 42*(6), 520–534.

Bean, J. C. (1996). *Engaging ideas: The professor's guide to integrating writing, critical thinking, and active learning in the classroom.* San Francisco: Jossey-Bass.

Bell, P. (2004). On the theoretical breadth of design-based research in education. *Educational Psychologist, 39*(4), 243–253.

Bimes-Michalak, B. (1995, May). The "portfolio zone." *Education Digest, 60*(9), 53–57.

Birenbaum, M. (1996). Assessment 2000: Towards a pluralistic approach to assessment. In M. Birenbaum & F. D. P. Dochy (Eds.), *Alternatives in assessment of achievements, learning processes and prior knowledge* (pp. 3–30). Dordrecht, Netherlands: Kluwer.

Black, B. (1998). Using the SGID method for a variety of purposes. In M. Kaplan & D. Lieberman (Eds.), *To improve the academy: Vol. 17. Resources for faculty, instructional, and organizational development* (pp. 245–262). Stillwater, OK: New Forums Press.

Bloom, B. S. (Ed.). (1956). *Taxonomy of educational objectives, handbook 1: Cognitive domain.* New York: Longman.

Bransford, J. D., Brown, A. L., & Cocking, R. R. (Eds.). (2000). *How people learn: Brain, mind, experience, and school* (Expanded ed.). Washington, DC: National Academy Press.

Bringle, R., & Hatcher, J. (1999). Reflection in service learning: Making meaning of experience. *Educational Horizons, 77*(4), 179–185.

Brookfield, S. D. (1995). *Becoming a critically reflective teacher.* San Francisco: Jossey-Bass.

Brown, J. S., Collins, A., & Duguid, P. (1989). Situated cognition and the culture of learning. *Educational Researcher, 18*(1), 32–42.

Bruffee, K. A. (1993). *Collaborative learning: Higher education, interdependence, and the authority of knowledge.* Baltimore, MD: Johns Hopkins University Press.

Burch, C. B. (1997). Finding out what's in their heads: Using teaching portfolios to assess English education students—and programs. In K. B. Yancey & I. Weiser (Eds.), *Situating portfolios: Four perspectives* (pp. 263–277). Logan: Utah State University Press.

Butler, J. (1996). Professional development: Practice as text, reflection as process, and self as locus. *Australian Journal of Education, 40*(3), 265–283.

Cambridge, B. L. (Ed.). (2001). *Electronic portfolios: Emerging practices in student, faculty, and institutional learning.* Washington, DC: American Association for Higher Education.

Cambridge, D., Kaplan, S., & Suter, V. (2005). *Community of practice design guide.* Retrieved December 15, 2007, from www.educause.edu/ir/library/pdf/NLI0531.pdf

Campbell, D. M., Cignetti, P. B., Melenyzer, B. J., Nettles, D. H., & Wyman, R. M., Jr. (2001). *How to develop a professional portfolio: A manual for teachers* (2nd ed.). Boston: Allyn & Bacon.

Campbell, D. M., Melenyzer, B. J., Nettles, D. H., & Wyman, R. M., Jr. (2000). *Portfolio and performance assessment in teacher education.* Boston: Allyn & Bacon.

Candy, P. C. (1991). *Self-direction for lifelong learning: A comprehensive guide to theory and practice.* San Francisco: Jossey-Bass.

Centre for Co-op Education Program, Centre for Career Education, University of Windsor. (n.d.). Retrieved October 2, 2008, from www.uwindsor.ca/cce

Claywell, G. (2001). *The Allyn and Bacon guide to writing portfolios.* Boston: Allyn & Bacon.

Cochran-Smith, M., & Lytle, S. L. (1999). Relationships of knowledge and practice: Teacher learning in communities. *Review of Research in Education, 24,* 249–305.

Coles, R. (1993). *The call of service: A witness to idealism.* Boston: Houghton Mifflin.

Collinson, V. (1995). Making the most of portfolios. *Learning, 24*(1), 43.

Cooper, D. D. (1998). Reading, writing, and reflection. In R. A. Rhoades & J. P. F. Howard (Eds.), *New directions for teaching and learning: No. 73. Academic service learning: A pedagogy of action and reflection* (pp. 47–56). San Francisco: Jossey-Bass.

Couto, R. A. (1995). Defining a citizen leader. In J. T. Wren (Ed.), *The leader's companion: Insights on leadership through the ages* (pp. 11–17). New York: Free Press.

Cox, M. D. (2004). Introduction to faculty learning communities. In M. D. Cox & L. Richlin (Eds.), *New directions for teaching and learning: No. 97. Building faculty learning communities* (pp. 5–23). San Francisco: Jossey-Bass.

"Creating and using portfolios on the Alphabet Superhighway." (n.d.). U.S. Department of Education. Original site unavailable but retrievable from http://web.archive.org/web/20041210095045/www.ash.udel.edu/ash/teacher/portfolio.html

D'Aoust, C. (1992). Portfolios: Process for students and teachers. In K. B. Yancey (Ed.), *Portfolios in the writing classroom: An introduction* (pp. 39–48). Urbana, IL: National Council of Teachers of English.

Darling-Hammond, L. (2000). How teacher education matters. *Journal of Teacher Education, 51*(3), 166–173.

Dental Council of New Zealand. (2007). *The dental council.* Retrieved October 2, 2008, from www.dcnz.org.nz/dcAboutCouncil

Dental Council of New Zealand. (2007). *Registration—Overview.* Retrieved October 2, 2008, from www.dcnz.org.nz/dcRegistrationOverview

Dental Council of New Zealand. (2007). *Roles and functions.* Retrieved October 2, 2008, from www.dcnz.org.nz/dcAboutRoles

Dewey, J. (1910). *How we think.* Boston: D. C. Heath.

Dewey, J. (1916). *Democracy and education.* New York: Macmillan.

Duckenfield, M., & Swick, K. J. (Eds.). (2002). *A gallery of portraits in service learning: Action research in teacher education.* Clemson, SC: National Dropout Prevention Center.

Edgerton, R., Hutchings, P., & Quinlan, K. (1991). *The teaching portfolio: Capturing the scholarship in teaching.* Washington, DC: American Association for Higher Education.

Educational Development Centre, University of Windsor. (n.d.). *WindsorLEADS.* Retrieved October 2, 2008, from http://uwindsor.ca/leads (see "Professional Portfolio" at Program Outline link)

EduTools. (2006). *EduTools ePortfolio review.* Retrieved December 15, 2007, from http://eportfolio.edutools.info

Elbow, P. (1998). *Writing with power: Techniques for mastering the writing process* (2nd ed.). New York: Oxford University Press.

Elbow, P. (1998). *Writing without teachers* (2nd ed.). New York: Oxford University Press.

Elbow, P., & Belanoff, P. (1986). Portfolios as a substitute for proficiency examinations. *College Composition and Communication, 37,* 336–339.

Emig, J. A. (1971). *The composing processes of twelfth graders* (NCTE Research Report No. 13). Urbana, IL: National Council of Teachers of English.

Emig, J. A. (1977). Writing as a mode of learning. *College Composition and Communication, 28,* 122–128.

Eyler, J., & Giles, D. (1999). *Where's the learning in service learning?* San Francisco: Jossey-Bass.

Eyler, J., Giles, D., & Gray, C. (2003). At a glance: What we know about the effects of service learning on students, faculty, institutions and communities, 1993–2000: Third edition. In *Introduction to service-learning toolkit: Readings and resources for faculty* (2nd ed., pp. 15–19). Providence, RI: Campus Compact.

Faculty of Education, University of Windsor. (n.d.). *PhD handbook.* Retrieved October 2, 2008, from http://web2.uwindsor.ca/courses/edfac/morton/phd_handbook.htm

Fenwick, A., Assister, A., & Nixon, N. (1992). *Profiling in higher education.* London: Council for National Academic Awards.

Fenwick, T., & Parsons, J. (2000). *The art of evaluation: A handbook for educators and trainers.* Toronto, ON: Thompson Educational Publishing.

Fink, L. D. (2001). Higher-level learning: The first step toward more significant learning. In D. Lieberman & C. Wehlburg (Eds.), *To improve the academy: Vol. 19. Resources for faculty, instructional, and organizational development* (pp. 113–130). Bolton, MA: Anker.

Fink, L. D. (2003). *Creating significant learning experiences in college classrooms: An integrated approach to designing college courses.* San Francisco: Jossey-Bass.

Fink, L. D. (2003). *Designing courses for significant student learning: Making dreams come true.* San Francisco: Jossey-Bass.

Flores, R. J. O. (2007, January). *Engaged pedagogies, liberal learning, and sustainable civic outcomes.* Paper presented at the annual meeting of the Association of American Colleges and Universities, New Orleans, LA.

Fontana, J. (1995). Portfolio assessment: Its beginnings in Vermont and Kentucky. *NASSP Bulletin, 79*(573), 25.

Fournier, J., & Lane, C. (2006, November). *Transitioning from paper to electronic portfolios in beginning composition.* Catalyst: Office of Learning Technologies, University of Washington. Retrieved October 2, 2008, from http://catalyst.washington.edu/research_development/papers/2006/2006-eportfolio-report.pdf

Gordon, R. (1994, May). Keeping students at the center: Portfolio assessment at the college level. *Journal of Experiential Education, 17*(1), 23–27.

Greenberg, G. (2004, July/August). The digital convergence: Extending the portfolio model. *EDUCAUSE Review, 39*(4), 28–37.

Hannam, S. E. (1995). Portfolios: An alternative method of student and program assessment. *Journal of Athletic Training, 30*, 338.

Harward, D. W. (2007). Engaged learning and the core purposes of liberal education: Bringing theory to practice. *Liberal Education, 93*(1), 6–15.

Hayes, J. R., & Flower, L. S. (1980). The dynamics of composing: Making plans and juggling constraints. In L. W. Gregg & E. R. Steinbert (Eds.), *Cognitive processes in writing* (pp. 31–50). Hillsdale, NJ: Lawrence Erlbaum Associates.

Hayes, J. R., & Flower, L. S. (1980). Identifying the organization of writing processes. In L. W. Gregg & E. R. Steinbert (Eds.), *Cognitive processes in writing* (pp. 3–30). Hillsdale, NJ: Lawrence Erlbaum Associates.

Hillocks, G., Jr. (1995). *Teaching writing as reflective practice: Integrating theories.* New York: Teachers College Press.

Howard, J. P. F. (1998). Academic service learning: A counternormative pedagogy. In R. A. Rhoades & J. P. F. Howard (Eds.), *New directions for teaching and learning: No. 73. Academic service learning: A pedagogy of action and reflection* (pp. 21–30). San Francisco: Jossey-Bass.

Huber, M. T., & Hutchings, P. (2004). *Integrative learning: Mapping the terrain.* Retrieved October 2, 2008, from www.carnegiefoundation.org/Integrative Learning/mapping-terrain.pdf

Hutchings, P. (1990). Learning over time: Portfolio assessment. *AAHE Bulletin, 42*(8), 6–8.

Hutchings, P. (Ed.). (1998). *The course portfolio: How faculty can examine their teaching to advance practice and improve student learning.* Washington, DC: American Association for Higher Education.

International Society for Technology in Education. (2000). *National educational technology standards for students.* Eugene, OR: International Society for Technology in Education.

International Society for Technology in Education. (2002). *National educational technology standards for teachers.* Eugene, OR: International Society for Technology in Education.

Jafari, A., & Kaufman, C. (2006). *Handbook of research on ePortfolios.* Hershey, PA: Idea Group Inc.

Jasper, M. (1995). The portfolio workbook as a strategy for student-centred learning. *Nurse Education Today, 15*, 446.

Jones, B. F., Valdez, G., Nowakowski, G., & Rasmussen, C. (1994). *Designing learning and technology for educational reform.* Oak Brook, IL: North Central Regional Educational Laboratory.

King, P., & Kitchener, K. (1994). *Developing reflective judgment.* San Francisco: Jossey-Bass.

King, T. (2002, July). *Development of student skills in reflective writing.* Paper presented at the 4th World Conference of the International Consortium for Educational Development in Higher Education (ICED), University of Western Australia, Perth.

Knight, P. T. (1995). *Records of achievement in further and higher education.* Lancaster, England: Framework Press.

Kolb, D. (1984). *Experiential learning as the science of learning and development.* Englewood Cliffs, NJ: Prentice Hall.

Kottkamp, R. (1990). Means for facilitating reflection. *Education and Urban Society, 22*(2), 182–203.

Lankes, A. M. D. (1995). *Electronic portfolios: A new idea in assessment.* Syracuse, NY: ERIC Clearinghouse on Information and Technology. (ERIC Document Reproduction Service No. ED390377)

Learning and integrity: A strategic vision for Fairfield University. (2005). Fairfield, CT: Fairfield University.

Levine, A., & Cureton, J. (2002). What we know about today's college students. *About Campus, 3*(1), 4–9.

Light, R. J. (2001). *Making the most of college: Students speak their minds.* Cambridge, MA: Harvard University Press.

Lindemann, E. (1982). *A rhetoric for writing teachers.* New York: Oxford University Press.

Lombardi, M. (2007, May). *Authentic learning for the 21st century: An overview* (ELI Paper 1: 2007 EDUCAUSE Learning Initiative). Retrieved October 2, 2008, from http://net.educause.edu/ir/library/pdf/ELI3009.pdf

Lorenzo, G., & Ittelson, J. C. (2005). *Demonstrating and assessing student learning with e-portfolios.* Retrieved October 2, 2008, from http://connect.educause.edu/Library/ELI/DemonstratingandAssessing/39337

Lorenzo, G., & Ittelson, J. C. (2005). *An overview of e-portfolios.* Retrieved October 2, 2008, from http://connect.educause.edu/Library/ELI/AnOverviewofEPortfolios/39335

Lorenzo, G., & Ittelson, J. C. (2005). *An overview of institutional e-portfolios.* Retrieved October 2, 2008, from http://connect.educause.edu/Library/ELI/AnOverviewofInstitutional/39336

Martin-Kniep, G. O. (1999). *Capturing the wisdom of practice: Professional portfolios for educators.* Alexandria, VA: Association for Supervision and Curriculum Development.

Mazow, C. (2002). *Portfolio use questions.* Unpublished manuscript.

McGregor, J. (Ed.). (1993). *New directions for teaching and learning: No. 56. Learning self-evaluation: Fostering reflective learning.* San Francisco: Jossey-Bass.

McMahon, B., & Portelli, J. (2004). Engagement for what? Beyond popular discourses of student engagement. *Leadership and Policy in Schools, 3*(1), 59–76.

Mills, R. P. (1990). Using student portfolios to assess achievement. *Education Digest, 55,* 51–53.

Ministry of Health. (2006). *Health Practitioners Competence Assurance Act 2003.* Retrieved October 2, 2008, from www.moh.govt.nz/hpca

Moersch, C., & Fisher, L. M. (1995). Electronic portfolios—Some pivotal questions. *Learning and Leading with Technology, 23*(2), 10.

Moon, J. A. (1999). *Learning journals: A handbook for academics, students and professional development.* New York: Routledge.

Moon, J. A. (2005, November 28). *Guide for busy academics: No. 4. Learning through reflection.* The Higher Education Academy. Retrieved October 2, 2008, from www.heacademy.ac.uk/resources/detail/id69_guide_for_busy_academics_no4_moon

Murphy, S. (1997). Teachers and students: Reclaiming assessment via portfolios. In K. B. Yancey & I. Weiser (Eds.), *Situating portfolios: Four perspectives* (pp. 72–88). Logan: Utah State University Press.

Murray, J. P. (1995). *Successful faculty development and evaluation: The complete teaching portfolio* (ASHE-ERIC Higher Education Report No. 8). Washington, DC: George Washington University.

Newman, C., & Smolen, L. (1993). Portfolio assessment in our schools: Implementation, advantages, and concerns. *Midwestern Educational Researcher, 6*(1), 28.

Newman, M. (2006). *Teaching defiance: Stories and strategies for activist educators.* San Francisco: Jossey-Bass.

Nieto, R. D., & Henderson, J. L. (1994). Using portfolios to assess student performance. *The Agricultural Education Magazine, 66*(9), 22.

O'Neil, C., & Wright, W. A. (1991). *Recording teaching accomplishment: A Dalhousie guide to the teaching dossier.* Halifax, NS: Dalhousie University, Office of Instructional Development and Technology.

Palmer, P. J. (1998). *The courage to teach: Exploring the inner landscape of a teacher's life.* San Francisco: Jossey-Bass.

Partnership for 21st-Century Skills. (2004). *21st-century standards*. Retrieved October 2, 2008, from www.21stcenturyskills.org/index.php?option=com_content&task=view&id=351&Itemid=120

Perry, M. (1997). Producing purposeful portfolios. In K. B. Yancey & I. Weiser (Eds.), *Situating portfolios: Four perspectives* (pp. 182–189). Logan: Utah State University Press.

Perry, W. G. (1970). *Forms of intellectual and ethical development in the college years: A scheme*. New York: Holt, Rinehart, & Winston.

Price, M. (2006, December 4). What is the purpose of an electronic portfolio? Is the answer the key to your successful implementation? *Campus Technology*. Retrieved October 2, 2008, from http://campustechnology.com/articles/41320

Ramsden, P. (2003). *Learning to teach in higher education* (2nd ed.). London: Routledge Falmer.

Regan, T. (2007). *Commencement address, Fairfield University, May 20, 2007*. Retrieved October 2, 2008, from www.fairfield.edu/pr_index.html?id=2107

Rhem, J. (1995). Close-up: Going deep. *The National Teaching & Learning Forum, 5*(1), 4.

Rogers, E. (1995). *Diffusion of innovations*. New York: Free Press.

Rogers, G. M., & Williams, J. (2001). *Promise and pitfalls of electronic portfolios: Lessons learned from experience*. Accreditation Board for Engineering and Technology. Retrieved October 2, 2008, from www.abet.org/Linked%20Documents-UPDATE/Assessment/Promise%20and%20Pitfalls%20of%20Electronic%20Portfolios_2001.pdf

Schön, D. (1983). *The reflective practitioner: How professionals think in action*. New York: Basic Books.

Schön, D. (1987). *Educating the reflective practitioner: Toward a new design for teaching and learning in the professions*. San Francisco: Jossey-Bass.

Seldin, P. (1991). *The teaching portfolio: A practical guide to improved performance and promotion/tenure decisions*. Bolton, MA: Anker.

Seldin, P. (1997). *The teaching portfolio: A practical guide to improved performance and promotion/tenure decisions* (2nd ed.). Bolton, MA: Anker.

Seldin, P. (2004). *The teaching portfolio: A practical guide to improved performance and promotion/tenure decisions* (3rd ed.). Bolton, MA: Anker.

Seldin, P., Annis, L., & Zubizarreta, J. (1995). Answers to common questions about the teaching portfolio. *Journal on Excellence in College Teaching, 6*(1), 57–64.

Seldin, P., Annis, L., & Zubizarreta, J. (1995). Using the teaching portfolio to improve instruction. In W. A. Wright & Associates, *Teaching improvement practices: Successful strategies for higher education* (pp. 237–254). Bolton, MA: Anker.

Seldin, P., & Associates. (1993). *Successful use of teaching portfolios*. Bolton, MA: Anker.

Shore, B., Foster, S., Knapper, C., Nadeau, G., Neill, N., & Sim, V. (1986). *The teaching dossier: A guide to its preparation and use* (Rev. ed.). Ottawa, ON: Canadian Association of University Teachers.

Shulman, L. (1998). Course anatomy: The dissection and analysis of knowledge through teaching. In P. Hutchings (Ed.), *The course portfolio: How faculty can examine their teaching to advance practice and improve student learning* (pp. 5–12). Washington, DC: American Association for Higher Education.

Shulman, L. (1998). Teacher portfolios: A theoretical activity. In N. Lyons (Ed.), *With portfolio in hand: Validating the new teacher professionalism* (pp. 23–37). New York: Teachers College Press.

Slater, T. F., & Astwood, P. M. (1995, May). Strategies for using and grading undergraduate student assessment portfolios in an environmental geology course. *Journal of Geological Education, 43,* 216.

Springfield, E. (2001). A major redesign of the Kalamazoo portfolio. In B. L. Cambridge (Ed.), *Electronic portfolios: Emerging practices in student, faculty, and institutional learning* (pp. 53–59). Washington, DC: American Association for Higher Education.

Stassen, M. L. A., Doherty, K., & Poe, M. (2004). *Program-based review and assessment: Tools and techniques for program improvement.* Amherst: University of Massachusetts.

Stein, S. J., Isaacs, G., & Andrews, T. (2004). Incorporating authentic learning experiences within a university course. *Studies in Higher Education, 29*(2), 239–258.

Stephenson, J., & Laycock, M. (Eds.). (1993). *Learning contracts in higher education.* London: Kogan Page.

Stronge, J. H. (2002). *Qualities of effective teachers.* Alexandria, VA: Association of Supervision and Curriculum Development.

Sunstein, B. S. (2000). Be reflective, be reflexive, and beware: Innocent forgery for inauthentic assessment. In B. S. Sunstein & J. H. Lovell (Eds.), *The portfolio standard: How students can show us what they know and are able to do* (pp. 3–14). Portsmouth, NH: Heinemann.

Swaner, L. E. (2007). Linking engaged learning, student mental health and well-being, and civic development: A review of the literature. *Liberal Education, 93*(1), 16–25.

"Technology briefs." (n.d.). National Education Association. Original site unavailable but retrievable from http://web.archive.org/web/20020803225931/www.nea.org/cet/BRIEFS/brief4.html

Thompson, A. D. (2007). TPCK: A new direction for technology in teacher education programs. *Journal of Computing in Teacher Education, 23*(3), 78.

Trowler, P., & Hinett, K. (1994). Implementing the recording of achievement in higher education. *Capability, 1*(1), 53–61.

University of Otago. (2007). *Bachelor of oral health (BOH).* Retrieved October 2, 2008, from www.otago.ac.nz/courses/qualifications/boh.html

University of Otago. (2007). *Dental students get their teeth into new oral health degree.* Retrieved October 2, 2008, from www.otago.ac.nz/news/news/2007/23-02-07_press_release.html

Villano, M. (2006, August 29). Electronic student assessment: The power of the portfolio. *Campus Technology.* Retrieved October 2, 2008, from www.campustechnology.com/article.aspx?aid=41130

Walvoord, B. E. (2004). *Assessment clear and simple.* San Francisco: Jossey-Bass.

Walvoord, B. E., & Anderson, V. J. (1998). *Effective grading: A tool for learning and assessment.* San Francisco: Jossey-Bass.

Waters, J. K. (2008, June 1). Unleashing the power of Web 2.0. *Campus Technology.* Retrieved October 2, 2008, from http://campustechnology.com/articles/63551_1

Waterson, K. (2001). Did Socrates have transferable skills? Or Dalhousie University's skills transcript project. In G. Tucker & D. Nevo (Eds.), *Atlantic universities' teaching showcase 2001: Vol. 6* (pp. 21–33). Halifax, NS: Mount Saint Vincent University.

Weiser, I. (1997). Revising our practices: How portfolios help teachers learn. In K. B. Yancey & I. Weiser (Eds.), *Situating portfolios: Four perspectives* (pp. 293–301). Logan: Utah State University Press.

Wenger, E. (1998). *Communities of practice: Learning, meaning, and identity.* Cambridge: Cambridge University Press.

Wenger, E., McDermott, R., & Snyder, W. M. (2002). *Cultivating communities of practice.* Boston: Harvard Business School Press.

Wetzel, K., & Strudler, N. (2006). Costs and benefits of electronic portfolios in teacher education: Student voices. *Journal of Computing in Teacher Education, 22*(3), 69–78.

Wilhelm, L., Puckett, K., Beisser, S., Wishart, W., Merideth, E., & Sivakumaran, T. (2006). Lessons learned from the implementation of electronic portfolios at three universities [Electronic version]. *TechTrends, 50*(4), 62–71.

Williams, J. D. (2000). Identity and reliability in portfolio assessment. In B. S. Sunstein & J. H. Lovell (Eds.), *The portfolio standard: How students can show us what they know and are able to do* (pp. 135–148). Portsmouth, NH: Heinemann.

Wolfe, E. W. (1996). *A report on the reliability of a large-scale portfolio assessment for language arts, mathematics, and science.* Paper presented at the annual meeting of the National Council on Measurement in Education, New York.

Wright, W. A. (2001). The Dalhousie career portfolio programme: A multi-faceted approach to transition to work. *Quality in Higher Education, 7*(2), 149–159.

Wright, W. A., & Barton, B. (2001). Students mentoring students in portfolio development. In J. E. Miller, J. E. Groccia, & M. S. Miller (Eds.), *Student-assisted teaching: A guide to faculty-student teamwork* (pp. 69–76). Bolton, MA: Anker.

Wright, W. A., Knight, P. T., & Pomerleau, N. (1999). Portfolio people: Teaching and learning dossiers and innovation in higher education. *Innovative Higher Education, 24*(2), 89–103.

Yancey, K. B. (1997). Teacher portfolios: Lessons in resistance, readiness, and reflection. In K. B. Yancey & I. Weiser (Eds.), *Situating portfolios: Four perspectives* (pp. 244–262). Logan: Utah State University Press.

Yancey, K. B. (2001). Digitized student portfolios. In B. L. Cambridge (Ed.), *Electronic portfolios: Emerging practices in student, faculty, and institutional learning* (pp. 15–30). Washington, DC: American Association for Higher Education.

Young, J. R. (2002, March 8). "E-Portfolios" could give students a new sense of their accomplishments. *Chronicle of Higher Education, 48*(26), A31–A32.

Zeichner, K., & Wray, S. (2001). The teaching portfolio in US teacher education programs: What we know and what we need to know [Electronic version]. *Teaching and Teacher Education, 17*(5), 613–621.

Zlotkowski, E. (1999). *Pedagogy and engagement.* In R. Bringle, R. Games, & E. Malloy (Eds.), *Colleges and universities as citizens* (pp. 96–120). Boston: Allyn & Bacon.

Zubizarreta, J. (1994). Teaching portfolios and the beginning teacher. *Phi Delta Kappan, 76*(4), 323–326.

Zubizarreta, J. (1995). Using teaching portfolio strategies to improve course instruction. In P. Seldin & Associates, *Improving college teaching* (pp. 167–179). Bolton, MA: Anker.

Zubizarreta, J. (1997). Improving teaching through portfolio revisions. In P. Seldin, *The teaching portfolio: A practical guide to improved performance and promotion/tenure decisions* (2nd ed., pp. 167–179). Bolton, MA: Anker.

Zubizarreta, J. (1999). Evaluating teaching through portfolios. In P. Seldin & Associates, *Changing practices in evaluating teaching* (pp. 162–182). Bolton, MA: Anker.

Zubizarreta, J. (2004). *The learning portfolio: Reflective practice for improving student learning.* Bolton, MA: Anker.

Index

Note to index: An *f* following a page number denotes a figure on that page; a *t* following a page number denotes a table on that page.

Credits

p. 8	Bulleted list from Dorothy M. Campbell et al., *Portfolio and Performance Assessment in Teacher Education,* published by Allyn and Bacon, Boston, MA. Copyright © 2000 by Pearson Education. Reprinted by permission of the publisher.
p. 12	Extract and bulleted list from L. D. Fink (2001), Higher-level learning: The first step toward more significant learning. *To Improve the Academy: Resources for Faculty, Instructional, and Organizational Development, 19,* Bolton, MA: Anker. Reprinted with permission of John Wiley & Sons, Inc.
p. 12	Bulleted list from *Situating portfolios: Four perspectives.* Utah State University Press, 1997. Reprinted by permission.
pp. 15–16	Bulleted list from Moon, J. (1999). *Learning journals: A handbook for academics, students and professional development.* London: Kogan Page, p. 34. Used by permission of Taylor & Francis Books (UK).
p. 27	Figure 2.2 from Moon, J. (1999). *Learning journals: A handbook for academics, students and professional development.* London: Kogan Page, Fig. 2.1, p. 35 as adapted in King, T. (2002, July). Development of student skills in reflective writing. Paper delivered at 4th World Conference of the International Consortium for Educational Development in Higher Education (ICED), University of Western Australia. Used by permission of T. King. Used by permission of Taylor & Francis Books (UK) and T. R. King.

composition. Catalyst Research and Development, Office of Learning Technologies, University of Washington. Used by permission of the authors.

pp. 62–63   Extract and bulleted list from Technology briefs. "Technology and Portfolio Assessment." Reprinted by permission of the National Education Association (www.nea.org).

pp. 64–66   Numbered list from "Electronic Student Assessment: The Power of the Portfolio" by Matt Villano, *Campus Technology*, September 2006, www.campustechnology.com.

pp. 66–67   Bulleted lists from Yancey, K. B. (2001). Digitized student portfolios. In B. L. Cambridge (Ed.), *Electronic portfolios: Emerging practices in student, faculty, and institutional learning* (pp. 15–30). Washington, DC: American Association for Higher Education. pp. 84–86 & pp. 86–87. Copyright AAHE, 2001; Stylus Publishing, 2005. Used by permission.

p. 85   Numbered list from Regan, T. (2007). *Commencement address, Fairfield University, May 20, 2007.* Reprinted by permission of Thomas J. Regan, SJ.

p. 111   Bulleted list from "Portfolio Use Questions" based on conversations with EPAC members, authored and compiled by Cynthia Mazrow. Used by permission of Cynthia Mazrow.

p. 113   Figure 8.1 from *Community of Practice Design Guide* by Darren Cambridge, Soren Kaplan, and Vicki Sutter, 2005, which was developed based on shared experiences of EDUCAUSE, AAHE, and iCohere.

pp. 128–129   Table 9.3 from NETS for Teachers: National Educational Technology Standards for Teachers, Second Edition © 2008 ISTE ® (International Society for Technology in Education), www.iste.org. All rights reserved.

p. 159   Epigraph from a quote from a conversation with Michael Gombola, PhD. Used by permission.